D0700039

PLAYING IN ISOLATION

PLAYING IN
A HISTORY OF BASEBALL IN TAIWAN
ISOLATION

JUNWEI YU

University of Nebraska Press • Lincoln & London

♾

Library of Congress Cataloging-
in-Publication Data
Yu, Junwei.
Playing in isolation : a history of
baseball in Taiwan / Junwei Yu.
p.   cm.
Includes bibliographical
references and index.
ISBN-13: 978-0-8032-1140-7
(cloth : alk. paper)
ISBN-10: 0-8032-1140-6
(cloth : alk. paper)
1. Baseball—Taiwan—History.
2. Baseball players—Taiwan—
History. I. Title.
GV863.795.A1Y8   2007
796.35709512'49—dc22
[B]
2006100127

For my parents,
Yu Minxiang and Zeng Yueer,
who offered unconditional support to me,
thus making this project possible.

CONTENTS

ILLUSTRATIONS

PREFACE

Ever since Taiwan captured its first Little League Baseball world series title in 1969, baseball has been a sport in which the Taiwanese people have taken deep pride. Over the next twenty-seven years Taiwan appeared in the annual tournament twenty-one times and captured seventeen titles.

I have followed Taiwanese national teams since I was small. Like many fellow islanders, I watched live Little League tournament games on television late into the night as I sipped instant noodles, a favorite snack in Taiwan. Thankfully, tournaments were held during summer vacations so that I didn't have to worry about school. I was filled with excitement and joy at that time, but as I grew older and learned more about the inner world of baseball, I found the game no longer as simple and beautiful as it had once seemed.

My interest in baseball research was sparked by playing amateur baseball during senior high school. As with just about every high school in Taiwan, mine did not have a formal baseball program. Thus for three years my classmates and I organized games in the sports fields behind our school until one day the principal posted a sign on the fence that read "Baseball, softball, and other dangerous sports are forbidden." Such signs are frequently posted in Taiwanese schools, the common notion being that baseball, unlike running or swimming, is quite unsafe.

Unable to play the game I loved, I found alternative ways to be around the diamond. At many amateur baseball games I had the opportunity to talk extensively with players, coaches, and other individuals who were deeply involved in the sport. In 1997 I was the scorer for the under-16 International Baseball Federation competition, which was my first contact with government officials involved in the game.

In 2001, thanks to help from friends, I was fortunate enough to be the U.S. team's interpreter during the baseball World Cup.

Eventually my deep fascination with all things baseball led to my adoption of the game for my PhD dissertation, in which I explored politics in Taiwanese baseball. This current book has been adapted from that work, as well as drawing upon recent events in Taiwanese baseball and from my lifelong obsession with the sport. Relying on thousands of hours of formal and not-so-formal research and interviews, I present an alternative perspective on Taiwanese baseball to the one commonly held on the island. The Taiwanese public tends to view governmental intervention in sports, specifically baseball, as good and special physical education classes as normal. But in this book I argue that it is such practices that led to the decline of Taiwanese baseball.

To understand fully the development of Taiwanese baseball, one must have some knowledge of the island's history. Taiwan's geographic location has made it a strategic base for those who sought access to China and for China when it wished to exert its influence over the Pacific Rim. Consequently, the island has changed hands many times. Because each ruling people possessed a different culture and language and represented a different ethnic group, each period of Taiwanese history has had its own unique characteristics.

It was one such ruling people, the Japanese, who introduced baseball to Taiwan in the early twentieth century. By the time Japan had ended its Taiwanese rule, thousands of islanders played the game.

The sport continued to gain popularity after the Kuomintang regime arrived. The level of participation was highest during this era, especially for adult baseball. Still, antiphysical Confucian ideas did prevent some parents from allowing their children to play baseball but not all since schools required athletes to study.

Grassroots baseball reached its peak in the 1970s because of the success of Little League teams at Williamsport and to the fame and fortune bestowed on successful Little League players, thanks in large part to the baseball policies of the Kuomintang. Despite these factors, another decline in baseball's popularity followed, with the lowest level of baseball participation occurring during the 1980s. During this decade many of the incentives disappeared, Confucian ideas resurfaced, and widespread reports of corruption in baseball soured parents' attitudes toward the game.

Against such a complex background, baseball, the largest spectator sport on the island, has been given specific meaning and purpose according to who has been in power. Thus, an overarching goal of this book is to trace the development of the game and the cultural and political forces that have influenced public perception of the sport. I chose to take a chronological approach because it best illustrates the dramatic swings in popularity of the game. Each chapter therefore covers a period in Taiwanese history that profoundly affected the game.

To date no academic work has explored Taiwanese baseball in its social, cultural, and political settings. In this book I will present a balanced view of Taiwanese baseball, even discussing thoroughly the cheating and corruption that have plagued the game. Because of the latter portrayal I have already felt pressure from island baseball authorities telling me not to expose the underbelly of our national pastime. However, I believe that my actions are justified and that only by seeing the dark side of the sport can the baseball world begin taking this negative side seriously, rather than turning a perpetual blind eye to the problems of baseball on Taiwan.

ACKNOWLEDGMENTS

I have been watching baseball since childhood, but it was Lincoln Allison, my PhD supervisor at Warwick University, who gave me the intellectual guidance needed to research Taiwanese baseball. The depth of gratitude and respect I have for him is immense. Other teachers, such as Terry Monnington and Ken Foster, at the Center of Sport in Society also deserve my thanks.

Further, this book would not have been started without the interest and enthusiasm shown by the University of Nebraska Press, to whose editors I am grateful for their consistent patience and support. I am especially indebted to Sara Springsteen and Rob Taylor, who acted on behalf of the press. Michael Haskell of Columbia University Press copyedited my manuscript, making it more readable. Most important of all was Dan Gordon, who spent hundreds of hours developmentally editing the manuscript.

I am indebted to both the Brother Elephants pro club and the Chinese Taipei Baseball Association. Jianong alumnus Cai Wuzhang deserves special thanks for not only providing valuable insights into Taiwanese baseball during the Japanese occupation but also offering precious information about the early development of Taiwanese baseball that is rare and difficult to obtain. Thanks go also to the Central News Agency for invaluable photographs that add color to this book.

My gratitude goes as well to such friends as Zeng Wencheng who helped me sift through ideas and provided intellectual support and friendship. George Gmelch of Union College offered advice. Riccardo Schiroli, Harry Wedemeijer, and Michal Hanus provided insight into European baseball, while Jamey Storvick talked about his scouting experience in Asia.

During my fieldwork in pursuit of this project, my associates in Taiwan were very helpful. I wish to offer sincere thanks to the many institutions and individuals who have provided assistances. Yang Rongjian and Huang Guanxiong, both of whom are responsible for www.playballx.com and who gave me the opportunity of being a trainee reporter, thus enabling me to interview players and coaches without the slightest problem. Zhang Huiyan, Yang Renjie, Lin Guanhong, Zhai Zhengming, Lin Haoqiang, Zhong Mengwen, and Qiu Wenyuan and other friends on telnet://bbs.aidsbbs.net provided additional information needed for this work.

Special thanks go to my interviewees Xu Weizhi, Tang Panpan, Peng Chenghao, Li Juming, Lin Huawei, Wei Laichang, Cai Qida, Lin Zongcheng, Xu Yashu, and Jonathan Hurst, as well as to several anonymous interviewees, all of whom have made a lifetime of contribution to baseball and all of whom provided important insights into the game.

Thanks also go to the students majoring in athletic training and health at the National College of Physical Education and Sports. They offered invaluable information about medical treatments of Taiwanese players, many of whom suffered serious injuries due to overuse during their careers.

Additionally, I offer my appreciation to the staff of the National Library for teaching me how to use microfiche and for solving mechanical problems while operating microfiche readers. The time and the money spent on watching and printing out old materials supplied a solid foundation for the project. In addition my subscription to the Society for American Baseball Research enabled me to gain access through ProQuest to several old newspapers, each of which offered me insights into Taiwanese baseball.

In this litany of thanks my family deserves my deepest gratitude. Over the years my parents Yu Minxiang and Zeng Yueer have given me constant encouragement and unconditional support, both spiritually and financially. This book would not exist without their love and assistance.

Finally, I would like to thank the following people: Zeng Weilin, Zhong Mingfeng, Xie Shiyuan, Xie Jiafen, Lan Peiyu, Cao Peiying, Chen Liangyue, Liao Fanbei, Wu Xuzhe, Qiu Guangzong, Huang Xiuyu, Huang Suyu, Lin Shuxian, Hong Jinfu, Cai Kunzhen, Xu Heling, Xu Yashu, Cheng Ruifu, Lin Jianyu, Li Bingzhao, Chen Liangyue, Cai Youlin, Lin Guanghong, Zhang Sheng, Chen Xianwei, Zhang Huiyan, Yang Zhiguo, Lin Jiang, Huang Zhaoxi, Tang Zhimao, Andrew Morris, Wang Jiaan, Wang Yueyu, Tu Youcheng, Wei Ziyao, Qiu Guobin, Leslie R Kriesel, Qi Laiping, Su Yanzhang, Huang Min, Fan Hong, Yu Bowei, and Yu Jiayi.

ABBREVIATIONS

BCUC	Bank and Corporation Union Cup
CBA	Chinese Baseball Association
CBL	China Baseball League
CPBL	Chinese Professional Baseball League
CTBA	Chinese Taipei Baseball Association
IBA	International Baseball Association
IOC	International Olympic Committee
KMT	Kuomintang (Nationalist Party)
LLB	Little League Baseball
MAAG	Military Assistance and Advisory Group
NPB	Nippon Professional Baseball
PONY	Protect Our Nation's Youth
PRC	People's Republic of China
ROC	Republic of China
RSEA	Retired-Serviceman Engineering Agency
SBL	School Baseball League
TML	Taiwan Major League

NOTE ON ROMANIZATION OF CHINESE NAMES

There are four common ways to render Chinese names into English: (1) the Pinyin system used by mainland China; (2) the Wade-Giles system invented by the Qing dynasty and used on Taiwan; (3) the Tongyong system developed during the late 1990s and used on Taiwan; and (4) idiosyncratic spellings and English Chinese name combinations adopted by individuals (for example, P. P. Tang). The situation on Taiwan is very confusing because all four types of romanization are used on the island. A foreigner can easily get lost on Taiwan because the names of roads and streets are often written using one system along one stretch but written in another system along another section. Likewise, the same person can appear to have three different names depending upon the system being used to spell that name. The United Nations accepted the Pinyin system as a standardized Mandarin romanization system in 1986. Thus, to avoid confusion, the entire book will use the Pinyin style. For example, U.S.-based players Tsao Chin-hui and Chen Chin-feng are written as Cao Jinhui and Chen Jinfeng, respectively. However, because of common usage, some names and terms will be rendered using traditional spellings. Thus the reader will encounter Chiang Kai-shek, Taipei, and the names of Chinese Professional Baseball League teams, among others.

INTRODUCTION

The first Europeans to reach Taiwan came in the early sixteenth century and were Portuguese sailors, who called the place *Ilha Formosa* (Beautiful Island). The island's name was possibly more appropriate in the days when it was covered by virgin forest and not by the factories of the present day.

Taiwan lies off China's coast, separated from the mainland by the Taiwan Straits. Shaped roughly like a tobacco leaf, the island is about two hundred and fifty miles long and at its broadest point around ninety miles wide. The Central Mountain Range bisects Taiwan from north to south, and about two-thirds of the island is covered with forested peaks. The island enjoys an oceanic and subtropical monsoon climate influenced by its topography. Summers are long and accompanied by high humidity, while winters are short and usually mild. Generally speaking, weather and climate render the place eminently suitable for baseball.

From the popular pickup games in the eastern provinces to the professional outings in Taipei of such teams as the Brother Elephants, island baseball has developed a culture that is uniquely Taiwanese. At the ballparks, which are comparable in size to Minor League stadiums in the United States, players chew watermelon seeds, fans bang drums, and cheerleaders sing songs through a microphone for the entire game. Fans also hang pineapples outside the home team's dugout when the team suffers a losing streak. This custom derives from the Taiwanese for "pineapple," *wanglai*, which means "bring us good luck." Sometimes whole teams are brought to Buddhist or Daoist temples to worship and ask for good luck. One may label this practice as superstition, but it is a part of Chinese culture. Large groups of diehard Internet fans, such as the Internet Elephants, attend games together. Alcohol is rarely consumed at Taiwanese games; vendors sell local Taiwanese delicacies, such as Taiwanese fried chicken, oyster omelets, pigs' blood cakes, Taiwan sausages, and pearl milk tea (tapioca milk tea).

Uniquely Taiwanese is also the custom among players of making and drinking tea to calm their nerves after an exciting or exhausting game. Some players spend large sums of money for tea sets that produce a high-quality tea. Typically one player prepares the tea, and his teammates surround the table, talking and chatting. The occasion becomes a small social gathering.

In the clubhouse players rarely use Mandarin, the island's official language, but rather speak Taiwanese, which is a dialect of Chinese. The reasons for using this dialect can best be understood from an outline of Taiwanese politics and culture.

Demographics

Taiwan has a population of roughly twenty-three million, making the population density the second highest in the world after Bangladesh. About fifty-nine percent of the population is concentrated in four cities: Taipei, Gaoxiong, Taizhong, and Tainan. Four ethnic groups inhabit the island: aboriginal peoples, Fujianese, Hakka, and mainlanders. The latter three belong to the same Han-speaking family of immigrants.

The eastern part of Taiwan has the highest proportion of aborigines on the island. These people, who came from southern China and Austronesia, comprise thirteen ethnic groups, with their population of four hundred and fifty thousand accounting for only about two percent of the total Taiwanese population. There are large differences in the size of each aboriginal group, which are spread over a large area.

The aboriginal peoples have been marginalized and isolated politically, economically, and culturally. Indeed, it was only a century ago that the tribal societies were integrated into the system of the modern nation. Consequently, the aborigines constitute an underclass and are overrepresented in the ranks of the socially and economically disenfranchised. For them baseball has become a means for social and economic advancement.

Spread throughout the rest of Taiwan are the Fujianese and the

Hakka, descended from Chinese settlers that began arriving on the island some six hundred years ago. The fourteen million Fujianese make up approximately seventy percent of Taiwan's population, and the three million Hakka account for around fifteen percent.

The final group, the mainlanders, are Taiwan's newcomers. The mainlanders arrived in 1949 when Kuomintang or Nationalist Party (KMT) military troops and their followers from every province in China migrated to the island in what may be the largest elite immigration of the last century. The mainlanders' two and a half million account for eleven percent of Taiwan's entire population.

The Han Chinese imported their culture with them. Thus the religious and cultural life of Taiwan is dominated by a polytheistic blend of ancestor worship, Buddhism, Daoism, and folk religions. Buddhism is the most popular religion, with approximately three and a half million followers and over four thousand temples. Daoism is viewed as an indigenous religion and has around four and a half million practitioners.

Although viewed by many foreigners as a religion, Confucianism is more a philosophy than a religion. Accordingly, Confucian temples are halls to honor Confucius rather than places of worship. A main tenet of Confucianism is respecting seniority in the family. Further, social roles and children's obligations to do well in academic study are strongly emphasized, especially in Han Chinese families. As a result, Confucianism cultivated an antiphysical or sedentary culture that profoundly affected the development of sports in Taiwanese society. The Confucian influence will be thoroughly examined in later chapters.

History

The root of Taiwanese population and cultural diversity lies in the island's history, marked by the arrival of several waves of immigrants. Taiwan was originally settled by the ancestors of the aborigines, who inhabited the low-lying coastal plains of the island. They called the island Pakan. From the fourteenth century through the eighteenth, the aborigine peoples were joined by large numbers of Chinese settlers from the Holo-speaking province of Fujian and the Hakka-speaking province of Guangdong. Although they were Han Chinese, their purpose for emigrating was not for territorial expansion of China but to flee local living conditions and taxes.

Throughout the Ming Dynasty (1368–1644) Taiwan was insignificant in the eyes of the imperial government, who had no intention of claiming sovereignty over the island. The imperial court was busy countering the threat posed by the northern nomads, especially the Mongolians.

This lack of mainland interest permitted foreign powers to set up trading stations in Taiwan. In 1642 the Dutch East India Company, for example, as a part of Holland's expanding global mercantile activities, established a fortress named Fort Orange on Taiwan. First, however, the Dutch had to drive out the Spanish, who had occupied the northern part of Taiwan.

Two years later a leading Ming general named Zheng Chenggong (also known as Koxinga) decided to cross the straits to occupy Taiwan. Zheng had suffered a crushing defeat at the hands of the Manchus, who then established the Qing Dynasty in China in 1644. Zheng planned to use Taiwan as a base from which eventually to recover the mainland. His fleet landed on the island and eventually drove out the Dutch in 1662. Zheng's motto, "Overthrow Qing, Restore Ming," made him a sacred symbol and a national hero for the KMT three centuries later. The reign of the Zheng family on Taiwan finally ended when they surrendered to the Qing Dynasty, who launched a surprise attack on the island in 1683.

Over the next two centuries the increasingly sinicized Manchus promoted Confucian practices on Taiwan. As Han Chinese families and permanent settlements grew during the nineteenth century, life on the island gradually came to resemble that of the mainland. Some island families had their sons trained in classical learning in order to enable them to take civil service examinations and thereby enter the state bureaucracy, which held the most cherished status in Chinese society.

After nearly two hundred years of peace and self-sufficiency, China suffered a series of humiliations inflicted by foreign powers. Most importantly for Taiwan, in 1894 China was defeated by Japan and ceded the island to the victor. As a result, Taiwan's development diverged from that of China, and it was during the fifty-year Japanese occupation that the notion of modern sports was introduced to the island's population. Thanks in large part to an aggressive assimilation plan by the Japanese, baseball took root on the island and gradually won over a skeptical public.

Japan's reign on Taiwan was brought to an end with the Japanese defeat by the allied forces in World War II, and on October 25, 1945, Taiwan was officially handed back to the Chinese KMT government, which had overthrown the Qing Dynasty in 1911.

Relations between the KMT and Taiwan's inhabitants soon ran into trouble. The 2/28 incident occurred less than a year and a half after Taiwan was returned to China. It erupted when antitobacco-smuggling KMT agents attempted to confiscate black market cigarettes from an elderly Taiwanese woman. She resisted and was pistol-whipped by the agents. As a result, a crowd gathered, and a warning shot fired by one agent went astray killing an onlooker.

This incident led to a petition by the people of Taipei to demonstrate on February 28, 1947, thus the name 2/28. On that day government troops shot at the petitioning crowds, and the demonstration turned into a fight against the government and went on to become a bloody conflict between Taiwanese and mainlanders. Once fighting had broken out, it spread across the island like a fever. The island-wide program of arrest and slaughter that followed became known as country sweeping. Many of the native elite of Taiwanese society were killed, and there were other heavy Taiwanese causalities, with a death toll somewhere between ten and twenty thousand (figures vary).

On the mainland the KMT was faced with another crisis when war broke out in China between the KMT and the Communists. In October 1949 Chairman Mao declared victory, formally establishing the People's Republic of China (PRC). General Chiang Kai-shek and his remaining six hundred thousand troops and over one million loyalists fled to Taiwan, which was declared to be an anti-Communist and free China.

As a government in exile the KMT essentially displaced the entire governmental and social infrastructure that had previously existed on Taiwan. Those who fled to Taiwan were for the most part ultrapatriotic soldiers and members of the government who viewed their retreat as a temporary setback. It was their belief that they would soon reclaim the mainland and return to their rightful positions. But months turned into years and then into decades. Yet the KMT still clung to the firmly held belief that there was only one China. Its leaders believed that they were the legitimate rulers of all of China (even Mongolia). The PRC, likewise, viewed itself as the only legitimate government of China. Both sides, however, agreed on one point: Taiwan was part of China.

The issuing of the "Temporary Provisions Effective During the Period of Communist Rebellion" on May 9, 1948, and the imposition of martial law on May 20, 1949, put Taiwan under the thumb of extreme authoritarianism and compromised the rights of Taiwan's people—freedom of assembly, freedom of association, freedom of speech, freedom of the press, and freedom of movement. Military rule would drag on for thirty-eight years—the longest continuous martial law rule in world history.

The KMT's first cultural objective in Taiwan was to eradicate any vestige left by the Japanese and to make the Taiwanese people Chinese. Thus the educational system that was established and the values that were promoted came from China and contained no trace of Taiwanese culture. It is understandable that the mainlanders wanted to transplant Chinese thinking to Taiwan. In so doing, they not only integrated the Taiwanese into the Chinese system but also suppressed the possibility of a call for Taiwanese autonomy or even independence. The aim of the KMT was to instill in the public an affection for the Chinese homeland and a filial loyalty to the paramount leader. Consequently, beginning in extreme youth, children were taught to be "righteous Chinese"; otherwise, they risked shaming themselves, their families, and their country. The implementation of an official language policy that called for the speaking of Mandarin and prohibited the speaking of Holo in public was also intended to compel the Taiwanese to think of themselves as Chinese.[1]

Throughout the 1960s and 1970s the KMT government promoted the Chinese Cultural Renaissance Movement. This movement restored traditional Chinese culture and articulated that Taiwan was the sole legitimate representation of China in order to counterbalance the Cultural Revolution trumpeted by Mao on the mainland. The purpose of the Cultural Revolution was to destroy Confucianism, which Maoists accused of being a feudal philosophy that would obstruct the creation of a Communist society. The Chinese Cultural Renaissance, on the other hand, tried to restore traditional Confucian culture by emphasizing family and ethics. An integral part of the movement was overseas cultural propaganda, which sought to solicit members of the Chinese diaspora to identify with the Republic of China (ROC). In these years Taiwan's first Little League Baseball championships provided the perfect arena for the KMT to manipulate and control Taiwanese national identity domestically and internationally by using the myth of the world championship won by Taiwanese teams.

International Pariah

After the Korean War began in 1950, President Truman pledged that the United States would protect Taiwan against possible attack from mainland China. However, American foreign aid would not last forever. In April 1971 the PRC invited the American national team playing at the World Table Tennis Championship in Japan to visit China. This invitation was dubbed "Ping-Pong diplomacy," and it produced extensive U.S. press coverage that proclaimed this step as the precursor of China's opening itself to American visitors. Henry Kissinger visited the PRC and announced that President Nixon would visit the following year.

These visits presaged a change in Taiwan's international image and relations. And indeed, those changes were soon in coming with the United States announcing that it favored United Nations membership for PRC-run China. Shortly thereafter, Taiwan was voted out of the UN via Resolution 2758.

Taiwan suffered further setbacks. Beginning in the mid-1970s, it became an international pariah as most nations chose to recognize the PRC as the sole legitimate government of China. Taiwan even lost U.S. recognition in 1979.

After the PRC normalized relations with the United States, it proposed "one state, two systems." But Chiang Ching-kuo, then the leader of the KMT, countered with the "three nos" (no negotiation, no contact, and no compromise). Despite these differences, the two sides began developing a peaceful relationship.

During this time economic development moved to the top of the KMT's national development agenda. Taiwan adopted a more reflective and pragmatic approach to its foreign policy. Chiang Ching-kuo outlined a strategy of total diplomacy in February 1973. He envisioned a mobilization of every kind of resource—political, economic, scientific, technological, cultural, and sporting—in order to develop substantial links with other states with which Taiwan no longer had official relationships.[2]

As the situation deteriorated after the United States withdrew recognition in 1979, the KMT no longer vied for the governance of China. Taiwan began adopting so-called sporting diplomacy in order to enhance its international visibility. In this way it reminded the international community that the ROC still existed in the world. Thus the KMT started to intervene politically and financially in baseball in order to create a myth of Taiwan as home to world champions, and consequently, baseball teams in one sense became diplomatic vanguards to the rest of the world.

Additionally, the government used satellite transmission to make the Taiwanese people feel that they were part of the competition and, most importantly, to be proud that they were Chinese. Even though international society had already chosen the PRC as the sole legitimate government of China, the KMT used Little League Baseball (LLB) triumphs to solicit overseas Chinese support and to comfort domestic Taiwanese.

The Separation of Taiwanese Identity

Even as the KMT wrestled with bolstering its international image, it faced domestic challenges. In the late 1980s President Chiang was forced to reevaluate the continuation of martial law. Externally a popular revolt expelled Philippine President Marcos, and government opponents in South Korea were calling for elections there. Domestically in 1985 political and financial scandals occurred that tarnished the KMT's image. As a result, Chiang allowed retired soldiers to visit their relatives in mainland China. Subsequently, on July 14, 1987, the government lifted martial law. The move ultimately paved the way for the formation of the island's first professional baseball league.

Further changes followed. When Li Denghui came to power in 1988 after Chiang's death, he announced that the KMT could not exercise authority over mainland China and should admit to that fact; he argued that from such an admission pragmatic policies could result. In May 1991 Taiwan terminated the "Temporary Provisions," thus formally ending the forty-two years of civil war with the PRC and recognizing the Communist regime on the mainland. The PRC was more than willing to broaden relations with Taiwan, but it refused to denounce the possible use of force against the island. The two sides reached an impasse when the Democratic Progressive Party candidate Chen Shuibian, who supports Taiwanese independence, was elected president in 2000.

Despite being less dogmatic and more agile than in the past, Taiwan could not hide the difficulty of its diplomatic status, which has official relations with only twenty-four countries. Being shut out of major international organizations, Taiwan focuses on second-track diplomacy, that is, taking part in economic, social, sporting, and cultural organizations that would not provoke protests from the PRC. Thanks to the International Olympic Committee (IOC), Taiwan was able to participate in sporting events under the name Chinese Taipei, a policy later known as the Olympic formula. To this day, Chinese Taipei adorns the uniform of Taiwanese squads playing abroad.

The KMT's acceptance of baseball was eventually accompanied by a more general shift in the government's attitude toward things Taiwanese. This alteration—an abandonment of de-Taiwanization and de-Japanization—began with the lifting of martial law in 1987. The governmental about-face sharply accelerated when President Li took power and began to launch programs of Taiwanization. In 1992 the legislature passed a resolution that newborn children would have their birthplaces registered instead of their provincial homes.[3] This measure was designed to diminish ethnic division and to promote social integration. In 1997 an educational reform was announced that required junior high students to study Taiwanese history and culture in their first year. Courses on China and the rest of the world would be in the second and third years, respectively. This step was a bold one in the process of sweeping pan-Chinese or greater-Han chauvinism aside.

Under the leadership of proindependence presidents Li Denghui and Chen Shuibian, baseball became a useful tool for the construction of a Taiwanese national identity that is distinct from that found in the PRC, which prefers soccer and basketball. More evidence of the growing sense of nationalism on Taiwan is the reform of banknotes, which traditionally only bore portraits of Chiang Kai-shek and Sun Yat-sen. The new banknotes contain strong images of Taiwanese identity and local flavor, such as Formosan sika deer, Mount Morrison, and, of course, baseball, with notes showing the players of Nanwang Elementary School jumping in delight after winning the national championship.

Like the history of Taiwan, the history of Taiwanese baseball has had a number of distinct periods, each possessing a slightly different character and all contributing to the current state of the game. The first of these periods was the introduction of baseball to the island by the Japanese.

ONE

Wooden-Ball Finds a Home, 1895–1945

Shortly after the Japanese occupied Taiwan in 1895, they were amazed to discover that the Taiwanese had neither folk dancing, which existed in most other parts of the world, nor modern sports.[1] Along with the Japanese, westerners must find it odd that a nation could live without any form of physical exercise. Yet such was the situation on Chinese-influenced Taiwan before the Japanese brought the concept of modern sports to the island.

In order to understand how the island could exist in a sports vacuum, one must understand the tenets of Confucianism, whose philosophy and ideology had been followed by several Chinese dynasties stretching as far back as 206 BC. Confucianism imposes a hierarchal order on the world in which sons obey fathers, women obey men, subjects obey rulers, and so on. Peace and harmony are maintained when everyone sticks to his or her position and does his or her job. Citizens revere their governmental leaders, and the leaders, being the elite of society, treat the populace with fairness and dignity.[2] The Han Dynasty (206 BC to 219 AD) adopted Confucianism as an official ideology because it emphasized subordination of the ruled and thereby legitimized and perpetuated the vested interests of the imperial rulers.

The Confucian saying "Those who labor with their minds govern others, and those who labor with their strength are governed by others" led to the culture of *wen* (sedentariness) over *wu* (physicality or martial prowess). This Confucian-inspired attitude rendered physical exercise trivial compared to academic study. Furthermore, the national civil service examination (*keju*), formally institutionalized during the

Tang Dynasty (618–907 AD), designated any profession related to physical strength as fit only for the lower class. The examination remained essentially unchanged until 1905. Since all civil officials were trained in the ideals of Confucianism, their Confucian ideas and manners permeated the entire culture and were consequently adopted by the masses.[3]

Prior to Confucianism, physical activity was acceptable. Indeed, the first record of physical exercise in a Chinese classroom dates back to the Western Zhou dynasty (eleventh century BC to 771 BC) when aristocrats were required to receive both academic and physical education at schools. However, after the Han dynasty ushered in Confucianism, physical education was virtually driven out of the schools, which emphasized moral and academic teaching. Other dynasties followed suit by adopting Confucianism as the sole legitimate ideology. The consequence was that for over two thousand years physical education was nonexistent in Chinese schools.

It is this sedentary culture that for centuries stifled the development of physical activities, including sports. Even when there was athletic competition, the main focus was on the cultivation of virtue and on the process rather than on outcome. These goals are compatible with the Confucian notion that men should live in a harmonious, patriarchal social structure. The only way to climb the social ladder was not through the use of raw strength but through a display of intelligence, manifested by passing the civil service examination. The athleticism of ancient Greece or the gladiatorial games of the Roman Empire would not be appreciated by Chinese society.

Since most Taiwanese settlers had emigrated from mainland China, Taiwan had long been a part of Chinese civilization politically, economically, and culturally. Consequently, Confucianism and Chinese tradition all contributed to Taiwan's attitude toward physical work, which was thought suitable only for the dregs of society. One Taiwanese headmaster went so far as to state that "students have to walk genteelly to classrooms. If a student is seen by a teacher running to the classroom, the perpetrator's bottom will be spanked five times. Then he will be told that students are not allowed to run."[4] This statement shows how despised the use of body was in the past.

Additionally, the Taiwanese also inherited from mainland China three habits that hugely hindered the development of sport: opium smoking, footbinding, and the pigtail. According to statistics from 1900, there were one hundred and seventy thousand Taiwanese who were legal opium users. Two-thirds of Taiwanese women had their feet bound. This ratio was identical to that of men with a pigtail.[5] The pigtail or queue, introduced by the Qing Dynasty, was very inconvenient for a man who wished to participate in sports because he had to tidy it before and during a game.

The contempt for physical activity remained a part of Taiwanese culture until the Japanese occupation. One of Japan's first acts was to establish modern schools, which promoted physical education and singing. Taiwanese parents fiercely objected to both activities. They thought these activities were unproductive and meaningless exercises that would compromise their children's academic work, even if the children liked these activities.

Taiwanese parents also objected to another Japanese educational practice: Japanese teachers always joined their students in games and singing. The Taiwanese people could not believe teachers would act so because playing with students was seen as inappropriate behavior for teachers, whom the Chinese prized for their intellects.

The Wooden-Ball Era

As soon as the Taiwanese heard that the motherland had given the island over to the Japanese, they decided to create the Taiwan Democratic Republic, hoping to drive out the Japanese and return to Chinese rule. However, the republic was short-lived. The Japanese, armed with modern weapons, quelled the regional revolts one by one from north to south. Over the next seven years thirty-two thousand Taiwanese were killed, over one percent of the island's population. After the pacification a dual educational system was established on Taiwan: one for children of the Japanese and the other for native Taiwanese. Though not forbidden from participating in Japanese schools similar to those of the Japanese homeland, the Taiwanese were not accepted for admission in large numbers. Based on the thinking that "education is the sword with a multisided blade," Governor Shinpei Goto was afraid that full education would equip Taiwanese youth with knowledge that might threaten colonial control.[6]

During this tumultuous time baseball was introduced in Taiwan, though only the Japanese played it. In 1906 three high schools in Taipei formed baseball teams and competed with each other. The game appeared in the south in 1910 when Japanese staff working in a Tainan post office formed a team and Japanese soldiers followed suit. These teams were the first adult baseball squads in Taiwanese history. By the time the Japanese founded the Taiwanese Baseball Federation in 1915, the sport had spread throughout the island.

To Japanese officials, however, baseball was more than simply recreation. The new Japanese governor, Samata Sakuma, believed that the promotion of modern sport was crucial to imperial expansion.[7] The game encouraged physical fitness, thus preparing youths for and keeping adults ready to serve in the Japanese army. Wanting to let Japanese children have regular baseball training, Sakuma recruited from the homeland specialist coaches, who gave guidance to various schools between 1911 and 1914.

Baseball remained the prerogative of the Japanese during the early years of the occupancy. The colonists, who were arrogant about their national sport and thought of the Taiwanese as an inferior race, prevented locals from playing the game. One Japanese headmaster pointed out that "the existence of a baseball team at our school is a small issue. But if the game ignites the awareness of colonized youth, it will be a big problem."[8]

In turn, most Taiwanese parents discouraged their children's natural curiosity about the sport. Heavily influenced by Confucianism, Taiwanese adults regarded baseball as a meaningless game that would jeopardize their children's academic work. Additionally, they viewed the baseball itself as a "wooden-ball," which was solid and hard and which might lead to fatalities if someone was hit by it.[9] The younger generation was more accepting of modern sports since they were less steeped in Confucianism. Still, deeply ingrained cultural values and stringent colonial policies made development of a Taiwanese game impossible.

Assimilation and Accommodation

At the end of the First World War President Woodrow Wilson's liberal ideals and internationalism combined with a change of government in Japan to create a new era of political liberalization in Japan under the Taisho Democracy. As a consequence, the Japanese petty bourgeoisie and working classes found themselves increasingly able to participate in national policy debates. For the first time a true two-party system existed in Japan, as the Seiyukai party and the slightly more liberal Minseito party traded cabinets for a decade. Both parties courted the favor of the masses, repealing odious labor laws, allowing the spread of unionization, and passing the universal manhood suffrage bill of 1925.

Taisho Democracy was also a starting point for reform in Taiwan, but a far stronger impetus came from Korea, where a rebellion forced the Japanese to ease harsh colonial policies. In October 1919 Kenjiro Den was appointed by the Japanese cabinet as the first civil governor in Taiwanese history to propagate incremental assimilation and to end racially biased colonization.

Realizing that the elder Taiwanese were hostile to assimilation, the Japanese concentrated their efforts on education, hoping that Taiwanese children's thinking could be shaped and cultivated. With the adoption of the assimilation policy, the Japanese abolished the dual educational system, which was replaced by a single system.[10] Accordingly, the Japanese expanded the educational opportunities available to the Taiwanese, who were now allowed to attend high school and vocational school.

In June 1920 the Japanese Ministry of Education decided to promote public physical education and in September 1924 ordered all schools to hold a National Physical Education Day as an annual event. This day served the purpose of indoctrinating "collective behavior, moral training, [and] aspiration of national spirit" in the students.[11] The colonizers obviously wanted to use sports as a tool to integrate the Taiwanese into Japanese culture and to weaken the possibility of armed resistance. A similar tactic was used in Korea, where Japan used baseball for amelioration and cultural conciliation.[12]

Some Japanese feared that including Taiwanese in baseball competition would raise their national awareness. According to the island's main newspaper, at one primary school competition, Japanese school officials worried about Taiwanese cheering during a game.[13] Nevertheless, the trend of Taiwanese participation was unstoppable, and baseball continued to play a significant role in the assimilation policy, which demanded that both peoples play together and be treated as equals.

With the systematic introduction of baseball in schools after 1919, Taiwanese children were soon playing the game in every corner of the island. Since Taiwanese youth possessed less anti-Japanese sentiment than their parents, they had few qualms about baseball. Ichizuo Muramatsu, a Japanese banker working in Taiwan, recorded the transformation in a journal: "Now in Taiwan, even cats and dogs talk about balls, bats, and baseball-related things, . . . but in the first two or three years of occupation, if you took a bat and tried to swing, it made people think of a stick-carrying crazy guy wandering at night, which could cause misunderstanding and alarm."[14]

Student participation was thus robust, and antisporting sentiment among the population gradually faded as students discovered the pleasure of playing baseball. Further, Japanese teachers convinced parents that sports built physical strength, and athletic festivals held regularly at schools educated communities on how to play sports.

Students Teaching Mentors

In 1925 Japan sponsored a stage performance by Wu Feng, who allegedly sacrificed himself to eliminate headhunting practices among aboriginal tribes. This myth was invented by Japanese officials to justify the policy of educating the aboriginal tribes. At almost the same time the Japanese were using baseball for the same purpose, that is, to teach what were perceived as bloodlusting savages to be modern Japanese.

Four years before the Wu Feng play, a group of aboriginal children from Gaosha formed a baseball team, the first ever created voluntarily by Taiwanese. However, this embryonic baseball autonomy was short-lived. Japanese officials co-opted the team, renaming it Nenggao and offering players the opportunity to attend Hualian Agricultural School. The intent was obvious. No voluntary organization was allowed to exist at that time lest it become a means for spreading anti-Japanese sentiments. The aborigines had an especially long history of armed resistance to the occupation. By assuming control of the team, the Japanese hoped that baseball could divert aboriginal energy from armed resistance to nonviolent competition. Hualian governor Saburo Eguchi, who had assisted in co-opting the team, pointed out that "teaching barbarians to play baseball is an astonishing thing. However, barbarians are still human and also accept Japanization and education. By letting them get in touch with civilization, maybe some of them will become famous scientists or statesmen one day. . . . I want to correct these barbarians born with violent blood and let them feel the true spirit of sport. In addition this will demonstrate extensively to the world that we had a positive effect of teaching and civilizing barbarians."[15]

According to Eguchi, the aborigines were natural ballplayers. Having relied for generations on stone throwing to catch birds, they were endowed with good pitching mechanics. They possessed base-running speed and tremendous power at the plate. The governor worried though that the players were impulsive and confused in key game situations, perhaps due to their limited exposure to the sport. He further suspected that low self-esteem also factored into their inconsistent performance. "Barbarians psychologically think of themselves as an inferior race used to being manipulated," he noted. "Therefore they do not play with their full potential in front of a packed crowd. This part will have to be improved in future training."[16]

In 1924 Nenggao toured the island to test their strength. The result was satisfactory, with 5 wins and 4 losses. Their high level of competitiveness drew the attention of the masses in Taipei, where over twelve thousand spectators watched these "barbarians" with curiosity. The most touching moment came when the president of the Tainan Baseball Association cried as Nenggao finished the tour by waving goodbye to him. The boundary between different ethnic groups was diminished by what others saw as the innocence, toughness, and prowess that Nenggao showed in baseball games. As the *Taiwan riri xinbao* put it, "as time goes on, the barbarians are not a foreign race but cute compatriots. They were just living in remote areas that stagnated their cultural development, thus making them become violent barbarians. If taught properly, they are innocent companions."[17]

The following year, the Japanese government brought Nenggao on a tour of Japan to see how they would match up against eight Japanese schools. Much to the host country's surprise, the aborigines won three games, drew one, and lost four. The third match, against Aichi Icchu, attracted over twenty thousand people. When the team returned to Taiwan, four of Nenggao's players, Axian (Teruo Inada), Jisa (Dazo Nishimura), Luoshaweili (Masao Ito), and Luodaohou (Jiro Ito), were recruited by Japan's Heian High School to continue their baseball careers. Luodaohou even made it to the Japanese professional league. The performance of the Nenggao team boosted Taiwanese confidence, proving that they were not inferior to the Japanese in baseball.

The aborigines gradually lost their cultural identity as armed resistance was crushed and cultural indoctrination and systematic education were implemented. After being incorporated into the state machine, the aborigines used their headhunting courage on the diamond and played an important role in the development of Taiwanese baseball. In addition their baseball games helped to enhance understanding among Taiwan's diverse ethnic groups.

The Flowering of Baseball

The success of the Nenggao team encouraged more islanders to practice the sport. In 1929 the Japanese baseball association held the first ever National Elementary School Tournament. Five schools took part, and the only squad consisting entirely of Taiwanese players was that of Gaoxiong First Public School, now Qijin Elementary, who claimed the title. The Taiwanese team's upset victory over the colonizers created an islandwide groundswell of pride and laid a solid foundation for the further development of baseball in the Gaoxiong area. Two years later, in 1931, Taidong's Mawuku Public School team, made up entirely of aborigines, won the national championship, a feat achieved thirty-seven years before the stunning victories of the legendary Hongye.

Of the twelve Gaoxiong players Li Shixiong was the most famous. He eventually joined the Gaoxiong Port-Building club, the only Taiwanese on the team. Playing third base and hitting third, he even traveled with the team, taking part in the highly competitive Industrial League in Japan; this accomplishment was quite rare for an ordinary Taiwanese.[18]

Though the Taiwanese had won championships at the primary school level, they still could not challenge the superiority of their colonizers at the senior high school level, for which playing in the Japanese National High School Championship (Koshien) in Nishinomiya was the highest glory.[19] The Jiayi Agriculture and Forestry Institute (Jianong) finally shattered this glass ceiling.

The dominance of Jianong in the 1930s challenged the Japanese stereotype of the Han Chinese being unsuited for playing baseball. Manager Hyotaro Kondo, a former outstanding player who had toured the United States with his high school, dreamed of taking a triracial team (consisting of Han Chinese, aborigines, and Japanese) to the hallowed Koshien tournament. Although Taiwanese students constituted the majority at school, Kondo adopted an impartial policy, under which anyone who excelled could be on the team. His only goal was winning on the field. Each day, every player was asked to run two thousand meters and swing at least three hundred times during practice. There were also restrictions placed on the players. Kondo, for instance, prohibited players from going to the cinema.[20] The austere training regimen was hardest on players who attended school in the morning and worked on the farms or in factories in the afternoon before going to practice. They had to keep training until it was dark. Addressing the team, Kondo always said that "baseball is spirit. If your spirit is straight, you will play well; if not, you will play badly."[21]

Under this spartan leadership Jianong won the island championship four times between 1931 and 1936. Kondo's most successful team was that of 1931 when Jianong finished runner-up at Koshien, losing only in the finals. The team made such an impact at the world's most celebrated schoolboy sporting event that Jianong still evokes nostalgia in Japan.[22]

Jianong's performances in Japan created a fever in Taiwan. The following newspaper report demonstrated the fanaticism of the Taiwanese public:

> On the 20th [August 1931], for Jianong against Oruga Kougyo, the entire Jiayi city, around sixty thousand citizens, were very confident about this game. . . . When the victory came out

through the radio at half past two in the afternoon, all of Jiayi city indulged in absolute joy. Some fans even drove cars or rode bicycles around Jiayi city spreading this exciting message to other Jiayi citizens. . . . On the fourth day of the tournament fans around the island crowded in the Taipei branch of the *Asahi* newspaper, which sponsored the game.[23]

The passion of the Taiwanese public for Jianong clearly revealed that baseball had rooted itself deeply in Taiwanese culture. It was such passion that would propel the game onward even after the baseball-loving colonizers left the island.

The star of the 1931 Jianong team was Wu Mingjie who almost single-handedly brought the squad to the Koshien final. Since Wu was the ace pitcher, his manager relied extensively on him and used him as a starter in each game until the Koshien final, in which Wu finally lost 0–4, more than likely due to fatigue. Overall in the tournament however, the pitcher won three and lost one and batted .412.

Subsequently, Wu entered Waseda University, which had an excellent reputation in baseball circles, and continued to shine as a player. In the 1936 Tokyo Big Six Baseball League Tournament he had the best batting average and bashed out 7 homers.[24] His record would stand for twenty years until Shigeo Nagashima, one of Japan's most famous hitters, surpassed it while playing for Rikkyo University. Although Wu could have gone on to pro ball in Japan, he instead opted for the relative obscurity of a white-collar job.

Compared with the tri-ethnic Jianong, the Taizhong First Senior High team, nicknamed *Youshi* (young lions) was unique because it was composed completely of Taiwanese players, who created the team in 1930 with local support. Youshi's greatest goal was to beat Japanese teams, such as Taizhong Commercial School and Taizhong Second Senior High. Suddenly there was rivalry in the air. Overall Youshi's accomplishments were unimpressive, with 1 win and 9 losses. But their one victory was over their sworn enemy, Taizhong Commercial School. The Youshi victory once again fueled confidence that Taiwan could hold its own against Japan. Some Youshi players, such as Wang Feizhang and Hong Jianchuan, became ambassadors of the game, sharing their baseball knowledge with younger ballplayers after the KMT took over.

By 1939 there were numerous high schools located in the central and southern parts of Taiwan whose teams had several Taiwanese players. However, there was not a sign of Taiwanese players in the north, which was the political and economic center of Taiwan. The colonizers in the north preferred not to let the Taiwanese play baseball, while in other parts of the island a connivance adopted allowed some players to compete evenly with the Japanese.

Imports and Exports

Being a Japanese colony, Taiwan was home to many Japanese clubs, shipyards, railway companies, and universities with sports exchanges, including for baseball. The most famous baseball exchange occurred in 1921 when Herbert Harrison Hunter, an unimportant U.S. Major Leaguer, organized the first of a series of barnstorming tours of the Orient by professional players. He recruited part-time big leaguers and members of the Pacific Coast League. In January the U.S. team played seven games on Taiwan against mostly collegiate teams and won all of them.[25] In the first match the Americans demonstrated their devastating offensive power by thrashing the Taiwan Coalition 26–0. Despite the name Taiwan Coalition, all of the Taiwanese teams were made up of Japanese players. Notwithstanding the high ticket price, over five thousand people filled the ballpark, and many of them climbed up on the outside fence trying to catch a glimpse of the match. On the next day a newspaper used the headline "Sumo between Big Man and Little Child" to describe the outcome.[26] During the entire exhibition series the Japanese and Taiwanese witnessed the mighty power baseball played by the Americans.

In 1936 Japanese professional baseball was established with the help of Matsutaro Shoriki, who founded the famous Tokyo Giants, the most popular team in Japan.[27] Another team, the Tokyo Senators, immediately signed former Nenggao pitcher, Luodaohou, who was already twenty-seven. Although his professional career was unremarkable, winning only one game and having a batting average under the Mendoza line, he was the first Taiwanese-born player to compete in professional baseball. Ye Tiansong, who was a reserve player on the famed Nenggao team, followed in his former teammate's footsteps, joining the Nankai professional team. His best year was 1944 when he won the league batting title. Wu Xinheng, a product of Jianong, joined the professional team Dai-Tokyo and was then transferred to the Tokyo Giants. Over his eight-year professional career he hit .255, with 14 homers and 125 steals.

Without question Wu Bo was the most successful of the Taiwanese professional baseball pioneers. The former Jianong star athlete played seven years with the Tokyo Giants, then moved on to the Hanshin Tigers and the Mainichi Orions, finally retiring in 1957. Wu won batting titles in 1942 and 1943 and earned League MVP in 1943. He even pitched a no-hitter in 1946 and retired with a career .272 batting average. Owing to his distinguished twenty years as a professional, Wu became the first Taiwanese-born player to be selected for the Japanese Baseball Hall of Fame.

It is also worth mentioning that numerous Japanese players who grew up on Taiwan had distinguished baseball careers. Hiroshi Oshita, for example, dubbed Japan's Babe Ruth, later became a professional star. Other Japanese, such as Sunao Imakurusu, Isao Imakurusu, Seiji Sekiguchi, and Teruo Shimabara, also successfully made inroads in Japanese pro baseball.

The Japanization Movement

For the Japanese, Taiwanese baseball was a means to an end, for throughout the Japanese occupation the colonizers were molding the character of the Taiwanese to make loyal imperial subjects of them. Nations are bound together by common historical memory. After fifty years of occupation the colonists gradually cut the cultural bond between China and Taiwan by promoting their official language and degrading sinology. The Japanese also built a sporting legacy with the Taiwanese and a collective history. Fostering a sense of common memory for the Taiwanese to follow was a scheme through which the Taiwanese would be made loyal to the Japanese Empire and would fight for the emperor.

While the colonizers attempted to make the Taiwanese character more Japanese, their homeland saw significant political change. When the Great Depression spread to Japan in 1930, the political parties began to bow to the military, for whom raw materials and markets had to be protected at all costs. In 1931 Manchuria, endowed with abundant resources and many Japanese-vested interests, was invaded by the Imperial Army on the basis of a fabricated incident. After being condemned by the League of Nations, Japan immediately withdrew from that international body. By 1937 Japan was waging a full-scale war against China after the Marco Polo Bridge Incident. In September 1941 Japan joined the Axis with Nazi Germany and fascist Italy. Three months later the attack on Pearl Harbor ensued, and Japan implemented the Southward Policy, whose objective was the occupation of Southeast Asia.

As the situation grew worse, the Japanese assigned Taiwan a new role. Where before Taiwan was mainly a supplier of resources and materials, it now became a home to the heavy industry associated with munitions manufacture. As industrialization progressed, the infrastructure was further modernized.

In addition to gearing up Taiwan's economy to help fight the global war, Japan also militarized the island politically and socially, most notably through the Japanization Movement. The Japanese objective was to instill the spirit of imperial nationalism by promoting education, by encouraging the learning of Japanese language and customs, and by cultivating the character of loyal imperial subjects. By April 1942 Japan began to draft Taiwanese as "volunteers." Approximately eighty thousands were drafted as soldiers, and over a million more enlisted or were drafted as laborers. As the war dragged on, particularly in China, Japanese policies toward the Taiwanese became more aggressive and ferocious.

In the tense war environment it became untenable for baseball to continue normally. In Japan the Tokyo Big Six Baseball League stopped its activities in 1943. Professional baseball ceased to exist in 1944. In a totalitarian country gearing itself entirely toward war, military-oriented sports, such as the martial arts of judo and kendo, were added to school's PE curricula. In 1941, even before the Pacific war began, the New School Ordinance transformed physical education into physical training, which became a part of military practice.[28] As a result, recreational sports gradually gave way to military training.

In the early years of the Pacific war Taiwan's baseball was not significantly affected. For example, during this period Jianong created its third golden era (1938–1943), producing many outstanding Taiwanese—as well as Japanese—players who later became the foundation of Taiwanese baseball immediately after the Second World War.[29] In 1944 the drafting of Taiwanese youths put a temporary end to the island's baseball. According to Jianong player Huang Changxing, "two years before the retrocession . . . [I was] enrolled in Jianong school, . . . [and] the Second World War had entered its final stage. Actually, after the spring game on January 18 this year [1944], Taiwanese baseball was virtually put on hold."[30] Another player, Chen Lunbo, remembered that "ancient Samurai flags appeared in the ballpark; a grenade-throwing competition occurred during the game. Baseball was no fun anymore."[31] In spite of the deteriorating state of baseball in the closing years of the occupation, Taiwanese attitudes toward sports had already been transformed. After fifty years of Japanese occupation the Taiwanese people no longer regarded physical education and sports as meaningless and useless activities. Nor did the passion for baseball die out after basketball- and soccer-loving mainlanders took over Taiwan after the Second World War. The Taiwanese baseball players who came of age during the Japanese period provided the nucleus for amateur baseball during the KMT reign.

TWO

The Golden Era of Baseball, 1946–1967

L ate one autumn evening in 1952 KMT secret agents stormed the houses of all the players on the Miaoli county baseball team, an accomplished and famous squad sponsored by the China Oil Company. Although the KMT was targeting center fielder Xie Yufa, whom they considered a Communist, the entire team was taken into custody and given reformatory education for several years. In the end the players were released but had to live with shame and disgrace. It took the China Oil Company baseball team more than ten years to reenter the baseball world.[1]

Surprisingly, this incident was one of the few incursions of the authoritarian KMT government into the world of baseball during its first twenty years in power. After the retrocession of Taiwan the KMT, who had just fought a bloody eight-year war with Japan, was eager to rid the island of anything related to Japan. Thus in 1946 Japanese books were banned, and the following year newspapers printed in Japanese were punished. Further, all the names of streets, schools, and public places were now represented by Chinese characters or usage. Mainlanders even forced students to take siestas after lunch: such was not a custom during the Japanese occupation.

In light of these and other KMT actions, many on the baseball scene worried that Japan's sporting tradition would also be suppressed. True, after the bloody 2/28 incident school principals from the mainland may have initially discouraged baseball on campuses because of its Japanese link. However, objections to baseball were short-lived. Bosses of public corporations and schools who, although virtually all mainlanders, allowed their institutions to form teams. These teams created one of the great eras of Taiwanese amateur baseball. As long as the players and spectators did not involve themselves in any Communist conspiracy, the KMT had no reason to oppose the game; KMT officials even turned a blind eye to players speaking Holo or Japanese. At the time Chiang Kai-shek was more afraid of socialism than of a Taiwanese independence movement.

In a small way Chiang saw baseball as aiding in his goal to retake the mainland. That goal was always important to him. Despite harsh economic conditions after the Second World War, he spent eighty-five to ninety percent of the entire government's budget on defense.[2] At the same time he shouted the slogan "One year of preparation, two years of conquest, three years of mop up, and five years of success" in order to boost the morale of mainlanders on Taiwan so that they would not give up hope of returning home. The military strongman aspired to retake the mainland and thus created an attitude of "citizen militarism." It was therefore understandable that he emphasized military combat and physical exercise like baseball in order to fulfill his dream.

Mainlanders and Sports

Although the KMT tolerated baseball, the mainlanders, particularly the military, preferred soccer and basketball. This mainland preference for other sports than baseball led the KMT to dispense with the Yuanshan Baseball Ground, a holy symbol for all schools fighting for the ultimate championship in the finals during the Japanese occupation. The KMT transformed it into the headquarters of the U.S. Military Assistance and Advisory Group (MAAG). After MAAG withdrew from Taiwan, its headquarters was turned into a soccer stadium.

Soccer came to Taiwan when the KMT fled to the island in 1949.[3] Chinese soccer was now split in two, one branch being supported by the People's Republic of China on the mainland and the other by the Republic of China on Taiwan. Some famous players, such as Dai Lin-jing, chose to stay on the mainland, whereas Li Huitang swore allegiance to Taiwan. At the same time Hong Kong also divided into two factions, supporting either the ROC or the PRC. Hong Kong players who recognized the ROC, or so-called Free China, as the legitimate

Chinese government represented the ROC in international games; those who played for the PRC, however, could not participate in international competitions.

Joined by this Hong Kong foreign legion, Taiwan was able to secure satisfactory results internationally and promoted the sport domestically.[4] In 1954 and 1958 the Taiwanese soccer team, with the help of Hong Kong players, was able to win consecutive gold medals in the Asian Games. In addition the soccer team also participated in the 1948 and 1960 Olympic Games. Because of these soccer successes the international soccer tournament held in Taipei has always been played in front of sellout crowds. Nevertheless, the Merdeka Cup in 1971 was the last time Hong Kong participants played on the Taiwan national team.[5] Taiwanese soccer glory has never come back.

The mainlanders' other favorite sport, basketball, according to a historical overview published in *Minshengbao*, was brought to Taiwan in 1947.[6] Basketball was often a propaganda tool for Chiang and the KMT. The Overseas Chinese basketball teams from Hong Kong, Macao, the Philippines, Cambodia, Myanmar, Vietnam, Malaysia, and Indonesia always came to Taiwan in October to celebrate Chiang's birthday and to play friendly matches. This tournament was named the *Jieshoubei* (literally meaning "wishing a long life for Chiang Kai-shek").[7] The games were used as propaganda to show that overseas Chinese were supporting the ROC as the sole legitimate government of China while at the same time demonizing the Communist regime.

In 1951 General Zhou Zhirou assisted in the construction of the Trimilitary Basketball Court under the auspices of the mainlanders. The completion of the state-of-the-art Chinese Sports Hall stadium, with a capacity of twelve thousand, further boosted the popularity of basketball in Taiwan. Consequently, Taipei hosted the second Asian Basketball Championship, at which basketball fever rose to such a pitch and resulted in so much chaos that thousands of military police were required to maintain order.

Whether intentional or not, mainlanders supported and sponsored basketball over baseball. Nearly all of the basketball coaches and players were mainlanders or Americans of Chinese descent. Unlike Taiwanese baseball, the language used by participants was always Mandarin, with no Holo being spoken either through custom or prohibition. In short, there was an unwritten law that the mainlanders should play basketball, and the Taiwanese should play baseball. These choices showed in the ethnic differences on the national basketball team. Even in the 1970s over fifty percent of the team members were descended from mainlanders, and in earlier times the percentage was even higher.

Several factors dictated the mainlanders' preference for basketball, particularly as a school activity designed to promote sports. First, basketball is easier to play than baseball, whose rules are often too complex for beginners to understand. Second, baseball is more expensive and time-consuming than basketball. Third, Taiwanese, the product of two generations of playing baseball, also picked up the more easily mastered basketball, while mainlanders just could not cross the cultural gap to play baseball. As a result, from 1955 through 1975 the national baseball team had only one mainlander. Mostly the team was composed of Taiwanese and aborigines along with several Hakka.

Mainlanders' ignorance of baseball was also shown by the appointment of Xie Dongmin to the Taiwan Provincial Baseball Committee (later named the ROC Baseball Committee), which controlled all baseball affairs on the island.[8] Xie was a Taiwan-born financier who left for China at the age of eighteen and had his university education on the mainland, where he stayed for twenty-two years. His appointment showed that the mainlanders had neither the interest in nor the knowledge of baseball needed to appoint a person who was born on Taiwan and educated in Japanese schools so as to be familiar with the game. Xie Guocheng, the so-called Father of Youth Baseball, succeeded Xie Dongmin. Unlike his predecessor, Xie Guocheng was thoroughly Taiwanese, raised and educated under the Japanese. This appointment was an anomaly during this period when mainlanders controlled all the important political, economic, and cultural positions. But in baseball, mainlanders eventually allowed the Taiwanese to manage themselves, as long as the islanders did not advocate policies against the government.

Although basketball was less glamorous than soccer, Taiwan still won two silver medals in the Asian Games and took part in four successive Olympics beginning in 1948. These basketball victories, along with those in soccer, were good propaganda for the KMT as they solicited the aid and approval of overseas Chinese and proclaimed the KMT's legitimate status as the government of China. Baseball, on the other hand, wasn't an official Olympic event until 1992, and the KMT considered the game to lack the international prestige of basketball and soccer. So although baseball was not discouraged, it was not encouraged, as it lacked value in the eyes of the KMT ruler. It was not until Taiwan was ostracized from every international body in the 1970s that baseball became the most important means of promoting Taiwan's international visibility.

A Flourishing Pastime

Although grassroots baseball was not nurtured by the KMT government until the 1970s, the first twenty years of KMT rule marked an important era in which baseball actually flourished without help either from the state or from the business community. Taiwanese parents were willing to let their children play baseball because they were fans or had been players themselves during the Japanese occupation. Additionally, the game provided average people with stable jobs that were precious during periods of high unemployment. Thus players could both enjoy participating in the game and also have above-average salaries.

Baseball was also an important means for the Taiwanese to preserve their culture and in particular their language. The Holo language, popularly spoken on the street and in homes, was despised during the KMT era because it was viewed as a second-class dialect. People of status would only speak Mandarin to display their superiority. However, during this period baseball teams were still allowed to speak Holo and Japanese, which in general mainlanders were trying to stamp out. Since most baseball players had learned Japanese in school and grew up speaking Holo, they reasonably had to use both languages to communicate, as few knew a word of Mandarin. As a consequence, the publicly forbidden Holo and Japanese languages—both part of Taiwanese culture—could be spoken freely and proudly and without fear of punishment during baseball games.

Owing to Japanese influence, Taiwanese baseball jargon includes such Japanese terms as *picchah* (pitcher), *kyacchah* (catcher), *homuran* (home run), *fasutoh* (first base), *sekandoh* (second base), *sahdoh* (third base), and so on. These terms, of course, are variations of the original English terms, but it was the Japanese monikers that first took root in Taiwanese baseball.

During the KMT period amateur adult baseball reached its highest peak on Taiwan. The game continued to flourish in the south where the majority of Taiwanese lived. However, even in the north, although filled with mainlanders who clung to their original culture and values, highly skilled ball clubs developed and achieved satisfactory results.

Economics dictated the existence of these northern teams. Agriculture was the main industry in the south, which had many foresters, sugar factory workers, and agricultural union members who organized baseball teams. In the north, on the other hand, as soon as the KMT arrived on Taiwan, it made Taipei a political, economic, financial, and cultural center where commercial and financial institutions were established. The banks and corporations in the north could provide higher salaries and more stable jobs than business in the south. Thus promising players were willing to go to the north for those jobs and, consequently, to play amateur baseball there as well.[9]

As a result of this northern migration, the national squad in the 1954 Asian Championship had fourteen out of its eighteen players from the south but with most of them playing for banks and corporations in the north. Further, in the National Provincial Games, the island's largest sporting event, baseball teams from northern cities dominated. Taipei city, which fielded teams consisting mostly of players from the south, was formidable in the late 1950s, winning six titles in a row. Eligible players did not need to represent the cities in which they lived or were born. As long as a player could transfer his registered residence to a different locale by a given date before the Games, he was entitled to represent any city on Taiwan. This relaxed residency requirements resulted in some highly controversial baseball recruiting practices in Little League Baseball in the years to come.

In a sign of things to come the Games had some not-so-subtle political overtones. The first Provincial Games were held in 1946 when Chiang Kai-shek and his wife flew all the way from the mainland to Taiwan in order to host the opening ceremony. From then on the Games had to be held in October in order to commemorate Retrocession Day on the twenty-fifth. The Games' torch relay also had a political meaning because it had to be started at Koxinga's Shrine, a temple built in honor of the storied Ming warrior, Zheng Chenggong, who had driven the Dutch out of Taiwan in the seventeenth century.[10]

Yet despite such ulterior purposes, the tournament attracted athletes from Taiwan's two major cities (Taipei and Gaoxiong), five provincial municipalities, and sixteen counties. Baseball games were tremendously popular and were often played in front of sellout crowds.

In 1948 the increasing popularity of the sport in the north led to the formation of the Bank and Corporation Union Cup (BCUC), the first organized baseball league created after the retrocession. The league initially consisted of six state-owned bank and corporation teams that played soft-core baseball once every year in Xinsheng Ballpark. (Soft-core baseball uses a rubber ball instead of the regulation hard ball.) In 1960 the BCUC ended, signifying the demise of the Six Banks and Corporations era.

During its peak years the league was a living example of the massive popularity of baseball at that time. As one league player recalled,

> Each team was very amateur in the sense that they only practiced after work and on weekends. They did not get paid and just played because of their passion for baseball. Economic poverty and material shortages forced them to search for equipment used during the Japanese era. When they played games in Xinsheng Ballpark, it was packed with people wanting to watch the games. There was no fence or lines that separated [the spectators] from players. That was why spectators felt so close to them. No fee was charged to watch the games.[11]

The BCUC created a baseball fever in the northern part of Taiwan and was able to attract large crowds to its games because the skill level displayed was high.

In addition to the BCUC squads, other teams also were formed by regional sugar factories, electricity companies, railway corporations, and the Taiwan Tobacco and Wine Board that inherited a love of baseball from the Japanese.[12] All of these organizations were publicly owned corporations or monopolies controlled by the KMT and provided financial and occupational opportunities to players.

The private sector also organized teams that took part in various tournaments, but employee salaries in these companies was more modest than those of public corporations and thus private companies were less attractive to players. Yet two teams sponsored by private firms stood out during the 1950s: Daliang Soda and Weibao Gourmet Powder. The former provided each player with a private suite, a practice unheard of in the day. The latter offered excellent wages to its players and even organized a cheering squad made up of company staff. Although both teams soon vanished because of financial difficulties, their efforts to lure players can be seen as the precursors of the extravagant baseball commercialism of the latter half of the twentieth century.[13]

Military Teams

When the KMT imposed compulsory military service in 1951 for the purpose of preparing to reconquer the mainland, it forced all the men on the island to join the army once they turned twenty. Since eighty-five percent of the draftees were Taiwanese, it was inevitable that baseball was brought to the army, navy, and air force. Although senior officers were mainlanders, they still gave the green light to units that wanted to organize baseball teams. This move fit with a general military policy that each unit engage in sports so that every military man would be strong and healthy for future battle. As a result, along with baseball, basketball, soccer, tennis, and volleyball teams were created.

The navy and the air force fielded the strongest baseball teams in the early 1950s. During the intramilitary competitions of 1953 the navy won the championship in division one by beating the air force. In division two, the lower level of the competition, the navy was again champion, followed by the army, the air force, the Combined Forces Service, and the Ministry of Defense. The navy continued to show its dominance by winning several divisional titles in the mid-1950s, and they were the team to beat for the next ten years. Looking again at geography, it is not surprising that the navy at this time had the strongest teams in the military. As mentioned above, baseball is more popular in the south than in the north, and geographically KMT naval forces were concentrated in Zuoying, a military port in the southern part of Taiwan.

Military teams had lively competitions for the next twenty years. Moreover, the ROC Military Sports Association occasionally invited foreign counterparts to have friendly matches with military teams. In 1968, for instance, the Military Association invited U.S. servicemen stationed in Okinawa, four of whom had pro experience; the Philippine's Canlubang Sugar Barons; and three Taiwanese service teams for a three-nation tournament. The Filipinos, who had eight national team members on its squad, crushed the Taiwanese naval and air force teams 17–2 and 10–2, respectively. The Filipino squad finally lost 1–2 to another Taiwanese team, the Cooperative Bank, which had nine national members; still the losing team had led the match for the first seven innings.[14]

The navy's humiliating defeat signaled its downfall and led eventually to its folding in 1973. The naval players had to join the air force. However, the air force subsequently encountered player shortages and merged with the army team in 1990, since which time the army has been the sole military unit training baseball players.

Foreign Connections

Military teams were not the only Taiwanese squads playing foreigners. Civilians were also playing exchange teams, particularly from Japan. Xie Guocheng, a graduate of Waseda University, used his personal connections to persuade his alma mater to come for cultural and sporting exchanges in 1953. These friendly matches not only increased goodwill between both Japan and Taiwan but also raised the skill level of Taiwanese baseball. Waseda coasted to easy victories over a series of island opponents. Xie observed that "these games were not spectacular to watch. But the arrival of Waseda University had brought baseball fever to every part of the province, forcing the locals to repair the baseball parks."[15]

Four years later Waseda came to challenge again but achieved far more modest results, with 3 wins, 3 draws, and 2 losses. As Xie recalled, "it showed our baseball team's defensive skills had reached a certain quality. The only difference was the offense. In other words, batting and base-running needed to be improved."[16] The popularity of these sporting exchanges encouraged the Baseball Association to invite foreign teams on a regular basis, a tradition that still endures today.

The American connection with Taiwan was very important. With the outbreak of the Korean War, the United States sent MAAG, which exposed Taiwan to aspects of American culture, particularly baseball. American soldiers often used their spare time to play baseball among themselves and with Taiwanese teams. Some island players improved their skills through these ad hoc games with American soldiers. At the time the United States had nothing in common with Taiwanese either racially or culturally. The only thing the two countries shared was baseball and an anti-Communist policy.

Beginning in 1950, the U.S. Navy's Seventh Fleet, which was safeguarding the Taiwan Straits, sent naval baseball teams, as well as basketball, to Taiwan for sporting exchanges that attracted thousands of fans.[17] In 1953 the American office in Jilong invited Seventh Fleet teams, led by Rear Admiral T. B. Williamson, to play baseball, basketball, and volleyball in order to enhance Taiwan–U.S. relations.[18] According to Huang Renhui, a pitcher for the Taiwanese naval squad,

> At that time American soldiers liked to challenge our navy baseball team. Every game they brought a big box full of beer and Wilson baseball equipment, but each time they took all those back after the match. We were very bewildered; we thought the stuff should have been given to us for free. One person asked whether it was because we won every game, thus upsetting the Americans, who then did not want to leave us anything. Therefore we deliberately lost a game, and the Americans gave us everything. From then on, we never won against the Seventh Fleet teams, but we took a lot of equipment and drank a lot of beer.[19]

American influence in baseball extended beyond playing Taiwanese teams. The nationwide Provincial Competition was even renamed the Golden Statue Cup because of the MAAG, whose chief, William C. Chase, donated a Golden Statue sent in 1952 by the U.S. National Baseball Congress as a goodwill gesture.

Other Competitions

In addition to nationwide competitions, local sponsors and government also organized baseball events extensively. The Minsheng Cup was one such popular tournament that attracted many of the major teams in its twenty-one years.[20] Sponsored by a local newspaper, the *Minsheng ribao*, the tournament was first held in 1951, after which games were played every May until 1972. The Minsheng Cup certainly succeeded in its original objective of attracting good teams to the competition. Not only did adult teams and schools join the feast, but also the U.S. Seventh Fleet baseball team, which participated in the eighth Minsheng Cup and won the title. In 1966 the sponsors invited the Japanese professional team Tokyo Giants to Taizhong for spring training.

A Tainan newspaper, the *Zhonghua ribao*, which was a KMT party newspaper and thus an organ for government propaganda, subsidized a politically-themed tournament, the Chinese Cup. The first Chinese Cup was held in 1965 with the assistance of *Zhongguo Qingnian Fangong Jiuguotuan* (The Anti-Communist and National Salvation Corps of Chinese Youth) and the Taiwan Provincial Baseball Association. Xiao Zicheng, chairman of *Zhonghua ribao*, claimed that the event's objective was to "fully promote sport in order to enhance public health for the sake of national rejuvenation and strength."[21] The scale and ambition of the Chinese Cup was unprecedented in Taiwanese baseball because no other sponsor had the ability to host a competition encompassing every level of island baseball from children to adults.

Another competition worth mentioning is women's soft-core baseball, which was first played in 1954 and which was a groundbreaking event in Taiwanese baseball history. The state-controlled newspaper *Taiwan Xinshengbao* called it "pioneering in Free China."[22] The public was curious about female soft-core baseball, and the tournament accordingly attracted a great many spectators. There were three teams competing, with Shulin High School winning the championship. However, this competition lasted only three years, but the advent of female soft-core baseball demonstrated that a baseball-loving atmosphere had permeated the island.[23]

While the public focused primarily on adult baseball, school baseball went under the radar. Still the number of student teams mushroomed. For example, twenty-four out of the twenty-five area elementary schools took part in the Taipei City Cup in 1946. As a famous island politician Kang Ningxiang recalled, "during that time kids playing baseball had no pressure to win the world championship, nor [had they] the onerous mission of becoming a professional player when they grew up. The biggest wish in playing a ball game was to make papa and mama happy, have relatives in the neighborhood praise them, and surprise those little girls, who had just quarreled with them, and make those girls admire them."[24] Li Yuanzhe, the 1986 Nobel Winner in chemistry, remembered that he was so crazy about baseball during the late 1940s that he had to put the cow to graze in the outfield while playing the game.[25]

During this period baseball was a genuine pastime among the public, who enjoyed it with deep passion and affection. The unlinking of baseball, state, and market ironically helped Taiwanese baseball grow in a more robust and normal way, as people organized teams freely and voluntarily. As a part of civil society baseball was immune from state and commercial encroachment. Taiwanese players were allowed to speak Holo and Japanese, both of which were banned publicly by the government, without fear of being punished. Baseball was thus an unorthodox, but effective, way of preserving native language and culture. The amateur ethos in baseball was maintained until the Little League Championship that led to large-scale state support and completely changed the essence of Taiwanese amateur baseball.

THREE

The Myth of Hongye and the LLB Championship, 1968–1974

During the late 1960s and early 1970s the international environment gradually turned hostile for Taiwan, which found its legitimacy in jeopardy. The first blow came in 1971 when the UN expelled the ROC in favor of the PRC. Subsequently, President Nixon's visit to China in 1972 triggered a domino effect as other countries, such as Japan, started cutting off diplomatic relations with Taiwan. It was during this time that the KMT government hijacked baseball, transforming it into a nation-building tool to offset these debacles on the political and diplomatic fronts. The outcome was extreme. On the one hand, the state put massive resources into a sport that had been neglected for twenty years. On the other, it sowed the seed for the eventual disastrous decline of amateur baseball.

The Hongye Legend

The metamorphosis of Taiwan's elementary school baseball began after a team from Hongye, a little village in Taidong County in the eastern part of Taiwan, beat a Japanese team. Taidong County is the least developed region of the island, with aborigines making up the largest percentage of the population. The team of Hongye elementary school, which had only around one hundred students, was made up of Bunun aborigines living at high altitudes. No one expected the quiet village to create such an important—indeed permanent—impact on Taiwanese baseball.

Many Taiwanese still wrongly regard Hongye as a pioneer. They assume that there were few, if any, elementary school teams prior to

1968 and that it was Hongye that triggered baseball fervor on the island among such schools. This assumption is erroneous. As has been discussed previously, elementary school baseball flourished during both the Japanese and the KMT eras. Furthermore, by 1967 over three hundred elementary school teams had been organized, despite the absence of Little League glamour.[1] These were teams playing mainly for fun, with no awareness that international glory could be won on the diamond. Nor did academic workloads deter schools from organizing teams, even though these workloads were heavy. One has to bear in mind that the junior high school entrance examination exerted enormous pressure on schools, parents, and students because children had to study long hours to pass the joint examination in order to get into a good junior high school.

As early as 1960 Hongye already had a baseball team. It was not until 1963 when principal Lin Zhupeng took charge of the school that baseball was developed systematically. During Lin's first days on the job, he discovered that, although ninety-six students were enrolled, only thirty to forty regularly came to class. The family hardships that most students endured outside of school made them reluctant to attend classes, particularly since there was little prospect for their entering junior high school. Even those in class showed little interest in academic work. One day Lin was bemused to discover that absent pupils were actually at school but on the playground playing and watching baseball rather than attending class. This discovery inspired him: Why not organize a baseball team to attract kids to the school permanently?[2]

Two months later Lin encountered a serious problem not so much related to baseball itself as to intertribal conflict.[3] Taidong was the most problematic and complex aboriginal area on Taiwan and was inhabited by six tribes in addition to the Han Chinese. Occasional violence and unrest occurred in the county. The Puyuma aborigines, who lived in another village, had historically feuded with the Bunun aborigines of Hongye. Armed conflicts frequently took place as a result. The feuding petered out following years of pacification by the Japanese and the KMT.

Still old tensions simmered beneath the surface and caused problems for Lin's baseball program. The principal often took his Hongye team over to the Puyuma village for matches. However, during one period many of the Hongye players experienced digestive problems, prompting the Hongye adults to suspect that Puyuma wizards had cast spells over their children. No matter how hard Lin explained that there was no such thing as black magic, the villagers refused to believe him. As a result, parents would not allow their children to participate on the team, which in turn was forced to disband temporarily. Lin immediately invited in a doctor to provide a diagnosis. The problem was found to be hookworm that resulted from unsanitary conditions in the Hongye village. Assisted by the village doctor, Lin was able to defuse the situation by personally providing proper food to the village. As the players recovered, their parents' opposition to their playing ceased.

Lin eventually invited veteran Gu Yi, who had played baseball during the Japanese occupation, to work as a voluntary coach. Under Gu the team commenced dawn-to-dusk training, even during break times. In their debut season the Hongye squad won the Yanping village champions, followed by victory in the Taidong Mayor Cup. However, the first significant triumph came in 1966 when Hongye defeated all the competitors in the Eighteenth Children's Cup held in Taidong. Many people celebrated the team's victory.[4]

Though Hongye qualified for the Twentieth Children's Cup, the school, with little or no money, announced it was withdrawing from the national tournament.[5] Fortunately, Cai Kunlin, the general manager of Wangzi Publisher (whose target audience were little children) came to Hongye's rescue. He himself was a legendary figure, who had been jailed for ten years after being wrongly convicted of Communist espionage. After learning about the plight of Hongye, he remarked that the Hongye players "are readers of our youth magazine; if we don't give them a helping hand, who will?"[6] Cai sent his brother to drive a minivan all the way from Taipei to Taidong—a sixteen-hour trip—to pick up the young players and bring them to Taipei for the competition. Cai further ordered his staff in the publishing house to house the players so as to cut costs.[7]

Hongye instantly became the fans' favorite in the tournament. The drama culminated in the championship game between Hongye and Chuiyang. Hongye trailed 0–1 for six innings, and then Jiang Honghui's two-run homer gave the team the victory. Cheering crowds swarmed over the young Hongye players, with fans pouring down gifts and setting off firecrackers in the stands.[8] On the next day the *Lianhebao*'s headline read "The weeping willows (Chuiyang) of the mountain fully covered by red leafs (Hongye)."[9]

That same year, Hongye also won the Provincial Children's Cup championship, the most important competition for elementary schools, and followed that victory with a winning streak of thirty-five games. At the same time, Xie Guocheng, the president of the Chinese Baseball Association (CBA), invited to Taiwan a Japanese all-star squad of elementary school students from the densely populated urban Kansai region to play five friendly games against Hongye and a few other schools. It was, however, the first time that Japan had sent a Little League team to Taiwan. The exchange proved to be a milestone in Taiwanese baseball history, and most Taiwanese attribute current baseball achievements to Hongye's success.

It is difficult to assess the level of this Japanese Little League team. Japan had joined the Little League in 1966, during which year they sent a team to Williamsport, capturing fourth place. The following year, a squad from Wakayama, which was in the Kansai region, won the Little League world series by beating the U.S. team 4–1. The Taiwanese public mistakenly identified the Kansai visiting squad as the world champion, mainly because of media exaggeration. In reality only one of the Japanese players, Kazumasa Kiyotsugu, had been on the 1967 squad. Still the team sent by Japan was a coalition of players and should have had a leg up in competition against a village elementary school. Moreover, sixteen of the players on the Kansai team were clearly older than LLB rules permitted.[10] The head of the Japanese delegation, however, was honest about his players' ages. Since the contest was only a friendly one, the age limit was not an issue.

The Taiwanese had a number of advantages of their own. First, according to Xie, "the Japanese all-star team was physically strong and had better hitting and stamina than us. But the Japanese pitchers rarely threw breaking balls, a weapon that the Japanese regarded as dangerous because it could hurt a pitcher's arm. Therefore our pitcher had an advantage in this respect."[11] Second, Japan was forced to give up their familiar regulation ball and had to adopt the rubber ball commonly used in Taiwan. Third, in order to prepare for the games, Taiwanese officials arranged for Hongye and Chuiyang to be trained at a military base near Linkou for over a month. Finally, Hongye recruited one of its elementary school graduates, Gu Jinyan, to the team.

In the first game Japan scored a solitary run against Chuiyang in the first inning, thus winning 1–0. The following day, it was Hongye's turn against Kansai. The game attracted over twenty thousand fans to the Taipei stadium and was covered live by the Taiwan Television Enterprise. Hongye's pitcher, Jiang Wanxing (also known as Hu Wu-han), threw 14 strikeouts without conceding any runs. Hongye scored 2 runs in the fifth inning. In the next inning Jiang Wanxing and Jiang Honghui hit back-to-back home runs, scoring 5 more runs. Hongye won the game 7–0.

The Taiwanese spectators, along with the whole nation, were ecstatic. A newspaper account vividly captures the fans' excitement after Hongye scored its first run: "At twelve o'clock the game entered the fifth inning. Hongye scored the first run. The 'first' run caused a sensation among the crowd. Ladies and young girls were no longer afraid of the burning sun, taking down parasols and clapping on the stand. Young students were even more excited. Bamboo hats and handkerchiefs were thrown into the air. One umpire took a four-year-old boy in his arms, shouting 'Who's son is it? Who's son is it?'"[12]

In the third game Chinese United, mainly composed of Hongye players, played against Japan. After only a day of rest Jiang Wanxing again pitched a complete game, beating Kansai 5–1. He and Jiang Honghui each homered. The former hit a grand slam, which was said to be the play of the game.[13]

The fourth game was played at Jianhua Junior High School in the Xinzhu county. Over thirty thousand fans were present, even though, according to the organizer, only ten thousand tickets were sold. Those without tickets tried to catch a glimpse of the game by climbing up onto the balcony of the school dormitory and the roofs of nearby houses.[14] This enthusiastic response contrasted sharply with the lackluster Provincial Games, which attracted less than one thousand spectators per game. The starting pitcher was again Jiang Wanxing, who pitched the first five innings and added to his tally of twenty innings in only four days. Hongye won the game 5–2. In the last game Kansai finally beat Jiayi United 5–3.

Jiayi United defeated Hongye the following day, thereby ending the latter's winning streak at thirty-five. Despite the loss, the small Hongye village was sleepless that night as the aborigines danced and sang in celebration of their local heroes' triumph.

With its victories against the Japanese Little Leaguers, Hongye set its mark on Taiwanese baseball, and its influence was quickly felt. When the team began a series of around-the-island tours after its Japanese victories and stopped at Jiayi, it attracted over one hundred thousand fans.[15] The retired professional player Zeng Zhizhen admitted that it was after watching Hongye play that he vowed to become a baseball athlete.[16] The Hualian Baseball Association even asked Hongye for compensation because the team refused to take part in the planned friendly games with local teams, thus resulting in large financial losses for the organizers.[17]

The Power of Television

Hongye's islandwide fame rested squarely on the team's victories over the Japanese, despite its having won the Eighteenth Provincial Children's Cup two years before. Nonetheless, this accomplishment attracted little attention. With the Japanese competition, however, it was the first time Taiwan and Japan had held such a student baseball contest. Additionally, the Japanese team was touted as world champions.

Yet there was another important reason for Hongye's new-found fame: live coverage of the Japanese games on television. Such coverage was new because in the past baseball games had only been broadcast live on radio. Television provided a sense of being there that radio could never achieve. Viewers could see, not just imagine, a game, and the players became more than just names as fans could now watch the players' faces and their actions. To the Hongye villagers the games in Taipei appeared tantalizingly close and real, as if they were actually there, and the same sense of reality was true for all Taiwanese who watched the games on TV. Thus state-controlled television proved to be a powerful tool that beamed live pictures all over the country.

Media coverage of sports often plays a significant role in the construction of national identity, which comes to be an imagined community, as Benedict Anderson terms it.[18] The audience is positioned to become a group of patriots. Through television, with its hermeneutic narrative, a covered sport generates this sense of national belonging.[19] Thus the Hongye boys became surrogate warriors for a country that could not succeed on political and diplomatic fronts. One Taiwanese newspaper dubbed those players little soldiers, fighting against the mighty Japanese. This same newspaper's headline read "[Hongye] did not let the country down; little soldiers shocked Japan."[20] This headline reveals the extent of the nationalism that Hongye-Japanese games had engendered in the public. Indeed, public need to view the games was so great that the Taiwan Television Enterprise was forced to delay other programs and to broadcast thirteen hours of baseball in a single day.

In addition to creating a sense of national identity, TV had other effects: it personalized and dramatized. For instance, Hongye, a little-known village, suddenly became one of the hottest tourist spots on Taiwan thanks to media exposure.[21] Additionally, Hongye's ace pitcher, Jiang Wanxing, became a well-known figure overnight as he won three victories against Japan. The media praised him and attributed his wonderful performances to a hard-working attitude common to the aborigines.

Further, the players' economic hardships on and off the field were widely reported on TV, as well as in newspapers, and large state and private donations were the result. For example, the Taipei Import and Export Union gave four graduating Hongye players $30 each so that they could pursue academic work in junior high school. Xinzhu Commercial Vocational School gave the Hongye general manager $100 in appreciation of the team's winning against Japan. Taiwan Governor Huang Jie ordered the Taiwan Provincial Department of Education to allocate to the Hongye school $2,500 as a reward for Hongye's performance. It is interesting to note that though the government praised Chuiyang's performance, it only offered the team $60 since the squad failed to beat Japan.[22]

Television consequently brought Hongye into the public eye as the team played against the right opponent. What could be better than to defeat Japan, with whom the KMT had fought during the Second World War and who had occupied Taiwan for fifty years? And what could be better than to watch that defeat live on television? It is therefore this TV exposure that explains why most Taiwanese are convinced that island elementary school baseball began with Hongye, while remaining ignorant of the seeds that the Japanese long ago sowed.

The Overaged Player and the Forgery Scandal

Hongye's glory was soon tarnished by scandal, although the details mostly remained hidden from the general public. Indeed, in conversations over the years with fellow baseball fans, I have discovered that only a small number of people know about the scandal.

The key to the scandal lies in the names of the players. Looking at the Hongye roster reveals that several squad members played under assumed names.

LINEUP OF THE TWENTIETH PROVINCIAL CHILDREN'S CUP

1. Qiu Chunguang, left fielder
2. Yu Youren, second baseman (under the name Hu Fulong)
3. Jiang Honghui, catcher (under the name Hu Yonghui)
4. Qiu Desheng, shortstop (under the name Wang Zhiren)
5. Jiang Wanxing, pitcher (under the name Hu Wuhan)
6. Xu Heyuan, first baseman (under the name Gu Jincai)
7. Hu Mingcheng, third baseman (under the name Hu Xianzhou)
8. Gu Renyi, right fielder (under the name Qiu Jinzhong)
9. Yu Hongkai, center fielder

In addition to the regulars, Hongye had two reserve players: Jiang Yuanxing, who used the name Yu Jingong, and Hu Xianzhou, who used the name Chen Jinzheng. Another team member, Lai Jinmu, did not register but took part in the competition, replacing Gu Renyi and playing under the name Qiu Jinzhong. Apart from Lai, who was an Amis aborigine, the players were Bunun aborigines.

The reason for the players' use of pseudonyms, a practice sanctioned by the school, was that many of them were older than twelve, the official LLB age limit: Xu Heyuan was fourteen, while Jiang Wanxing, Jiang Honghui, Hu Mingcheng, Qiu Desheng, and Yu Youren were all thirteen.[23] Therefore in order to be eligible for the competition, team members used the names of other students who were under the age limit. In 1966 Taiwan had not instituted the nine-year compulsory educational system, and consequently, the six overaged players coming from disadvantaged family backgrounds could not enter junior high school. To do so required passing an entrance examination that these six did not have the education to pass. Instead, they worked part time in the mountains. Thus it was probably the case that the Hongye principal and coach exploited the situation by recruiting these older players under false names to circumvent regulations.

This name-borrowing process created some odd fallout. For instance, when the six overaged players came to the squad, Hu Xianzhou allowed one of them, Hu Mingcheng, to use his name. As time went by, Hu's playing skills improved. In order to provide him an opportunity to play the school officials assigned him another false name, Chen Jinzheng. A bizarre situation ensued in which Hu's teammate addressed him by his real name, while on the field he was known by his pseudonym.

Immediately after Hongye's victory over the Japanese, an informant told the authorities that Hongye had been using ineligible players as far back as the Twentieth Provincial Children's Cup. In response the Taidong district court prosecuted the principal Hu Xueli, the coach Qiu Qingcheng, and an administrator Zeng Zhendong on forgery charges and for producing fraudulent documents.[24] To prevent public humiliation that would surely have brought shame to the country, the matter was handled with as much secrecy as possible. During the trial the court deliberately met at night, and Hu, Qiu, and Zeng attended the trial six or seven times in secrecy to avoid media coverage. The scheduling proved to be successful, as very few people learned of the scandal.

On April 26, 1969, the Taidong district court sentenced the three defendants to one year of imprisonment but with two-year suspended sentences so that the men would not go to jail as long as they did not commit any crime within that two-year period.[25] The sentence was the most lenient possible because the court acknowledged the benign motives of the accused, who had promoted honor for their country and who had aroused baseball fever throughout the island.

Aftermath of Victory and Scandal

In a documentary film about Hongye, famous broadcaster Fu Daren observes that "we know of the forgery scandal of Hongye, but it does not diminish their important status in baseball. If it had not been for Hongye, Taiwan's baseball would not have developed so vibrantly."[26] This view is shared by most Taiwanese and thus perpetuates the myth of Hongye. But one columnist pointed out that "the sole purpose of victory prompted school officials to use false names and created an ominous philosophy of winning at all costs that paved the way for the future decline of Taiwanese baseball."[27]

The nationwide fame earned by the Hongye children was often replaced by tragedy. In later life many of the players involved became alcoholics when they could not find proper and stable jobs because of the poor education that they had received. Consequently, more than half of the Hongye team (seven out of thirteen) are dead. The famous pitcher Jiang Wanxing died quietly in 1991 of liver failure resulting from heavy drinking. Jiang's widow blamed the government for not taking care of these players adequately after they made such a contribution to the country.

And those contributions were very real, with the Hongye myth having two major effects. First, live TV coverage brought not only nationwide but governmental attention to baseball, which the government had ignored for twenty years. The government now noticed that the game was popular with the Taiwanese people, who played it freely and spontaneously. More importantly, the government realized that on the international stage baseball could become a powerful propaganda tool to promote a state that was being pushed aside in favor of the PRC. The result was the KMT taking an active role in Taiwanese baseball.

Second, the success of Hongye propelled other schools to organize teams that achieved unprecedented success. The victory of Hongye inspired the CBA to join Little League Baseball in 1969 and vie for a trip to Williamsport.

It is also interesting to speculate whether the Hongye myth inadvertently destroyed the autonomy enjoyed by elementary school baseball. Prior to Hongye, there were already three hundred teams, each of which had been developing normally and freely, though with some forgery incidents similar to that of Hongye. Although Hongye's success led to schools organizing teams, its role in promoting national honor meant that the sport was no longer played in the spirit of fun.[28] This change sowed the seed for a sharp decline in grassroots baseball, as shall be discussed later.

The Origin of the LLB Champions

The seriousness with which Taiwanese officials took the LLB can be seen in the way in which the teams that would compete at Williamsport were organized. From the outset the methods of selection were irregular. LLB regulations required that teams representing an entire country must be formed on the basis of community. An area with a population no more than fifteen thousand people needed at least four teams, from which an all-star squad could be formed after regional tournaments had been played. If the population was over fifteen thousand, a second league needed to be created along with another all-star team. However, the two leagues, though in the same community, could not form a combined all-star team.

When forming Taiwan's first national team, island authorities either ignored the rule or utterly failed to read the LLB regulations because the final squad was actually a national all-star team. In 1969 the CBA had set up the first ever National Youth Baseball Competition, dividing the island into four districts (east, west, south, and north). Each district sent its top two teams to the championship round. After five days of exciting contests, Jiayi Datong beat Taidong 7–6 to capture the championship. The national team was selected shortly thereafter, with nine Jiayi players selected as the backbone of the team, coupled with five players from other counties.

From mid-March onward, the team began a grueling training routine. In April they played two exhibition games with a Japanese squad from Wakayama. The results were shocking. Jiayi dropped both games, 2–6 and 2–9. Taiwanese baseball administrators lost confidence in being able to qualify for Williamsport unless the squad were strengthened. So the CBA changed the criteria of selection. According to the revised rules, a panel of baseball experts would select another fourteen players whose height was over four foot nine. These players would be thrown into a pool with the original team members of the all-star team, which was then divided into two teams, Red and White. The two sides competed in a best-of-three series, the winning team was then allotted nine spots on the national team, the losing team five. The result was a genuinely national all-star team, with nine players from the south, two each from the central and the east, and one from the north.

After the final squad was determined, the CBA had to decide on the name of the team. The LLB called for teams to be named for the districts or areas from which they hailed. Thus the team could not be called Chinese Jinlong, as islanders affectionately dubbed them, because "Chinese" is neither a district nor a county. Logically the team should have been named after Jiayi since Jiayi Datong had the most players (five) on the squad. But when the speaker of the Taizhong local council, Chen Qingxing, offered full financial support of the youngsters in their quest for the LLB championship, the team was named Taizhong Jinlong, although only two Taizhong players had been selected for the squad.

In late July the team headed to Japan for the Far East LLB Qualification, the winner of which would represent Asia at Williamsport. Just the experience of leaving the country was a treat for the Little Leaguers. Traveling abroad twice in one year was unusual for ordinary Taiwanese.[29] Under the island's martial law people were prohibited from easy international travel except for diplomatic and business delegations endorsed by the government. Political and economic measures were strikingly tight for fear of Communist subversion and capital outflow.

Jinlong's level of play was unbeatable, and they crushed Guam 16–0 and shut out Japan 3–0, thereby winning the trip to the United States. At Williamsport they went on to win the LLB world series by beating Canada 5–0, North USA 4–3, and West USA 5–0. All of Taiwan was euphoric. The media trumpeted how the Little Leaguers were models of Chinese citizenship. Lin Yiwen, president of overseas Chinese in Japan, said that "the performances of these little national heroes has left a deep impression on foreigners, who no longer think of us as the 'sick man' of East Asia."[30]

When the Jinlong players returned from Williamsport, the KMT honored them with an eight-hour parade in Taipei. Every player and coach was allocated a military jeep on which to stand and from which to wave to the crowd. Two-thirds of the city police force was mobilized to maintain public order.[31] The parade traveled along V Dunhua North Road, then snaked its way through major thoroughfares with more than half a million excited fans lining the streets, pedestrian bridges, and balconies of the famous Zhonghua Commercial Market. At the Military Officers Club and Presidential Hall the players rested and listened to politicians give speeches. In honor of perhaps their most ardent supporters, players lined up in front of Presidential Hall and shouted "Long live the Republic of China! Long live President Chiang!"

Despite the excitement and mania, those players now faced academic hurdles in high school since they had been playing baseball all year long and had hardly spent any time studying. Hoping to help them in school and to encourage them to continue their baseball careers, Song Meiling, Chiang Kai-shek's first lady, had them enrolled at Huaxing High School. This school had been established to look after orphans of military servicemen. The Jinlong players were the first nonmilitary students to enter it.

Little League Domination

The pressure on Taiwan's LLB representatives was immense. The Jiayi Qihu (Seven Tigers), who won the national championship and Far East Qualification in 1970, lost to Nicaragua in the team's opening game in Pennsylvania. It was widely reported that, when the game concluded, many Taiwanese watching TV or listening to radios threw the devices to the ground. Head coach Wu Mintian apologized to the nation, while coach Fang Shuiquan asked, "How can we face the public after we get home?"[32] Overseas Chinese mourned the team's loss by refusing to go to the stadium. Thus where thousands had crammed the stands at the opening Jiayi game, singing the ROC anthem and waving flags, only two hundred attended game two. To the Taiwanese the LLB was a crusade in which the duty of Taiwanese children was to bring home a victory.

The pressure only grew when U.S. President Richard Nixon visited mainland China in July 1971. His overtures to the PRC cast dark clouds over Taiwan, as looming on the horizon were the acceptance of the PRC into the United Nations and the expulsion of Taiwan.

Amid growing despondency over these events, the island pinned its hopes on a group of determined youngsters from Taiwan's national champion Juren to restore national pride and a sense of belonging to the international community. The entire nation stayed up through the early morning hours watching live telecasts of the games. Juren answered the nation's prayers by tearing through the competition, saving their most memorable performance for last. Juren's Xu Jinmu notched 22 strikeouts over nine innings, outdueling another brilliant young pitcher Lloyd McClendon of Gary, Indiana. McClendon would become a Major Leaguer and later the manager of the Pittsburgh Pirates. After Xu recorded the final out, many Chinese loyalists burst into tears, including Xie Guocheng, president of the CBA, and Shen Jianhong, ROC ambassador in Washington. After the game Shen treated the players to a full course western meal, which was rare for Taiwanese at the time. The ambassador also gave each player $20.[33]

Upon returning to Taiwan, Juren was treated to a victory parade similar to Jinlong's two years earlier. According to *Lianhebao*, after the players left the airport, the sound of firecrackers never stopped; the First Company department store set off a firecracker that, if stood upright, would have been seven stories high. Citizens left their work, markets closed down, and both the elderly and the young eagerly sought to shake hands with the players. One player, Li Wenrui, estimated that he shook hands with the crowd over two thousand times. Police escorts barely controlled the crowd and their motorcycles were toppled by fans pushing for a closer look at the procession.[34]

For days the players were showered with gifts, mostly from overseas Chinese living in the United States. These gifts included cash, bicycles, wristwatches, books, Parker pens (donated by China Airlines), milk, candy, sports shoes, and suits and other clothing.

The cash donations soon became the subject of controversy as embezzlement accusations were leveled at the general manager Lin Quanxing, who was suspected of pocketing some of the money.[35] Lin had announced to the players that the team had received cash rewards amounting to $7,835, of which every player was awarded $360 and the coach, manager, and general manager $486 each. (This kind of money was a great deal at the time since the GNP per capita in Taiwan in 1970 was only $389.)[36] Parents, however, had strong reason to suspect that donations by overseas Chinese may have been as high as $12,410. Since there was no mechanism by which to hold Lin accountable, the whole matter soon faded away.

The promise of fame and money created a baseball mania on Taiwan, and going abroad was suddenly the goal of every player, parent, and school. Even a trip to the Far East Qualification was a money-making opportunity. Parents and friends would instruct the Little Leaguers to buy lots of foreign products that were scarce or heavily taxed on Taiwan. The products were then sold in order to make extra money.

According to former Little League coach Tan Xinmin, the lure of these financial rewards led to much corruption:

> At that time parents gave money and presents [to coaches] so that their children would be on the team. Every coach wanted to take his team abroad because there were profits in it. When the overseas Chinese saw the national team, they threw U.S. dollars into the bus. Coaches would give a symbolic dollar or two to each player, who would be absolutely delighted. The rest wound up in the coaches' pockets. Unorthodox smuggling is another issue. When the team came back home, the authorities collectively granted fast custom clearance regardless of the restriction of two boxes of cigarettes and one bottle of wine. Players were told by their parents to purchase a dozen or twenty bottles, which would be sold at a higher price domestically.[37]

After Tainan Juren captured the 1971 world series, the eligibility of ace pitcher Xu Jinmu was called into question by LLB President Peter J. McGovern because Xu had represented Jiayi Qihu the previous year but had then jumped to Tainan the following year. To address the LLB's justifiable concern, Taiwanese baseball officials revamped their teams so that Taiwan appeared to be complying with the LLB rule that teams needed to be formed on a community basis. Taiwan had formed their national teams in 1970 and 1971 from regional all-star teams, a coalition of players from a particular region. From 1972 onward, the formation of the national team was assembled from county all-star teams. However, with a wink and a nod from Taiwanese government sports authorities and LLB officials, players continued to move around the country, although this movement was kept hidden.

This practice contributed to the establishment of an unassailable Taiwanese hegemony in the LLB. Over an eleven-year period the island's Little Leaguers amassed an incredible thirty-one straight victories at Williamsport. Many of the stars moved on to compete in the LLB's Senior League (age 13–15) world championship at Gary, Indiana. Here these seniors won nine straight games from 1972 through 1974, with most games being decided by a large margin. Beginning in 1974, Taiwan fielded teams for the LLB's Big League world series (age 16–18), held at Fort Lauderdale. Again, having an advantage over community-based teams, the Taiwan squad captured the world series in their first year in the tournament. Taiwanese LLB teams had a magnificent year in 1974, winning the championship at all three levels and thereby capturing the triple crown (*sanguanwang*), the holy grail of the LLB.

The degree to which Taiwanese baseball authorities moved around players just to field teams for the Senior League and Big League world series was astounding. In most years the island's best players at these levels were sent to one of three high schools—Huaxing, Retired-Serviceman Engineering Agency (RSEA), or Meihe—so as to look as though they were from the same school district. In reality, they actually came from every part of the island. For instance, the winning team of the Senior League world series in 1973 was from Huaxing High School, yet none of the squad was actually from the northern city of Taipei, the location of the school.[38] Eleven out of the fourteen players in the squad came from southern Taiwan.

Baseball with a Mission

Official sanctioning of this deceptive team-building was aided by the feeling of escalating international isolation. To counter this isolation, the KMT government resolved to dominate the international LLB scene.

Thus after the Juren victory amateur baseball came to depend less on a simple desire to play the game and more on heavy KMT involvement in a sport. Before 1970 there was no regular government budget for sports, let alone for baseball. What money was available was distributed according to the athletic preferences of KMT officials. These government grants to sports were therefore inconsistent, and the process was often opaque. That was why initially Xie Guocheng, dubbed the big beggar, had to raise funds himself in order that the national baseball squad could travel abroad to compete in international tournaments. So desperate was the funding shortage in 1969 that Xie even asked MAAG if a military jet could give the team a lift to Williamsport. MAAG had to decline because their jets could only be flown for military purposes, but in the weeks before the tournament it raised $7,598 in contributions from U.S. soldiers.

By 1971, however, the government had stepped up its subsidies and provided three-fourths of the cost of Juren's trip to Williamsport. The Ministry of Education, the Ministry of Defense, the Provincial Department of Education, and the Taipei City Council all contributed funds for the trip. This official KMT aid clearly demonstrated that the authorities took the necessity of Juren's playing in the LLB world series very seriously.

In addition state-controlled television was also willing to endure the high coverage costs, little of it paid for by advertising. In 1972 the China Television Company spent $4,500 to cover the Senior League championship final. That same year, the Little League final cost $95,000, in addition to over $18,250 in travel fees. Revenues, mainly from advertising, was only $60,000.[39] Though costs were massive, the KMT was more than willing to help meet television's end since the games were good propaganda.

In 1974 the Ministry of Education implemented a policy of fully subsidizing air fare for teams taking part in international competitions that had political significance. Accordingly, such international tournaments as the Asian camp games were deemed of less importance than summer camp-style competitions held in the United States. These latter competitions included Little League baseball, which received full government support.[40]

The money was considered well spent because the notion of "Chineseness" or the "Chinese nation" was embodied in the extravagant spectacle of the world championship, with which people were happy to identify as if they themselves were members of the team. Throughout history many nation-states with a culturally and linguistically divided population have had to manufacture a sense of national identity. Often the more unstable and divided a country is, the more likely its government is to use sports aggressively as a means to create nationalism.[41]

Baseball also served another KMT need. During the 1970s the hostile international environment made the Taiwanese uneasy; they felt vulnerable, as if the PRC might eventually take over the island. Clearly the ROC faced a legitimacy crisis. But from the beginning the advent of the LLB world champions was enough to transform the nation's dissatisfaction and despair into a fantasy of world victory.

The KMT exploited these LLB world championships to conduct its nation-building project, trumpeting the message that the Chinese on Taiwan were better than the Chinese on the mainland, and the capitalist regime was better than its Communist counterpart. A jingoistic rhetoric was used at the time, as seen in the following extracts from major newspapers of the day.

> Our Chinese nation had been a country of manners. But recently we have not been taking manners seriously, especially the rudeness and violence expressed by the Communist bandits [the PRC], whose aggressiveness and tyranny are the greatest shame of our Chinese nation. The proper manners manifested by our youth [baseball] team demonstrated the intrinsic value of the Chinese nation, further verifying the inhumanity of the Communist bandits.[42]

> Jinlong not only won glory for the country but also wiped out the humiliation of our nation. In the past the Chinese were bodily and physically inferior to others…therefore dubbed "the sick man of East Asia." The youth team demonstrated that the Chinese of the next generation have fit bodies and superior physiques. Their victories and glory belong to the country and the nation![43]

The Chinese Communist regime wanted to use hunger control and military-oriented methods to cultivate a few Ping-Pong players. These players were utterly tools without souls. We are not bothered though. The Taiwan Little League team are made up of purely innocent kids whose skills and tastes are better than those of Communist Ping-Pong players. They demonstrated the characteristics of free will and talent. Sport in the free world is far better than that of the Communist world.... The consecutive successes of the youth baseball team made it difficult for the Chinese Communists to use good Ping-Pong players to deceive overseas Chinese and wage infiltrative diplomacy.[44]

Symbolism was also used to emphasize and construct national identity. For instance, the Taiwanese national squad's uniform had to be either blue or white or a mix of the two, blue and white being the colors of the KMT party flag. The color red, which represented the Communists, could not be used. Even today, blue and white are still the only colors of the national team.

Diplomacy was another element in maximizing the propaganda value of Taiwanese LLB. The ROC ambassador to the United States in particular played an instrumental role in the process. When Taiwanese Little League contingents arrived, he arranged dinner meetings with overseas Chinese, prepared patriotic signs, drafted slogans, imported flags, and rented large buses to carry overseas Chinese and students to the game. That was why the LLB world series was filled with the national flags of the ROC. This overt display made Americans indignant because the U.S. fans felt that the Taiwanese teams were not only humiliating the U.S. teams on the diamond but that the Taiwanese were also transforming the stadium into a political battle ground.

The Taiwanese embassy in Washington had to send a report back to Taiwan about its success at promoting the ROC through the LLB world series. Such reports were expected from the embassy and the consulates in U.S. major cities on all efforts to create an international identity for Taiwan. These reports allowed ROC officials to assess the success or failure of the international propaganda war in their struggle against Communism.[45]

The KMT was not the only faction seeking to shape a national identity for Taiwan. Activists seeking to make Taiwan an independent country mobilized to challenge the Chinese identity that the KMT was using the LLB to construct. The activists hoped that they too could use baseball to advance their cause.

It was obvious that Williamsport, the only venue that could ensure a massive Taiwanese television audience, provided an ideal platform to trumpet independence. Thus in 1971 a small aircraft flew over Williamsport's Howard J. Lamade Stadium while Juren played West U.S. The plane towed a banner on which was written "Taiwan duli wansui [Long Live Taiwanese Independence], GO GO Taiwan!" KMT officials were stunned, yelling that "Taiwan independence activists even have an air force! Damn it!"[46]

Some Williamsport world series games witnessed violent fights between Taiwan independence activists and KMT loyalists, even though both were cheering for the same Taiwanese team. Tao Qixiang, the KMT official, accused Taiwanese independence activists of being rabble rousers who were responsible for the unrest.[47] To prevent further trouble, the KMT even dispatched its marines, who were training in the United States.

Ethnic Integration

Despite these cries for independence, the success of the world champions did much to integrate Taiwanese and mainlanders into one nation. Baseball was the only thing that pulled the country together. As author Gao Zhengyuan puts it, "the role played by Juren [in 1971] is historically significant…in that it was the only thing that made all the Chinese living on Taiwan throw away the shadows in their minds and forget troubling things surrounding them, thus integrating completely. . . . At the moment when Xu beat McClendon, people, whether speaking Mandarin or Taiwanese, unanimously said 'congratulations' to each other."[48]

Before 1968 the mainlanders and Taiwanese inhabited different worlds of sport, the mainlanders playing basketball and the Taiwanese, baseball. Mainlanders rarely played baseball since it had not been part of their culture on mainland China. Nationally, of course, the divide ran far deeper than sports preferences. The 2/28 tragedy had deeply scarred the entire country and led to a generation of Taiwanese who deeply resented the ruling KMT. The situation was further complicated in sports as baseball teams mainly spoke Taiwanese and Japanese, a practice that further drove mainlanders away. As a consequence baseball had a more specific ethnic identity than did basketball, an activity in which some Taiwanese took part. However, with the national publicity of Hongye and the winning of the world championship, mainlander children, encouraged by their parents, began to play baseball.

The first successful mainlander player during this period was Li Zongyuan, whose father came from Hebei province in North China. Li was a tall, big lefty pitcher who threw an extremely hard fastball. At the 1973 Senior League he struck out 17 hitters of the South U.S. team; by doing so, he equaled the record for strikeouts in a game. Because of a weight problem that absolved him from military service, a Japanese professional club, Lotte, signed him in 1980.[49]

Li did not make a big splash in the Japanese professional league, but he blazed a trail that a new generation of mainlander youth followed. Among the standouts was the famous slugger Zhao Shiqiang, who once attracted attention from American Major League clubs because of his home run-hitting.[50] There was also Lin Huawei, a multitalented third baseman, who later became the head coach of Chinese Taipei. Though Taiwanese and aborigines still made up the majority of players, more and more mainlanders were knocking on baseball coaches' doors.

One mainlander basketball player, Li Miao, lamented the erosive effects of baseball on basketball: "On a weekend afternoon during late April [1972] I unwittingly bumped into two national team basketball players, Cheng Wei and Ren Zhaoliang [both mainlanders] and had a chat. When talking about the development of youth baseball, the two players jokingly said. 'If we had known youth baseball was so popular, we would have been born ten years later and played baseball.' Although it was a joke, it showed how dominant youth baseball was in the country."[51]

Mainlanders entering baseball were forced to learn Taiwanese and even some Japanese. According to a former Huaxing player, "these mainlanders became assimilated . . . since they had to live with Taiwanese players day and night. Most people playing baseball had to gradually speak Taiwanese fluently; Mandarin instead became a secondary language. . . . Yin Jinglong [whose father was from the northwestern Shanxi Province] could not even speak Mandarin properly."[52] Thus baseball not only contributed to ethnic integration but also to the spread of Taiwanese culture, language, and perspectives among mainlanders, who now began to think like Taiwanese.[53]

Ethnic integration occurred off the baseball field as well. The famous store chain Yonghe Doujiang (Yonghe bean milk) benefited from the LLB world championship.[54] Yonghe Doujiang sold staple foods, such as *shaobing* (sesame seed cake) and *youtiao* (deep fried fluffy dough sticks), breakfast foods for mainlanders. Ever since its founding in the 1950s the eatery catered mostly to mainlanders because ethnic Taiwanese traditionally ate rice and were unaccustomed to *shaobing* and *youtiao*. However, in the early morning hours, after LLB world series games, hungry ethnic Taiwanese flocked to Yonghe Doujiang because it was the only eatery open for breakfast. The chain became so popular that its stores soon began staying open twenty-four hours; additionally, it spread out from Taipei. Taiwanese historians thus credit the LLB for introducing Taiwanese to mainland food, which later became common to every part of the island.

A Tragedy in Disguise

During this LLB period parents of even academically talented male students allowed their sons to play baseball rather than devote the time to study. These parents believed that participation in the world championship would bring fame and fortune denied to ordinary citizens. They, however, were not aware of the grave consequences for the young ballplayers following their stint in the Little League. Academic work and the physical training for championship teams were mutually exclusive, just like *wen* and *wu*. If one was chosen, the other had to be given up. Wu Chengwen, a member of the 1971 world championship squad, recalled why he gave up sports in junior high school: "It was for my future career! Baseball occupied most of my time then. My father considered that my academic work had always been very good and therefore did not allow me to play any more. Besides, I had always been a good boy. If I continued playing baseball and hurt my dad's heart, I would rather not play."[55] Wu later earned a PhD in computer science.

The gap between *wen* and *wu* widened during this period, but *wen* did not take dominance until the late 1970s. The government worsened the situation with the "Regulations of Non-examination for Students with Good PE Records," which allowed pupils who excelled in sports to be exempted from examinations. The passing of examinations was the standard method for students to move from junior high to senior high and eventually to university.

Athletes, however, were automatically promoted, and thus with no need to pass examinations, exempted ball players had no incentive to study or to learn. Indeed, players rarely had the chance to read books after their prolonged training and competitions. Consequently, many players, after having attended junior school, found it difficult to catch up with other students. Several members of the 1969 world champion squad were required to repeat their first year in Huaxing High School because they did nothing but play baseball in elementary school.

Championship Syndrome

Academic failure was not the only negative effect of playing Taiwanese LLB. Indeed, playing of the game became itself a victim of altered expectations. One sports reporter described how deadly serious the Qihu players were in Williamsport during the 1970 world series: "After arriving in Williamsport, foreign players went swimming, but Jiayi players were not allowed to touch the water. Ostensibly our kids are more disciplined, honorable, and driven to win; realistically, they were not as happy as other foreign kids. During the game Nicaraguan players were chewing gum, laughing in the field, and not really caring about the match. Jiayi players were very stern."[56] Winning was the only thing the Taiwanese players had in mind, and this focus meant that they could not enjoy the experience of playing on the world stage.

Such seriousness had not always marked Taiwanese baseball. During the first twenty years of KMT rule, baseball, still being under the influence of Japanese culture, had been voluntarily and spontaneously played for fun. However, the advent of Hongye and later the LLB world championships completely altered baseball, which children, parents, schools, the public, and the government now perceived as a means to an end, not an end in itself.

Almost all baseball researchers and writers praise Hongye for its role in motivating the government to finally take baseball seriously. But a strong argument can also be made that Hongye and the later LLB victories were the very reason for a precipitous drop in grassroots baseball in the 1980s and the gradual decrease in the popularity of youth baseball among the public. As soon as the government put massive resources into baseball, people started to rely on state support and no longer thought that the game could exist without that support. Additionally, the government treated the players as messengers of the country and the teams as a model for the Chinese nation, notions that made players national celebrities. Public enthusiasm for the sport was based solely on winning, which made an otherwise intrinsically interesting activity less involving, particularly if victory proved elusive.

Inevitably, with only one champion team going to Williamsport, there were disputes over roster spots on the local all-star teams. Before the preliminary rounds of the national championship, district champions were required to pick four or five players from other counties or cities within their district. In the southern district especially, where baseball was most popular, teams sometimes didn't want to kick original team members off the roster in order to accommodate players from other places. The requirement often produced disharmony, disputes, and cronyism, and sometimes parents pressed charges against general managers on the teams claiming unfair selection.[57] If Taiwanese baseball had abided by LLB regulations, in which leagues had to be formed on a stringent residency basis, every child would have had a chance of being selected for the team. Instead, the championship was the sole objective, forcing schools to find the best players possible to achieve that goal, whether they were local or not.

In short the rationale for school teams was now to win rather than to play. Pressures from schools and sponsors compelled teams to strive for results, as these pressuring groups intended to reap the benefits of backing champions. Victory alone was the major force that compelled people to sustain teams that had become expensive. The result of this attitude was vicious under-the-table recruitment and distorted practice schedules.

As part of their recruitment, schools shrewdly used a loophole in LLB rules by enticing promising players from other counties based on the Taiwanese law of freedom of movement.[58] As long as parents consented, their registration address could be changed to another county, and the children would therefore be eligible to be enrolled in and play for the recruiting school. Since the LLB could not identify those who had been in one county but moved to another county, Taiwanese schools were able to evade residency restrictions.

Many players became mercenaries, who would go to any school that was available to them; as mercenaries they lacked any loyalty to the school or its community. One extreme example was Jiang Kunsheng, whose nine-year school career made him a journeyman at eight different schools, three in elementary, two in junior high, and three in senior high. His travels took him to northern, central, and southern Taiwan. In 1979 the wandering eventually paid off in Jiang's last year in senior high school when his team won the national championship and went to Fort Lauderdale to compete in the Big League championship.

The government cooperated in school recruitment by turning a blind eye to how teams were formed and to fabricating facts. As Xie Guocheng observed, "we reported to the LLB that only eight teams could take part in the national championship. Therefore each district could only have one or two teams represented. We limited teams taking part in the national championship because we did not want to dilute our youth baseball's strength. The more teams in the national championship, the less trouble would occur, but the weaker the teams would be."[59] Moreover, ROC baseball authorities exaggerated the number of teams in a county or school in order for teams to be eligible to play. They also reported the names of many players who were not even playing baseball. For example, if a county had a population of thirty thousand, it was required to have two leagues and eight teams. In reality, it would have only one regular team and perhaps one reserve team. The authorities would simply report the names of six other teams, although none actually existed.

Schools were also held ransom by *houyuanhui*, booster associations made up of mostly parents and local entrepreneurs. *Houyuanhui* wanted championships so badly that they demanded schools implement full-time baseball training and hire a full-time coach, or else the boosters threatened to dissolve the team.

Because a coach's salary was often paid by the *houyuanhui*, who also could fire him, there was enormous pressure for a coach to win by any means possible.

Coaches for their part, having been taught and educated under the Japanese occupation, accepted a Spartan and military style of managing teams. Coaches thus went in for long practices, year-round competition, and the overuse of good players. They required players to stay in school dormitories and, if they were generous, allowed their squads to go home on holidays. During the year-round season coaches sometimes scheduled two games in one day just to gain match experience. Finally, coaches often used corporal punishment to make players obedient and fearful and to help them win games.

According to a former player, "we had to get up at six o'clock, or maybe earlier, in the morning to start drilling until lunch, after which we continued till the sky turned very dark."[60] Some players even got out of the bed in the middle of the night to practice their swing because they felt obliged not to let their country down. After being asked by a baseball commentator about his life in youth baseball, Zheng Baisheng, a member of the 1973 world champion squad, replied that "it is like hell!"[61] Small wonder many young players burned out at a very early age. They did not want to lose games by being average players, who might cost the team victory and the coach his job.

In the end many players received only baseball knowledge and harsh treatment from their coaches. The latter had no time for good sportsmanship or the well-being of their players. As models of behavior, many coaches often left much to be desired, their integrity and characters questionable. For instance, in the 1971 southern qualifying round Gaoxiong county simply threw the game away to Gaoxiong city in order to allow the other team to go onto the next stage of the tournament. Two years later, in Jiayi, match-fixing occurred.

Fueled by world championship mania and state support, Taiwan reached a point at which players became *daqiu jiqi* (playing robots), through whose minds ran only the concept of practice, practice, and practice. They were forced to abandon academic work, as baseball was no longer a pastime played after school. It was during this time that one sports writer did some soul-searching on Taiwanese baseball: "Their [the players'] little minds are bearing adult enthusiasm and expectation. Heavy psychological burdens and mental stress force them to have no smile during entire games. Children's innocence has long gone. . . . This is not their fault. Let the adults of the entire nation carry this sin."[62] This relentless pursuit of the LLB world championship would eventually exact a heavy price on Taiwanese baseball.

FOUR

A Drastic Decline in Baseball's Population, 1975–1989

I n 1975 President Chiang Kai-shek died, and his dream of retaking mainland China went into the coffin with him. On the diplomatic front the United States finally established official relations with the PRC in 1979, forcing Taiwan into further isolation. At the same time Chiang Ching-kuo, now Taiwan's president, promoted nongovernmental relations and exchanges with other countries while implementing the three-nos policy (no negotiation, no contact, and no compromise) toward Communist countries. Despite being an international pariah, Taiwan nevertheless experienced rapid economic growths in the 1980s, earning it the name of "Asian tiger." In addition the PRC no longer stressed using its military to recover the "rebel province" and instead proposed peaceful unification via one country, two systems.

The Taiwanese baseball scene also underwent change, both at home and abroad. After Juren completely destroyed their opponents in the 1973 Williamsport world series, scoring 57 runs in three games, allegations surfaced in American baseball circles that Taiwan had been circumventing the LLB rules. In response the LLB appointed an investigative committee of three LLB representatives from Japan, the Philippines, and Hong Kong. With the Japanese official reportedly sick, a two-person committee arrived on Taiwan on October 3 and stayed for three days, during which time they asked baseball authorities about local leagues, team organization, and practice times.

In many ways the committee faced an impossible task. Without living on Taiwan or speaking the language, these outsiders could not uncover the truth about Taiwanese LLB. For instance, although some ballplayers transferred from elementary to elementary school many times over, their parents had moved the child's residency registration in advance. Further, the KMT government also gave a helping hand. Finally, any islander divulging information to LLB officials would have been deemed a traitor.

In the end the LLB investigators certainly never gained the information needed to assess the validity of the accusation against Taiwan. So having barely scratched the island's surface, the committee turned in a report stating that they found no irregularities in Taiwan's LLB program. Although LLB President Peter McGovern told Xie Guocheng that the "allegation is unfounded," the LLB still put Taiwan on probation in 1974.[1]

That same year, after Taiwan captured the highly coveted *sanguanwang* (winning world championships at all three levels of LLB play), the LLB once again suspected foul play and the following year announced a closed-door policy that banned foreign teams from competing for the championships. The LLB's decision sent a shock wave through the Taiwanese baseball world. For the previous six years school teams were organized to win national championships and to go abroad. Play was never for play's sake; it was focused on winning. Without the world series incentive what then was the purpose of fielding a team? Consequently, the LLB's announcement created panic throughout the nation. The fallout was immediate: a decline in the playing of baseball. Sixty to seventy percent of schools lost interest in their baseball programs and disbanded their teams.[2] The attendance for the seventh national tournament was poor, and advertisers pulled their ads for an event that in past years had drawn high ratings. Although three national networks broadcast the finals, not one ran a commercial during the game.[3]

The Far East Qualification still occurred that year and coincidentally Taiwan was the host. The last time Taiwan had played host, the tournament had packed the stadium. This time, however, crowds were sparse.[4] Without the Williamsport incentive the Taiwanese showed no interest in going to games.

The Private Parts Incident

The level of participation in youth baseball continued to drop, even after the LLB rescinded its ban on foreign teams in 1976. The LLB's reversal was based on a survey of district managers, who believed foreign teams should be allowed to compete as long as they adhered fully to regulations.[5]

With this reversal the Taiwanese game logically should have revived. Such was not the case. Instead, the number of teams fell to fewer than one hundred for the first time since 1968.[6] The slide did not stop until the advent of professional baseball in 1990. Against a background of rising Confucianism, the public had grown weary of the emphasis on athletes rather than academics, the forgeries, the under-the-table deals, and the scandals. Furthermore, the 1976 private parts scandal brought to a head the government's apparent treatment of children as tools rather than as human beings.[7]

The incident involved southern LLB players and occurred after Taiwan's baseball authorities adopted a more guarded approach to the formation of teams following the lifting of the LLB ban. The southern regional qualification was held in May, and Gaoxiong Gushan, the national champion of the previous year, was again the favorite. The most prominent player on the team was the multitalented Zhao Liangan, who the previous year had batted .545 and cracked 4 homers during the four-game national championship. Additionally, Zhao was also the best pitcher in the tournament. All of these accomplishments earned him an MVP award. Continuing his hot hitting at the Far East Qualification, he batted .571 with 5 homers.

It was Zhao's size and strength that made him formidable both on the mound and at the plate. Indeed, these physical characteristics aroused the suspicions of rival Taiwanese teams who suspected that he might be over thirteen. Along with Zhao two other teammates, Cao Qinglai and Ma Shijie, were also regarded as questionable due to their size and strength.

Fearing that the trio would be found to be overage by the LLB, Xie Guocheng and his colleague Lin Fenglin launched an internal investigation. The players were taken to Taiwan University Hospital and were told to remove their underpants. After a visual inspection of their genitalia, the three players were proclaimed "legitimate overaged players" (*hefa chaoling qiuyuan*), meaning that they were legally legitimate but ruled ineligible. The term, to be discussed in detail below, was an invention of Taiwanese baseball. By looking at the size of the penis and the amount of pubic hair, the age of a player could be determined, or so it was claimed.

The methodology was unprecedented in the baseball world and so extreme that it raised anger in the Provincial Police Department, which kept birth records of all Taiwanese citizens. The police argued that birth registration is indisputable. How could a medical examination of private parts, a procedure that had no scientific foundation, be another means of judging someone's age?[8] Xie subsequently had to clarify that he did not dispute the authority of the police department. Instead, although the players were not overaged, their "body and physique were beyond that of natural children, and they were not suitable for playing baseball," thus the meaning of legitimate overaged players.[9]

As a result of the loss of the three players, Gushan lost to RSEA, a team that was widely considered inferior and that, despite eventually winning the national title, lost to both Korea and Japan at the Far East Qualification. Some people believed that had Zhao, Ma, and Cao not been ruled ineligible, they would have led Gushan to victory at the Williamsport world series.

The private parts incident may also have further increased parents' unwillingness to allow their children to play baseball. Additionally, the dreadful treatment may have deeply scarred the players. Zhao and Ma quit baseball after entering junior high school, while Cao never really lived up to expectations in the rest of his days in baseball.[10]

Widespread Cheating

The private parts scandal was only the tip of the iceberg. Taiwanese amateur baseball was rife with problems and a general disregard for LLB rules. As a former official of the CTBA confessed,

> There was not a single year that Taiwan played by the LLB rules. We simply cannot enforce such rigid regulations on our country. To make teams eligible, we had to contact and tell schools to make bogus numbers of teams and other things that would be within LLB regulations. If an LLB investigation team came to check things out, we had to create more lies to cover up original

lies. We were finally fed up with the cheating that really set a bad example to those little kids. That was why we decided to pull out from the LLB in 1997. Besides, we have other international organizations, such as the PONY League whose rules are less strict than the LLB, that we can attend.[11]

This statement sums up the abnormal development of Taiwanese baseball beginning in the late 1960s. Endeavoring to win national championships for a berth at Williamsport, schools, parents, and even the government tolerated and allowed corruption and scandal year after year.

Perhaps the most flagrant violation of rules was the schools' virtually ignoring the population parameters prescribed by the LLB, as discussed previously. The most extreme case was for the Big League; Taiwan always sent a national all-star team, a practice that lasted until 1995. Taiwan cleverly used a loophole in the LLB's Big League rules that required that a district must have a league with at least five but no more than ten teams. From the outset the whole of Taiwan never had more than ten senior high school baseball teams, from which a national all-star teams was always formed.

Vicious under-the-table recruitment was also a common practice. Those schools that did not want to be involved in a bidding war simply disbanded their teams because they could not be competitive against the big teams. Moreover, players developed in one school often defected to another with a more distinguished team. Many schools thus asked themselves, "Why squander so much time and money fostering players if they were going to leave?"

Sometimes a coach would make an under-the-table bargain to ensure his team's victory. Perhaps the most famous incident of game-fixing happened on live television in the 1979 junior high school tournament. Meihe, who had no chance of retaining the title, threw the game away. In exchange the opponent, Dongfeng, promised to give Meihe two players, Liao Jincheng and Dai Qingyang, for next year's tournament because Dongfeng planned to disband its team.[12] Meihe pitcher Wu Qingsheng was a submarine-style hurler who really confused Dongfeng's hitters. The game was scoreless until the top of the seventh inning when Wu suddenly slowed down his velocity and kept throwing the ball over the plate. In addition Meihe's center fielder Tang Zhihong deliberately slipped while chasing a routine fly ball. The match-fixing was so obvious that some Meihe supporters angrily scolded their team, throwing crumpled papers, paper cups, and other debris onto the field, shouting that the team threw the game away.[13]

Taiwanese baseball was also plagued by other corrupting practices, such as the existence of full-time players and coaches. Among other practices, the most infamous concerned the legitimate overaged players (*hefa chaoling qiuyuan*), of which there were two types. The first type arose by exploiting the LLB rule for determining a player's age of eligibility. This age determination is made on July 1. Players who turn thirteen after July 1 are still eligible but only if they are still enrolled in elementary school. However, many of the players who turned thirteen after July 1 had finished elementary school and were scheduled to attend junior high. Consequently, some schools asked talented and experienced players to repeat elementary school for another year in order to help the team win the championship. These so-called *chongdusheng* (elementary school repeaters) had more sophisticated skills than their younger LLB peers. This practice existed despite a ruling by the Taiwanese Ministry of Education that no child could repeat elementary school unless his or her academic record was extremely poor. The ministry, however, turned a blind eye to repeating players.

The other type of legitimate overaged players is more bizarre: delayed birth registration. To be understood, this practice has to be put into a wider historical and cultural context.

Before the National Calendar (also called the Foreign or New Calendar) was introduced in China in 1911, the Chinese always celebrated festivals according to the Farmers' Calendar (also called the Lunar or Old Calendar). The same applied to Taiwan. Rural villagers especially lived according to the Farmers' Calendar and in some instances weren't even aware of the National Calendar.

When the KMT arrived on Taiwan, they enforced strict household registration in order to squeeze out Communists. Part of this registration was the recoding of birth dates, which were calculated according to the National Calendar. The difference in the dating methods used by the National and Farmer Calendars meant that a person's birthday fell on different days under each system. Most Taiwanese, however, continued to depend upon the Farmers' Calendar to determine their birthdays, not on the official birth registration date.

When Taiwanese parents turned up to register a child's birthday, they could not easily convert the birth date of the Farmer's Calendar to that of the National Calendar. They therefore often recorded the birthday as the same day they registered the child. Because many factors, particularly farm work, might make them late in arriving at the registration office, the registered birth date of the child might be off by as much as a month, sometimes even several years.[14]

The consequence of these incorrect birth registrations was that children who were actually old enough to be in junior high school were, according to their registration records, of an age to be in elementary school. For example, Xu Jinmu, the famous 1971 Juren pitcher, had had his birthday reported late, and as a result he was eligible for LLB competition.

The most famous incident resulting from late birth registration occurred in 1982. Three extraordinarily talented players, Zheng Wuxiong, Zhang Mingbin, and Zhang Mingguo—the latter two claiming to be twin brothers—were announced as *hefa chaolin qiuyuan* and were thus ineligible to compete in the national tournament. The Zhang brothers were members of a 1981 Taiping team that won the LLB world series in 1981. Zhang Mingbin stood five foot ten, his brother five foot seven, and Zheng five foot eight. These three players raised suspicion among competing Taiwanese teams, who believed they should be in junior high school.

The CTBA began an investigation and discovered that Zheng was born much earlier than was recorded on his birth certificate. Terrified of possible accusations of fraud by the LLB, the CTBA decided to disqualify Zheng from the tournament. The two Zhangs, persuaded by local Taizhong people who believed their bodies were too conspicuous for elementary school kids, voluntarily withdrew from the competition.

Although few islanders spoke publicly about the age status of the Zhangs, many were skeptical that they were twins as Mingbin looked much older. And indeed, they were actually three years apart, and both were over thirteen, with Mingbin being seventeen and Mingguo four-teen. After Taiping had won the 1981 Far East Qualification, the team was invited on a program called Entertainment 100. The program's famous hostess Zhang Xiaoyan asked Mingbin why he and his brother looked different, if they were twins. Mingbin answered, "I look more like my dad, my brother looks more like my mother."[15] The implica-tion was that the two were fraternal, not identical, twins.

The widespread use of "gigantic" players such as the Zhang brothers exposed the ugly truth of *hefa chaoling qiuyuan*. Commonly *hefa chaol-ing qiuyuan* did not continue their baseball careers. The first reason is that these players were overused by coaches because they were taller and stronger than other players. Such overuse led to eventual burnout. The second reason is that their skills matured at a very early stage and could only be improved slightly, if at all. The final reason is that these players had to endure psychological pressure from outside and from within since virtually everyone knew they were *hefa chaoling qiuyuan*. One player, Lin Zhongqiu, has spoken about his experience: "I had never read a book properly for one day nor had the opportunity of learning other skills because parents, relatives, and opponents on the field wanted me either to get better or to confirm the view that 'Lin would fall very quickly.' I hope youth baseball can be normalized as soon as possible and do not want my ordeal to be reproduced for a new generation."[16]

The Myth of the Triple Crown

While unethical strategies hindered participation in the grassroots game, continued domination on the world stage riveted the public to their television sets. Taiwan established an unassailable hegemony among the three levels of competitions held by the LLB. Throughout the 1970s, 1980s, and even into the early 1990s, one of the most cher-ished collective Taiwanese experiences was staying up into the predawn hours to watch live broadcasts of Taiwanese youths "crusading" at the three levels of the LLB. These broadcasts were thanks to the three KMT-controlled television stations, which willingly televised the games de-spite the costs. Staying up late to catch these broadcasts thus became an annual custom, of which many Taiwanese were and still are proud and which they remember fondly.

As a consequence, a mythic image of *sanguanwang*, the triple crown, was invented and reinforced by the media and the government. People over the age of thirty always remember the term *sanguanwang* because it represents a sense of pride and prestige that Americans might find hard to understand. Taiwan achieved *sanguanwang* in 1974, 1977, 1978, 1988, 1990, and 1991. The government even issued memorial stamps and cards honoring these victories.

Unfortunately, the triple crown was another myth that was created just as that of Hongye. Student teams were recruited and trained professionally in order to bash their American counterparts, who were organized on a community basis with coaches and players who were devoted volunteers—amateurs in the true sense of the word.

The actual amateur nature of the LLB games and settings often came as a shock to Taiwanese players. Lin Yizeng, a famous outfielder and coach, recalled his disappointment about playing in the 1978 Big League world series:

> In my mind the ballpark in Broward County [Fort Lauderdale] should be very large if they were hosting the world series. But when I arrived in Fort Lauderdale, the so-called Big League world series was taking place in a surprisingly lackluster ballpark with no seats in the outfield and only a few seats made out of wood in the infield. Spectators were only parents from the local area, and the umpires were also local volunteers. The only thing that reached an "international standard" was those overseas Chinese in the cheering squad from Florida. They brought their young and elders and gave us soup and water. Furthermore, they waved national flags and beat drums happily cheering for these country kids who were homesick after leaving the motherland.[17]

For the under-19 age group the best international baseball competition was actually a tournament unaffiliated with the LLB. Dating back to 1981, the IBA (International Baseball Association) has hosted a youth AAA tournament whose level of play is far superior to that of the LLB because countries send their best under-19 all-stars to the contest. Indeed, Japan, Korea, and most other Asian countries did not send their teams to the LLB's Senior and Big Leagues Asia Qualification because they did not deem such competitions important. Taiwan and Guam were the only two Asian countries who always competed in the LLB Asian under-16 and under-19 qualifications. Of the two only Taiwan took the contest seriously; Guam merely played for fun.[18]

The two countries that have enjoyed the most success in the IBA are Cuba, with ten championships, and the United States, with six. It is sad to say that Taiwan only won one championship. The reason for this poor showing is twofold. First, every country put its best players into the competition, and Taiwan was outclassed and thus could not dominate as it did at the LLB world series. Second, although Taiwanese authorities realized that the IBA's level of play was higher than that of the LLB, they sent the national champion to the LLB tournament and the runner-up to the IBA's competition.[19]

Today, many people still believe that the LLB is the real world series because they have been deceived in a sense by the government's highlighting this tournament. Taiwan's appearances at the IBA are far less publicized and never broadcast on the island. To further enhance the prestige of the LLB in the eyes of the public, the government and media refer to the LLB as *shijie shaobang lianmeng* (World Little League Baseball) instead of the more proper *shaobang lianmeng* (Little League Baseball). Because the IBA does not have the grand-sounding "world" in its name, the public views the latter as a minor organization.

International Exposure to Adult Baseball

The Focus on Adult Baseball

Public perception aside, Taiwanese officials did not simply ignore the IBA. Rather, Taiwan joined the IBA in 1972 in order to compete in adult international tournaments. The most distinguished Taiwanese player during this era was a pitcher named Chen Xiuxiong, who beat Japan twice, in the 1971 Asian Championship, 3–2, and in the 1972 World Championship, 1–0. In the latter game Chen threw 12 strikeouts. The Nishitetsu Lions, a Japanese pro club, was so impressed with Chen's performance that they offered him a $3,000 bonus to sign with the team. Chen, however, was persuaded to stay in Taiwan by KMT general Yang Sen, who said to him, "Japan has just established official relations with the PRC and cut off ties with the ROC. I hope you do not go to Japan. Stay here, the country will treat you well."[20]

Another important IBA player was Tan Xinmin, who in the 1972 World Championship won 4 victories and threw 57 strikeouts and who in consequence was given the Best Pitcher and Most Strikeouts awards. Two years later, after Chen was persuaded to stay in Taiwan, the same Japanese club, now known as the Taiheiyo Lions, that had tried to sign him ironically recruited Tan when Taiwanese–Japanese relations improved. Later in 1974 Tan became the first Taiwan-born player to compete in the U.S. Minor League after being sent to the San Francisco Giants by the Lions.

Such players built a solid reputation for Taiwan's adult IBA teams and led to Taiwan's participating in several championships during the 1970s. After being invited to the Intercontinental Cup in 1977, Taiwan was rejected by the Baseball Federation of Asia after refusing to relinquish the team name "China," which was now being used by the PRC. Since there would be no international competition in the foreseeable future, Xie Guocheng encouraged talented players, such as Li Laifa and Gao Yingjie, to play pro baseball in Japan in the hopes that they would come back to Taiwan to pass on what they had learned.

This act was one of Xie's last as he died in 1980. Yan Xiaozhang, a mainland-born Chinese, replaced him as president of the CTBA. At the time Yan was head of the RSEA, which sponsored baseball vigorously by having a team at each educational level. Yan had gained the appointment because the KMT hoped that he could use his influential RSEA to expand Taiwan's international presence. Actually Yan's favorite sport was basketball, and he had wanted to become president of the Chinese Basketball Association. Nevertheless, his five-year reign in baseball was a complete success. It was he who brought pride to the national team, and he was later dubbed the Father of Adult Baseball.

As soon as Yan took charge, he began a series of long, difficult diplomatic maneuvers with important figures in the IBA. The former head coach of the national team, Wu Xiangmu, remembered that, when meeting with baseball officials, Yan often carried a 007-style suitcase filled with cash—presumably another kind of money diplomacy.[21] Through these efforts Yan successfully brought Taiwan back into the international arena at the 1982 Seoul World Championship, at which Taiwan seized the bronze medal. It was under Yan's leadership that Chinese Taipei beat the most awesome amateur team, Cuba, three times in official international games from 1984 through 1986. Further, the CTBA president saw that unofficial international tournaments were held every November or December starting in 1984.[22] "Big Unit" Randy Johnson even represented the U.S. team at the inaugural tournament, but he and his team were battered by Chinese Taipei, who won the game 8–1.

My most precious baseball moment while growing up was watching the 1983 Asian Championship, in which Taiwan's adult national squad beat South Korea and Japan on the same day and thus qualified for the 1984 Olympics. The China Television Company televised both games, an act that at the time was unprecedented for Taiwanese adult baseball. As a consequence, virtually every Taiwanese household tuned in.

Taiwan won the first game on a squeeze bunt in the eleventh inning. The winning pitcher Guo Taiyuan, who had relieved Liu Qiunong from the fourth inning, had pitched eight shutout innings. After the game tournament organizers announced that South Korea had qualified for the Olympics but that Taiwan and Japan, who had the same winning percentage, needed to play a tie-breaker. So after only a half hour of rest, Taiwan played their second match of the day for the other Olympic berth.

Taiwan again put the ace Guo Taiyuan on the mound. Both Guo and Japanese pitcher Chikafusa Ikeda held their respective opponents scoreless, and the game went very quickly as if the end promised something great. Eventually, in the bottom of the ninth inning, first baseman Zhao Shiqiang came up to the plate, swung at the first pitch, and sent the ball sailing over the left field wall for a walk-off home run. The marathon against Korea and Japan lasted over seven hours, with pitcher Guo Taiyuan tossing seventeen shutout innings in one day.[23] I recall that, when Zhao hit the home run, firecrackers were lit throughout my neighborhood, contributing to the general noise of celebration.

"China! China!"

Taiwan's involvement with international adult baseball set the stage for its confrontation with Cuba. It was an unlikely match because Chiang Ching-kuo's three-nos policy forbade all contact with Communist countries. Among the fallout of this policy was that Taiwan could not hold major international tournaments since it could not invite Communist countries to take part. True, individual athletes from Communist countries did come to Taiwan to appear in tournaments. Thus the Czechoslovakian-born tennis player Ivan Lendl was on the island in the late 1970s, and one Yugoslavian-born basketball player representing the UK in 1983. But neither was a part of a sports team.[24]

The three-nos policy also meant that Taiwanese teams could not travel to Communist countries in order to compete. There was a sporting delegation in Moscow at the 1980 Olympics. However, its members appeared only at a conference; they did not compete.

In 1984 baseball became an exception to Taiwan's anti-Communist policy when the national team was allowed to play in the IBA's World Championship in Cuba. Those Taiwanese older than thirty vividly remember the fantastic performance of Chinese Taipei as its squad beat the best amateur team in the world three times during a three-year period.

Until these Taiwanese victories the amateur hegemony established by Cuba in the baseball world had been unshakable. After the Cuban revolution in 1959 Fidel Castro had abruptly expelled U.S. Major League clubs operating in his country and created Cuba's own national league. The Cuban players were not considered professionals since under the Communist regime they did not receive a paycheck for their efforts. Accordingly, they were classified as amateurs and the Cuban league as an amateur association. Pro players were banned from taking part in international competition at this time.[25] However, since Cuba's players were supposedly all amateurs, it was able to muster all of its best players and send them to international games, even though they were actually trained professionally.

At first glance Cuba and Taiwan appear to be totally different entities, one Communist, the other capitalist. Still they have a number of things in common. Both are islands that maintain large standing and reserve armies to defend against continental neighbors whose perceived intent is to take over these island nations. Both Cuba and Taiwan are also situated in subtropical areas where baseball can be played year round. Further, for both baseball is a method of asserting themselves on the international stage. Therefore both preserved the amateur status of their players so that these players could participate in international tournaments for the national good.[26] Finally, rulers in both countries cared so much about international games that they cultivated a must-win attitude among their respective people.

Playing another team with this must-win spirit made the World Championship victories all the sweeter for Taiwan. The first encounter with the Cubans was at the 1983 Intercontinental Cup in Antwerp, where both teams met twice. Taiwan surrendered the first game, losing 3–12. Slugger Zhao Shiqiang and infielder Lü Wensheng, nicknamed "Peter Pan" because of his nimbleness, both hit solo homers for Taiwan.

It was the result of the second game that shocked the baseball world. This time coach Wu Xiangmu put in his ace pitcher, Zhuang Shengxiong. Zhuang, master of various breaking balls, threw a gem thanks to the American umpire's generous strike zone. Taiwan upset Cuba 13–1 in perhaps the most humiliating defeat in the history of the Cuban national team. Even the Soviet media reported this astonishing baseball result.

The following year the World Championship was hosted by Cuba. Traveling to Cuba meant enduring certain hardships. The host country confiscated the Taiwanese players' instant noodles so that Cuba could control the team's meal through rationing. Players were also not allowed to leave their hotel. According to skipper Wu Xiangmu, the only luxury the team was afforded in Cuba was "a big orange juice barrel kept in the dugout, which was supplied without limit to the players."[27]

For this championship Wu was pleased that he had ace Zhuang on the team along with several young arms—only eight of the players had been on the previous year's squad. Taiwan started the tournament ominously, losing to Panama, Korea, and the Netherlands. The prospect of going to the next round was bleak. However, the United States surprisingly lost to Taiwan, who thus barely made it to the next round.[28]

Wu now amazingly sent Guo Jinxing, an inexperienced and raw pitcher, to face Cuba in a game that Taiwan won by hitting 3 homers. The homer hit by Peter Pan especially amazed the thirty thousand Cuban spectators because he looked too short and thin to have the power to hit the ball so far. Subsequently, Wu sent in his ace Zhuang in the later part of the game to secure the victory.

When the silver medal was awarded in the closing ceremony, thirty thousand Cuban fans in Havana's Estadio Latinoamericano shouted "China! China!" out of respect. Despite ferocious protests from the PRC, Fidel Castro allowed the national flag of the ROC to fly in the ball-park.[29] Coach Wu even shook hands with *El Jefe* and had his picture taken; the photograph now hangs in Wu's home.

Although I was studying abroad in England during the World Championships and unable to experience the euphoria in my homeland, numerous friends and acquaintances shared their experiences with me. A student from Taizhong First Senior High School described the frenzied atmosphere at his school during the second game with Cuba: "Our teachers told us not to listen to the radio; instead, they would write the scores on the blackboard. No one wanted to go home after school. Then a loud bang was heard from the campus. We won!"[30]

In 1986 the World Championship was held in Amsterdam. Taiwan did pretty well, with 7 wins and 3 losses that culminated in the last game against Cuba. From the outset Taiwanese hitters were hopeless against Cuban pitchers, from whom they only managed three hits. Thanks to the ingenious tactics of Zeng Jien, several bunts and two squeezes were implemented to score runs. Meanwhile, Cuban hitters were quelled by relief pitcher Lin Kunwei, whose unorthodox submarine delivery confused the Cuban batting tempo. That game ended 4–3 in favor of Taiwan.

During the celebration an emotional scene occurred when team members received word that their beloved CTBA president, Yan Xiaozhang, had died of a sudden heart attack just before the game. Afraid the news might affect the players, officials had deliberately withheld the information until the game ended. The Taiwanese players, who had thought their leader was as usual in the stands, burst into tears when they heard the news. Perplexed foreign media captured the sudden change from joyfulness to woefulness. When Yan's body was brought back home, the four most senior Taiwanese baseball players escorted the coffin, showing their absolute respect for the person who had devoted so much to senior baseball.

The Taiwanese victory was a fitting tribute to Yan. It and the previous terrific performances against Cuba boosted national confidence. That confidence was further enhanced when Rob Smith, president of the IBA, granted that Taiwan was one of the "World's Top Five" (*shijie wuqiang*), along with Cuba, the United States, Japan, and South Korea.

In reality, however, *shijie wuqiang* was another Taiwanese baseball myth that came to permeate the public mind. It is an odd myth because *shijie wuqiang* only means that Taiwan was one of the five best amateur teams and speaks nothing of pro baseball. Countries such as the Dominican Republic, Venezuela, Panama, and so forth could not send their best pros and former pros to international tournaments, and so Taiwan had not played the very best possible teams with the very best players.

Still the performance of the Taiwanese national team during the 1980s and the early 1990s created a golden era for Chinese Taipei. Players were proud of being part of a national team that could go abroad and enjoy privileges and popularity.

Domestic Competitions

Taiwan's international success was founded on a series of competitions that resulted in the selection of the national team. Before 1978 the major domestic competitions for adult baseball were mainly the Provincial Games, the Chairman Cup, the Chinese Cup, and other sporadic tournaments held by local baseball associations. Yet by the late seventies the Provincial Games' glamour had plummeted, and other competitions were either unorganized or the skill levels of the participants was low.

Against this background of lessening interest in adult baseball, the CBA decided to make the games competitive by reforming the current system. In 1978 it set up two leagues: the Spring League normally played in March and the Fall League around October.[31] In general the season for both leagues lasted less than a month. Each league had two divisions. The champion of Division Two could challenge the last place team of Division One in a best-of-three series.[32]

At season's end the CBA named a squad of approximately forty players, who would be divided into two or three training teams. The players on these training teams battled for a place on the national team. Though called amateurs, they played nearly the whole year in order to take part in international games and minor tournaments.

Two national teams, National A and National B, would be produced by the CTBA selection. The former would take part in official international games, such as the Olympics, the World Championship, and the Intercontinental Cup, while the latter would be sent to Latin American countries to gain playing experience. But both teams would appear together in the International Invitation Tournament held in Taiwan at the end of the year and would be named Chinese Blue (*Zhonghua lan*) and Chinese White (*Zhonghua bai*), respectively.[33]

The number of teams in Division One varied between eight and fourteen. Division Two always had fewer than ten squads, sometimes falling to as low as six. Each team was sponsored by a public corporation, the most prominent of which were the Cooperative Bank, Taipower, the China Oil Company, and the RSEA. Teams were also fielded by the military, Chinese Cultural University, Furen University, and PE schools. Kekounaizi, a biscuit firm, was the first private company to organize an adult team. However, its team folded in 1980 due to financial difficulties. It was not until 1984 that another private enterprise-backed squad, Brother Hotel, was created that later became the major driving force of pro baseball.

Perhaps the most memorable game during the eight years of the two leagues' existence was the Fall League's Weichuan–Putaowang showdown that lasted twenty-one innings on September 15, 1979. Both starting pitchers, Huang Guangqi of Weichuan and Zhuang Shengxiong of Putaowang, pitched the whole game. Huang, while throwing a shutout, allowed 12 hits and struck out 18. Zhuang allowed 11 hits and surrendered the game's only run in the top of the twenty-first. During the game Zhuang threw 235 pitches, which smashed his own record of 215 from the previous year. The game lasted from 4:05 p.m. to 10:11 p.m., six hours and six minutes, which is also a record. The right field umpire was so tired that he had to be replaced by another in the nineteenth inning.

From the outset both the Spring and Fall leagues attracted many people to their games. However, fan attendance declined when Chinese Taipei was allowed to return to the international stage in 1982. Witnessing the drastic decline in attendance, the CTBA instituted a reform, trying to revive public fervor for domestic games. In 1986 Yan established a semiprofessional system with the creation of the Adult Baseball League (ABL). Now games had to be played on weekends, and twenty-five percent of the gate receipts from each game was awarded to the winning team, fifteen percent to the losing team, and the remainder to the ABL. The purpose of the ABL was to appeal to both spectators and participants.

Unfortunately, the grand project proved to be a catastrophe. The weekend schedule was often interrupted by rain, and consequently, some games had to be played on weekdays sometimes conflicting with those of some universities, such as Chinese Cultural University and Furen University. After only a year the ABL was abandoned altogether. It was the precursor to Taiwanese pro baseball created in 1990, but it failed because conditions were not yet right.

Civil Versus Martial: *Wen* Versus *Wu*

Modern Keju

As touched on earlier, *keju* (the civil service examination) had a unique place in Chinese history and is virtually unrivaled in other countries. Most aspects of Taiwanese life was affected in some way by *keju*, not the least of which was the island's baseball.

To understand that profound effect on baseball, one must first understand *keju* and its relationship to traditional Chinese society. The reason for *keju*'s importance was the system's fairness, in which people had faith. Other means of selecting officials were considered unfair, especially as the Chinese emphasized the importance of *guanxi* (informal personal relations), through which people could obtain advantages outside the law and from behind the scene.

This long tradition of examination was preserved in Taiwan after the KMT took over the island. One may argue that the Chinese on Taiwan accepted the exam-centered system more willingly than even past Chinese in order to preserve their Confucian heritage.[34] Kuling, a famous Taiwanese TV broadcaster and critic, vividly demonstrated the intensity of competitive examinations in modern Taiwan through a fictional dialogue between student and teacher:

> STUDENT: Teacher, this question in the history exam has a problem.
> TEACHER: How come? Let me see—it says "the Imperial Civil Exams were abolished in Guangxu 31 [1905 AD]. What is wrong with that?
> STUDENT: It is not true . . .
> TEACHER: Why not?
> STUDENT: They have not been abolished at all![35]

The first Joint University Entrance Examination (*daxue liankao*) was implemented on Taiwan in 1954, followed soon by the Joint Senior High School Examination (*gaozhong liankao*). These *liankao* were seen as modern *keju*, for which the acceptance rate was ridiculously low and which when passed virtually guaranteed people better jobs.[36] People who passed *daxue liankao* were the elite of society.

Under this traditional system parents wanted their children to be successful only in academics, not in matters, such as baseball, that were not included in the *liankao*. Children obeyed their parents because in order to work the examination system depended upon filial piety, a deeply regarded Confucian virtue in Chinese society. Traditionally children had no say in their futures; rather, their parents dictated what the children would do. Yet this arrangement was by no means a one-sided affair. As Francis L. K. Hsu suggested in his writings on the influence of Confucianism on the family,

> The son owes to his father absolute obedience, support during his lifetime, mourning after he passes away, burial according to social station and financial ability, provision for his soul's needs in the other world, and glory for the father by doing well or even better than he. But the father must provide for his sons when they are young, educate them in the ancestral tradition, find mates for them, and leave them good names and inheritances as well as he can. . . . They are both obligated to the generations that went before and those yet to come.[37]

This traditional system is based on the concept that parents will always know what is right and will thus make the decisions for their children, whether the children like it or not. Consequently, when parents believe that academic study is the only way to success, they force their children to ferocious studying because they must "glorify clans and exalt ancestors" (*guangzong yaozu*). This conduct, they perceive, is good for both family and individual.

Looking back, I find that Taiwan's education was just dreadful. To me personally, it was like going through examination hell all year long, especially in junior high school. On weekdays it was normal for me to get up at 6:00 a.m., arrive at school before 7:30, clean the school for half an hour, study for another half hour, and attend any assembly before lessons started at 9:00. The official school day ended at 5:00, at which time everyone had dinner at school and then studied for another three hours until 9:00. Students then went home and studied until midnight or 1:00 a.m. On Saturdays we'd have more classes in the morning and then attend cram schools for the remainder of the day as well as all day Sunday.

This schedule is still in effect today in practically every junior and senior high school. There was, and is, nothing but study. Parents told their children, "You don't want to study, so are you going to be a coolie all your life?" All this onerous studying was geared to taking and passing the final examination.[38]

This stress on examination has erected serious barriers to the promotion of sports. In *Guozhong jiaoyu gaige lun* (The Educational Reform of Junior High School), teacher Tan Yuquan writes that "pupils have been in an environment of reference books, test papers, and mock exams. Whether students digest or not, they have to memorize. How could PE develop in these circumstances?"[39] Joining sports teams meant carving out time from study, and such a loss was intolerable to parents, teachers, and principals. If sport is not included in the *liankao*, they asked, why bother wasting time on athletics since sports cannot help improve a student's score? Accordingly, parents would make serious complaints to school authorities if students were found playing on the playground.[40]

The disapproval of parents toward a physical culture made it impossible for schools to promote sports extensively. Consequently, the glamour of student baseball and the successes in senior baseball were not enough to maintain the popularity of the game. Although the government stepped up its subsidies for sporting activities, its money appeared to have little effect in reversing this decline of baseball's popularity. Apart from providing money, the state also established the PE strong-point school program. Under this program certain schools were selected to develop various kinds of sport. The program's aim was to allow players to advance from school level to school level through their sporting ability rather than through their academic aptitude. The strong-school regime became a way of circumventing the normal route of the *liankao*. However, the public stereotyped the athlete as having a "shallow mind, strong body" (*tounao jiandan sizhi fada*), which is an ancient Chinese proverb. The situation was similar to the martial service examination (*wuju*) in ancient China. Though *wuju* coexisted with *keju*, it was not valued by ordinary people because participants were rarely educated and frequently cheated on written exams.

This lack of education left many athletes ill prepared, and after finishing school, some could not find proper jobs. As a result of this failing, parents were easily deterred from letting their children take part in school athletics. People's interest in baseball simply could not be stimulated by the victories at Williamsport or the strong-point school program. Only those not interested in academic work now joined sport teams. According to the sibling of one player,

> To my knowledge those who came to play were often restless and overenergetic in normal classes and had not the slightest interest in studying. Only baseball could contain and control their restive behavior. It provided those boys with a way to release their energy. They were being guided by strict managers, who might use "special means" to make them listen obediently. If it had not been for baseball, my brother might have been a gangster now.[41]

These student athletes, however, found fewer school teams to join. The exact number of elementary school teams that existed in the 1980s is not known. Compared to the more than five hundred teams in 1969, there were only thirty teams active regularly in big competitions in 1983. In the following year thirty-four elementary school teams were playing because of strong-point school programs, without which the number of teams would have been fewer than thirty.[42] Unfortunately, the strong-point school plan was flawed because some schools, once allocated funds, spent the money for other sports than those authorized under the program or on school facilities. Some school officials even used the money for personal profit. These schools had no intention of developing baseball. Accordingly, the baseball slump continued until 1990 when the SBL was established, leading to the revival of grassroots baseball.

High School Baseball

The sports situation was even worse for high school teams. There were three main pillars of high school baseball: Huaxing, Meihe, and RSEA. These three alone graduated players who went onto to staff adult baseball teams during the 1980s and early 1990s.

Although the baseball triumvirate produced many distinguished players and captured countless world championships, they also suffocated the popularity of the sport by decreasing competition at the high school level. Since there was no residency restriction on Taiwan, especially in terms of baseball, players could move around the country as freely as they wanted. Many were like mercenaries and joined one of the three major baseball teams that had the best chance of winning the national championship and going to the LLB competition. These players would automatically receive promotion to universities if they won the world championship. As a consequence of the dominance of the high school triumvirate, newly established teams could only attract lesser players who had been rejected by the three.

These baseball mercenaries led a rigorous life. The following account by a former Huaxing High School ballplayer presents a good general picture of this life during the 1980s. In its presentation of an average day, the account reveals the sports training environment under the civil-over-martial regimen.

> 5:30 a.m. We have to wake up for morning drill. The third-year students of the senior high (normally the captains) would come to the room turning on the light and shouting, "Get off the bed!" We have to dress ourselves in one minute, putting on clothes, socks, and shoes. Then we have to run five to six kilometers for about thirty minutes. We do not run on Saturday mornings, but

it was used by seniors to make fun of juniors, who were, for example, forced to sing songs. In other words, they wanted to train the juniors' guts [to make them courageous].

7:00 a.m. Breakfast time. The dining room is called Spellman Hall, but we nicknamed it the "Spellman Grand Hotel." Seven or eight people sit at a table, with two juniors responsible for filling rice and cleaning up. One senior will allocate food to everyone. After breakfast students take turns washing up used bowls. But baseball players do not have to do that, which is our first prerogative.

8:00 a.m. After Breakfast. Cleaning up the pupils' living area. Compared to massive areas allocated to normal students, the baseball players' area is very small, which is our second prerogative. After cleanup there will be a flag-raising ceremony.

8:30 a.m.–12:00 p.m. Study time. I will briefly describe the studying situation of junior high players. In the first year players occasionally read some books. In the second year players occasionally cheat on exams. In the third year players are too lazy to cheat, and they sleep on the table during study periods, which is our third prerogative. Only when the class ends would players wake up and salute the teachers, showing a little respect; otherwise, they will be with *Zhougong* [a Chinese proverb for sleeping]. Teachers would only wake them up when saliva was all over the table or they snored too loudly. The basic attitude of the teachers is that as long as the players do not interrupt their teaching, it is all right. As for exams, players will automatically get a pass, which is sixty points, so long as they put their signature on the exam papers without filling in the answers. This is our fourth prerogative. As for senior high players, it is practically the same, sleeping in classes and signing exams.

12:10 p.m. Lunch time. To be honest, Huaxing's lunch is not that good. There are rarely any well-fed students in Huaxing. In summer there is watermelon. Everyone can have a piece of it, but it is so thin that you have to admire the chef's "knife skill."

1:30 p.m. After lunch. Break time. Normally juniors have no right to take siestas. We have to put all the gear in place for afternoon practice.

1:30 p.m.–5:40 p.m. Drill time. First there are warmups. We have to run for twenty minutes, after which there is stretching. After that we have to sprint twenty meters back and forth. After half an hour everyone is already pouring with sweat. Then we start tossing and catching the ball. Then there is batting practice, which is tantamount to a real game. Fielders have to concentrate. If there are too many errors, the coach would order punitive running, which lasts over an hour. Overall it is not uncommon to run twenty kilometers a day.

6:00 p.m. Dinner time. This is the time players have the greatest prerogative, which is a meat course, such as chicken, pork, beef, shrimp, and so on, that were interchangeably served every day. Normally we could finish it at one sitting. If not, we often gave it to regular students, making sure nothing was wasted.

7:00 p.m. After dinner. Showering and washing time. It goes without saying that seniors shower first.

7:00 p.m.–9:00 p.m. Evening study time. We often listen to music, write, fool around with teammates (not too loudly), or continue the interrupted sleep from the morning. We are not allowed to go back to our dormitories because the teachers will check on us.

9:00 p.m.–10:00 p.m. Weight-training time. We try to do something relaxing, such as holding dumbbells. But sometimes a few "abnormal" seniors would come and order special physical training, such as sprinting up a slope for twenty-five seconds, push-ups, or sit-ups, all of which left juniors speechless.

10:00 p.m. Bed time. Seniors come punctually to turn off the light. After that, the light is not allowed to be turned on, except under special circumstances. This is the sole free time everyone has. Some players wash their clothes or take showers (though no hot water is available). Some would stealthily get up to improve their batting skills, while others smoke while hiding somewhere they cannot be discovered by coaches or more senior players.[43]

This is the standard schedule without competition pressure. If major competition were looming, the school would cancel the players' morning academic classes so that they could concentrate on training. The practice would continue until it was very dark when the players would go back for a dinner prepared in advance for them. This kind of practice would start one month before a real tournament.

There is another characteristic of high school student baseball: the hazing system, under which juniors have to serve seniors unconditionally. As one Huaxing player stated, "running a baseball team is like running a military, with a strict senior-junior relationship. It is a kind of obligation. Hazing for seniors was to avoid being bullied without proper cause. Most things we did were to wash seniors' clothes, buy things, run errands, something like that, nothing serious. One or two seniors were very bad. For instance, they gave you NT$100 [$3] to buy NT$200 [$6] of stuff. But they are not very many. Seniors had rights to conduct corporal punishment when the coach was not present. But it was also rare."[44]

The Tragedy of Tong Renchong

Since there can be only one champion, the competition between the top high school teams became so fierce that they turned students into full-time players. Additionally, the schools overused certain talented players, especially ace pitchers, some of whom were injured so badly that they could not continue playing. Overusing players was especially common during the player-poor period of the 1980s, for as soon as a player was judged promising, he became a target for overuse. Such was the fate of Tong Renchong, the most tragic case of overuse in Taiwanese baseball history. Tong is an unfamiliar name to the newer fans and a forgotten name among the older, but his tragedy epitomized baseball development during the 1980s.[45]

Tong enrolled in Huaxing High School in 1983 with thirteen other players. In elementary school he had already been an ace pitcher, possessing a fastball, a curve, and a wicked slider. It can be said that he who lives by the slider also dies by the slider because it often injures the pitching elbow. However, coaches cared less about the individual player's welfare than they did for the accomplishments of their teams.

During his time at Huaxing Tong became an ace again in his second year even while his other teammates were still on the reserve team. In his third year Huaxing was on the verge of winning the precious national championship. Tong was in pain from his shoulder because, being the best pitcher on the team, he had been used relentlessly for the previous two years. Finally, his coach made the drastic decision to take him to a hospital, where Tong's arm was injected with a high-dose analgesic, called by the Taiwanese the "American panacea." The adjective "American" was used because the Taiwanese thought highly of all medicine produced in the United States. Tong went on to win against RSEA, thus helping Huaxing go to the United States in 1986.

Tong even appeared in the Regional Games, a tournament dominated by adult players. He faced Taipower that possessed many famous players, among them Zheng Baisheng, Song Rongtai, and Zeng Zhizhen. Armed with his sharp slider, Tong struck out Taipower's hitters one by one. They were absolutely shocked by this rookie pitcher and could not believe he was only sixteen years old.

Tong continued getting injections to ease the pain of his shoulder, but these treatments were masking the potential for serious injury. Finally, after five years on the mound with continual use of the American panacea, Tong suffered a ligament tear. Doctors told him to have an operation to repair his shoulder. However, he feared the operation would end his career and refused. After this injury, however, he was gradually forgotten as his injured shoulder caused a crisis of confidence within him about his ability to pitch. Thus although the Mercury pro baseball club tried to sign him and the University of Hawaii offered a scholarship, he rejected them both.

Eventually, in 1995, Tong agreed to have the shoulder operation. His postoperative recovery went well, and people expected that he would return to the mound. But then three months after the operation, he died suddenly due to complications caused by a bacterial infection. His death certificate showed that he died of acute meningitis cerebralis.

Tong started playing baseball when he was nine and died when he was twenty-five. Baseball brought happiness, pride, and responsibility to him, but it also contributed indirectly to his death.

Tong was a rarity in Taiwanese baseball because he did not smoke or drink, common habits among players. He did not even have a girl-friend. Everyone who knew him had nothing but praise for him. One parent said that "knowing so many Huaxing players, [he] never saw such a good, decent, and polite player." One of his teammates recalled that Tong was "the most decent and honest player" he had ever seen, with "none of the bad habits possessed by other players."[46] Wang Jin-yong, currently a pro player with the Brother Elephants, remembered that "at Huaxing the hazing system was popular. Therefore corporal punishment and special physical training exercised by seniors were normal. . . . But Tong was different. He always talked to juniors with reason and never used those horrible methods. Thanks to Tong, I was able to encourage myself and to continue on the baseball path."[47]

Unlike the passing of Lin Xiangrui, who was a member of the 1972 world champion team whose death from cancer a year later caused a national sensation, Tong's death did not produce the slightest stir be-cause people cared only about pro stars or international tournaments. The apathy shown by the media and the public really saddened some die-hard baseball fans like myself who lamented that a society obsessed with winning simply did not care about the well-being of its lesser-known players. In many ways the tragedy of Tong mirrors the tragedy of modern Taiwanese baseball.

Although Taiwan enjoyed continual successes in the LLB and at in-ternational tournaments, its amateur baseball had many dark aspects, including match-fixing, under-the-table recruitment, and disguised professionalism, just to name a few. These negatives caused a drastic decline in baseball's popularity, and it was not until the creation of a professional league that grassroots baseball revived.

一九三一年七月十九日〜廿三日全島中等學校野球大會以蓄音机向全島湧宴况轉播

1. Staff and reporters used radio to broadcast games to all of Taiwan during the Japanese occupation. Photo courtesy of Cai Wuzhang.

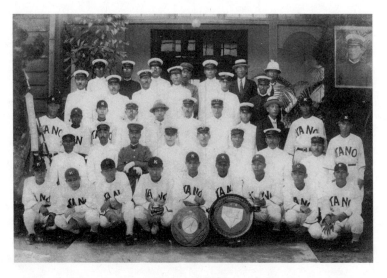

2. Jianong's glorious return to school with shields awarded to the team for winning the Taiwan championship and for being the Koshien runner-up. Photo courtesy of Cai Wuzhang.

3. Commemorating Jianong's participation in the three-day, forty-inning marathon of 1941. Photo courtesy of Cai Wuzhang.

4. Members of the U.S. Seventh Fleet hold up a souvenir banner given to them by the Taiwan Coal baseball team during a visit to Taiwan in 1952. Photo courtesy of Central News Agency.

5. On behalf of America's National Baseball Congress, U.S. Major General William Chase, chief of MAAG, donates the Golden Statue award to the Taiwan baseball association. Photo courtesy of Central News Agency.

6. Wearing simple T-shirts and torn trousers, young Taiwanese play baseball barefoot during the 1954 Children's Cup. Photo courtesy of Central News Agency.

7. The dugout of Taiwan Land Bank during the 1954 Bank and Corporation Union Cup. Photo courtesy of Central News Agency.

8. Taiwan hosted the Fourth Asian Championship, at which fans were packed so tightly into the partially completed Taipei Municipal Stadium that many had to sit on the wall. Photo courtesy of Central News Agency.

9. Sadaharu Oh exhibits his offensive power in front of a packed crowd in 1965. Photo courtesy of Central News Agency.

10. Hongye's catcher Jiang Honghui hits a grand slam against Japan's Kansai team. Photo courtesy of Central News Agency.

11. A jubilant crowd lifts the two Hongye heroes Jiang Honghui (*left*) and Jiang Wanxing (*right*) after the team's victory over Kansai. Photo courtesy of Central News Agency.

12. U.S. Major General Ciccolella donates money on behalf of MAAG to the Jinlong youth team, who needed it for the trip to Williamsport. Photo courtesy of Central News Agency.

13. A victory parade was held in downtown Taipei after Juren won the LLB world series in 1971. Photo courtesy of Central News Agency.

14. The national team and staff are shown here shouting patriotic slogans in front of Presidential Hall after the 1983 Asian Championship campaign. Photo courtesy of Central News Agency.

15. The 1992 Olympic squad that won the silver medal in Barcelona. Photo courtesy of Lin Huawei.

16. Chen Jinfeng (Chen Chin-feng) signs with the LA Dodgers in 1999 and becomes the first Taiwanese player to reach the Major Leagues. Photo courtesy of Central News Agency.

17. Fans cheer for Brother Elephants, the most popular team on Taiwan. Photo courtesy of Brother Elephants.

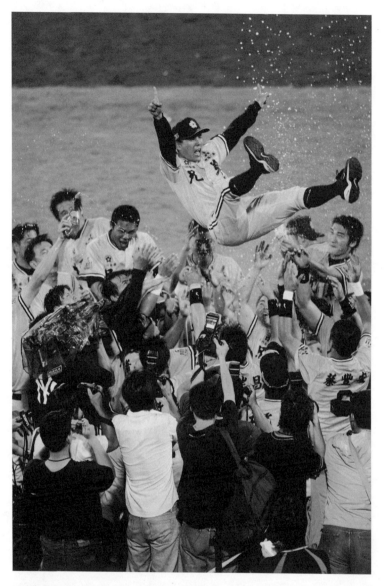

18. The Brother Elephants celebrating their second-half season title in 2003.
Photo courtesy of Brother Elephants.

公告

禁止打棒，壘球及從事

其他危險性體育活動

體育組 啓

No Ball Playing Allowed

Physical Education and Sports Office

19. This sign reads "Baseball, softball, and other dangerous activities are forbidden." Such signs are commonly found in many Taiwanese schools. Photo courtesy of Zhong Mingfeng.

20. In a landslide 13–1 victory over Cuba in the 1983 Intercontinental Cup, Zhuang Shengxiong (*far right*) was the winning pitcher, and Zhao Shiqiang (*far left*) hit two home runs. Photo courtesy of Central News Agency.

FIVE

The Birth of Professional Baseball, 1990–1995

In 1987 the government of Taiwan lifted the infamous martial law that had existed for more than thirty-five years. A year later Li Denghui succeeded Chiang Ching-kuo as the nation's leader and offered an entirely different approach to foreign policy. Li had no intention of encompassing mainland China as part of the ROC; rather, he sought equal status with the Communists. Incrementally barriers to cross-straits interaction were removed.

Economically Taiwan continued to have robust growth. Domestically not only were political reforms put into effect, but there were also calls for expansion of public expenditures on education, science, and culture. Additionally, explicit demands for greater state funding of sports were heard.

In reaction to these changes Taiwanese civil society, not surprisingly, came suddenly alive after being infiltrated by the state apparatus for decades. It is not a coincidence that the notion of creating a pro baseball league occurred in 1987 during this time of awakening.

Bringing Back Our Boys

The 1980s were marked by dismal participation in amateur baseball. This decline was not a result of the public's having tired of national teams victories. As discussed in the previous chapter, the underlying factors were the deterioration of the baseball environment and the re-emergence of the traditional sedentary culture.

The situation further worsened as star players found it difficult to continue playing baseball after they finished school, for during this period once student players graduated from senior high or university, they only had two options for remaining in baseball. The first was to join the public-corporation teams, such as Cooperative Bank or Taipower, which paid $500 a month. However, these teams took only a few players each year. The second option was going abroad and signing with foreign pro or amateur clubs that often paid high salaries. Since at the time there was no prospect of a domestic pro league, a host of good players left Taiwan.

Such players as Li Zongyuan, Li Laifa, and Gao Yingjie went to Japan to play pro baseball. Although they did not fare well in the Japanese leagues, their examples opened the floodgate for Taiwanese playing abroad. The most successful Taiwanese players were pitchers Guo Yuanzhi, Guo Taiyuan, and Zhuang Shengxiong. Guo Yuanzhi, an Amis aborigine, achieved 106 wins and 116 saves during his pro career in Japan. Guo Taiyuan, who has always been mistakenly identified by foreigners as an aborigine, was famous for his extremely hard fastball, recorded at 97 mph, enabling him to obtain 117 wins in the NPB. He was dubbed the "Oriental Express."

In general the Japanese pro clubs preferred signing Taiwanese pitchers to hitters. The latter often had trouble adjusting to the wooden bats used in the pro leagues after being accustomed to the aluminum bats required in amateur competitions. However, Chen Dafeng, a power-hitting outfielder from Huaxing High School, defied all odds. Chen went on to become the most successful Taiwanese batter to ever play in Japan, hitting 277 home runs in his fourteen-year career with the Chunichi Dragons and Hanshin Tigers.

Offers from Japanese amateur clubs were also very alluring to Taiwanese ballplayers. For example, Liu Qiunong, who was signed by the Yamaha amateur club in 1981, received $1,030 a month plus certain bonus fees.[1] Kang Mingshan, who was named the best right-handed pitcher in the 1986 World Championship, joined a Japanese amateur club that paid him $4,195 a month and that promised to release him immediately if any pro club became interested in him.[2]

The process of player outflow caused an emptying of Taiwanese baseball, which not only became shallow at the grassroots level but at the adult as well. It is therefore not surprising that adult games attracted fewer and fewer fans to the ballparks since the best players were gone. Despite winning the bronze medal at the 1984 Olympics, which drew the entire island's attention, Taiwanese baseball received no boost. The fiasco at the 1988 Seoul Olympics at which Chinese Taipei lost to the Netherlands, Japan, and Puerto Rico, thus being relegated to last place, did not help either.

Tang and Hong

Hong Qiaorong, a senior member of the Chinese Baseball Committee, audaciously proposed the idea of creating a professional league in the hopes of revitalizing adult baseball when the national team hit rock bottom in the 1971 Asian Championship, even as the Little Leaguers won the world championship at Williamsport.[3] But the public did not heed his suggestion. The entire country was focused on the LLB world series and was consumed by world championship fever.

The most opportune time to develop pro baseball would have been between 1977 and the early 1980s, during which period veteran players had yet to retire while new players cultivated after Hongye were beginning to come through the pipeline. Nevertheless, the opportunity was lost. Government officials, fans, and the general public all thought international results were more important than the creation of professional baseball, whose players were not allowed to take part in international tournaments. So many good players, such as Xie Lianggui, Xu Ronggui, and Huang Dongnan, retired early. Other stars went to Japan. Two presidents of the CTBA, Xie Guocheng and Yan Xiaozhang, tried to establish semiprofessional baseball, but both failed.

It was not until Tang Panpan took office in 1986 that a serious proposition for professional baseball was fielded. Tang, the general manager of the China Broadcast Company, was appointed to the CTBA job through the endorsements of the KMT secretary-general, the KMT social work president, and the education minister. He was a mainland-born Chinese who loved basketball and baseball. After being inspired by the successful commercialization of the 1984 Los Angeles Olympics, Tang first had the idea of professional baseball. As Tang recalled,

When I took office in 1986, many people asked me to develop pro baseball, but a lot more told me not to. They used South Korea as an example since that it had not had proper international results in the seven years following the creation of a pro league in 1982. But after IOC President Juan Antonio Samaranch began to allow pro athletes to take part in the Olympics, the division of amateur and professional was no longer important. That is why I made up my mind to develop pro baseball.[4]

The second figure in the creation of pro ball was the founder of the Brother pro club, Hong Tengsheng, dubbed the Father of Professional Baseball. The Brother Hotel baseball team was created in 1984 and was the second squad after Kekounaizi's to be sponsored by a private company that did not depend on the cooperation of universities or colleges. At the time Brother Hotel offered almost $880 in monthly wages to first-class players; this sum double the salary offered by the public corporations.[5] From the outset Hong was determined to make Brother the most popular brand on the island.

Motivated by the good pay, over forty players submitted their résumés to the club, whose chairman, Hong, and manager, Zeng Jien, jointly held interviews. Although the high salaries offered by Brother Hotel drew criticism from some who favored amateur baseball, most people basically thought the wages were a start in taking players' welfare seriously.

Apart from high wages, Brother also had different rules to govern its players. At the time all public corporation ballplayers were required to work as clerks for the company in the morning and train in the afternoon, while players with university teams had to attend school. Brother players, however, did not have to work for the hotel. The only thing they were required to do was play baseball.[6]

Zeng, the Brother coach, had spent most of his life in the air force and was a very strict team manager. It was his spartan ways and stringent discipline that made Brother the most popular team on Taiwan. As an example of the rigor of Zeng's training, infielder Lin Baiheng lost fifteen kilograms (going from ninety-nine to eighty-four) within two months. Still Lin fell short of his target weight of eighty kilograms and was thus grounded on weekends.

In 1987 Tang and Hong joined forces to form the Committee for the Promotion of Professional Baseball, with the former chairing the committee and the latter serving as executive secretary. The advent of pro baseball was not met with universal approval. Critics argued that pro ball might weaken the national team and thus affect its ability to win international tournaments. To counter this objection, Peng Chenghao, former president of the CTBA, suggested that instead of pro baseball Taiwan should have semipro ball just as the Cubans did.[7] The season would be long and the standard of play high, but all players would retain their amateur status and would be eligible for international games. Moreover, players' wages would be kept to a minimum and thus would not place a financial burden on the clubs.

Tang and Hong, however, did not accept Peng's proposal. Their objective was to provide relatively high salaries that would allow players to make a good living. They felt that pro baseball with its good wages would slow the player exodus and rescue the stagnated grassroots baseball by offering talented student athletes a future as professional ballplayers.

The Chinese Professional Baseball League

All of Hong and Tang's efforts finally bore fruit in 1990 with the inaugural season of the Chinese Professional Baseball League (CPBL). The new league featured four teams: the Brother Elephants, the Weichuan Dragons, the Mercury Tigers, and the President Lions. Originally Eva Green was to have been one of the four, but it eventually chose to pull out of the league because the team management felt league officials had too much say in team operations. Hong was forced to look for a replacement. Fortunately, he was able to convince former classmate Chen Junyi, head of Mercury Bank, to sponsor a team.

Weichuan and Brother had already had amateur squads for eleven and six years, respectively, with the latter especially having a huge fan base across the country. Mercury and President had the fewest fans because their teams had been created in 1989 by absorbing players from Cooperative Bank and Taipower, respectively. Although there were still doubts about the CPBL's prospects, the league was naively assured by the Committee for the Promotion of Professional Baseball that, if the average attendance was over twenty-five hundred per game, the bottom line could be met.[8]

Unlike pro teams, such as Daiei in Japan or Samsung in Korea, which were owned by large well-known corporations, Taiwanese teams were owned by small and medium-sized companies, which are common to the island. The only big companies on Taiwan were government-owned public corporations, which were still tiny when compared to those of Japan and Korea. Since the sponsors of the new Taiwanese pro teams could only offer modest budgets, their teams controlled costs by carrying no more than thirty players on a roster and forgoing minor league and reserve teams.

What was—and remains—unique to the CPBL was that no team had a local fan base. Although the President Lions stationed their team in the south, the Lions did not represent this region because the El-ephants actually had more fans than the Lions in the south. The pro clubs were like circus bands touring the island and playing in five ball-parks, a phenomenon exclusive to Taiwan.

One factor that led to this lack of regional identification was the way in which players were recruited by schools, which commonly brought in athletes from all over the island. Thus as soon as promising players entered high school, they would go either to Huaxing or RSEA in Taipei or Meihe in Pingdong. This dispersion meant that fans could not root for local boys since they had gone elsewhere. Even if people wanted to cheer for local stars attending any of the three high schools, they would feel strange because the athletes were playing for other counties. Additionally, although Huaxing, Meihe, and RSEA created a hegemony in high school baseball, local residents of Taipei and Pingdong did not possess any particular sentiment toward team players, regarding them as mercenaries from other counties instead of homegrown boys. This lack of regional identity became a part of Taiwanese baseball, even for senior and professional baseball.

The Golden Age of Pro Baseball

This lack of regional loyalty did not deter Taiwanese pro ball from getting off to a good start, for when Brother and President played the first-ever pro match, it was in front of a huge crowd of some fifteen thousand at Taipei Municipal Baseball Stadium. The game ushered in a new era in Taiwanese baseball. The league slogan was "Purity, Health, and Happiness," crafted to impart to the public that the CPBL's primary purpose was to provide a leisure-time activity; organizers did not want fans to skeptically view the league as commercialized.

The success of the opening game, however, did not keep the corporate sponsors from initially being pessimistic about the financial prospects of the league. The sponsors did not expect to achieve the target goal of twenty-five hundred per game, but to their surprise the CPBL got off to a flying start by drawing nearly nine hundred thousand fans, around five thousand per game, in the inaugural season. This initial success demonstrated that pro baseball was an enormous market waiting to be exploited. Apparently pro sports provided a whole new venture in which people could participate and engage. It became an entertainment; it was show business.

However, larger-than-expected crowds did not translate into profits for the owners. On the contrary, every club suffered losses each year of operation. The cost of players' salaries and travel could only be partially offset by ticket money and TV revenue, which in any case did not really exist until 1997. Yet this lack of profit was not a prime concern of the owners since their main objective was publicity for their corporations, the names of which could be seen virtually every day during the season by attending fans or on TV. Such publicity could not be measured in terms of money.

Of all the CPBL clubs none provided its owners with better publicity than that of Brother Hotel. Knowing from the very beginning that its goal was to create a pro baseball club, Brother was very aggressive in promoting its amateur team among Taiwanese fans. Brother strove to make its team the New York Yankees or Tokyo Giants of Taiwan. Its efforts successful, Brother attracted many loyal fans from every social class and gave new depth to domestic amateur baseball, which had been eclipsed by Little League Baseball and international tournaments. Although Weichuan established its team earlier than Brother, it had no long-term plan for wooing fans and found its team only the second favorite in the new pro league.

Brother was so popular because of its team's character and the squad's winning record that the company inspired a rare event in the world of baseball. On April 24, 1986, four thousand Brother fans seated in the stadium collectively called for the continuation of a game that had been interrupted by a relentless downpour. Fans hollered at league officials for the game to resume. In a state of panic the officials recruited players from four other teams, plus part-time workers to make the field playable. Brother won the game dramatically in the eighth inning to claim their first-ever title, an unforgettable moment for many fans.[9]

By the 1990s Brother had created a baseball dynasty; its success culminated in 1994 when the team won its third title in a row. That season Brother established a winning percentage of .727 (64 wins, 24 losses, and 2 draws) and a team batting average of .302, a record that has yet to be broken. In these peak years Brother drew nearly ten thousand fans per game.

When the Brother dynasty finally faded, the CPBL also went into decline. In 1995 the average attendance dropped for the first time, as Brother suffered one of its worst seasons. In 1996 the darkest era of Taiwanese pro baseball began.

The Return of the Taiwanese Diaspora

Brother, as well as the other CPBL teams, needed players, and in the beginning all looked to recruit those Taiwanese who were playing overseas. Indeed, when Tang and Hong announced that the pro league was to be launched in 1990, some members of the Taiwanese diaspora in Japan were tempted to come back immediately. After all, there is no place like home. As Huang Pingyang, a future megastar pitcher for Weichuan, said at the time, "although the Japanese baseball environment is better than that in Taiwan and salaries are also higher, I have personal and family reasons to consider."[10] Huang was a national hero who had made his mark in the 1987 Asian Championship, in which he'd started against Japan and South Korea, winning both games and thus leading Taiwan to its first-ever championship in the tournament. That same year he signed with a Japanese amateur club, who tried to re-sign him three years later by offering $6,640 a month. The CPBL's maximum wage was only $2,950 in its first season. Despite the better Japanese offer, Huang swiftly rejected it because Taiwan was his home and he wanted to play in front of Taiwanese fans. Weichuan fans were eternally grateful and came to adore the breaking-ball pitcher, who won twenty games in his inaugural CPBL season and earned the nickname *jinbiren* (Man with the Golden Arm). Commentators came to refer to him as having "seven pitches with rainbow colors."

However, most Taiwanese pros in Japan maintained a wait-and-see attitude, wondering how far the CPBL could go. They were suspicious about pro baseball development since it had not existed previously on Taiwan. The experiment might therefore go disastrously wrong. Nobody could know the ultimate outcome. Moreover, the Japanese amateur clubs played fewer games per season than the CPBL teams, and the salaries were better. The average wage for the Taiwanese contingent was $6,565 per month.[11] The Taiwanese players were not prepared to give up their salaries and positions in order to throw themselves into an unknown future, and as a result, most chose to stay in Japan.

This decision was soon reversed when, witnessing the enormous popularity of the CPBL's inaugural season, virtually all the Taiwanese playing on Japanese amateur clubs came back for the first draft in the CPBL's history. Chen Yixin, a former Japanese pro player, also chose to join the CPBL. He was strangely picked up through the backdoor by Brother Elephants via a foreign players' draft, even though he was not a foreign player. It is alleged that the CPBL secretary, Hong Tengsheng, who was also chairman of Brother Hotel, deliberately allowed him to join in this law-evading manner. Wu Sixian, a member of the 1992 Olympic squad, was the last Taiwanese playing for a Japanese amateur club to join the CPBL. Since then no Taiwanese player has been signed by an amateur club in Japan. Apart from a few players in the Japanese pro leagues, the CPBL was able to attract all the best Taiwanese players to itself.[12]

The most famous return from the Taiwanese diaspora was Lü Mingsi, who triggered the first player trade in CPBL history. Lü's decision to return from Japan in late 1992 started a war between Brother and Weichuan. Brother, which had finished in last place the previous season, obtained the first draft choice. Yet Lü's parent club was Weichuan, and he wanted to rejoin the team with which he was most familiar. Weichuan was equally adamant about reobtaining him; it even tried to circumvent the draft by signing him as a hitting coach, which would also have allowed him to play at the same time. Under fire from all quarters of the league, however, Weichuan finally conceded by parting with its best outfielder, Lin Yizeng, and catcher and good batter Chen Yancheng to Brother in exchange for "Cannon" Lü. As matters turned out, Brother received the better bargain. Lin and Chen went on to help Brother create its dynasty, winning three consecutive championships, while Lü's performance never lived up to the fans' expectations.

Government Policies on Sport

Sport for All

The influx of these diaspora players into the CPBL filled out the league's teams with good players. Still Brother Elephants' owner Hong Tengsheng knew that pro baseball could not last without wide participation in grassroots baseball from which future players must come. Unfortunately, as discussed in the previous chapter, grassroots baseball was in decline. At this point the government tried once more to revive school baseball programs, along with others sports.

For the first time the government officially admitted that sports were valuable other than for competition; they had a recreational value. This new declaration about sports shifted the emphasis from international competition to domestic play.

Since the establishment of the strong-point school program had not worked during the 1980s, at least in terms of increasing baseball participation, the government replaced it with the sport-for-all program and the School Baseball League (SBL). The new objective was to provide standard physical exercise for students in their spare time and to build character through sports. The government also hoped to convince the general public that the enjoyment of sports was more important than winning. Before the adoption of the SBL the CTBA launched a primary school and junior high school scheme, to which Elephants' owner Hong Tengsheng donated $209,790 annually starting in 1987. Like the later SBL, this program subsidized the purchase of baseball equipment for schools who wanted to organize teams.

The government's shifting its focus from international competitions to domestic popular sports can be discerned in terms of money spent. In 1986 the budget for international competitions was $8.41 million, while that for domestic sports was a minuscule $841,000. Three years later $153 million was spent on international competitions, but over $306 million was spent on domestic sport.[13] So while spending for overseas tournaments was eighteen times as great, that for domestic sports was thirty-six times as great—a growth rate twice that of international spending.

In the realm of grassroots baseball the government, through its Department of Physical Education, provided handsome incentives for schools interested in taking part in the SBL. It subsidized any school, whether bona fide or not, wanting to have a baseball team. Governmental regulations stipulated that a school that was organizing a team for the first time would receive $1,840 and that schools with existing teams would receive $1,105 if they continued to participate. Furthermore, transportation, meal, and drinking water expenses would be covered depending on how far away schools were located from the sites of competition. The plan immediately made a big impact, and over two hundred primary schools were funded.[14]

Not all participating schools necessarily coveted a baseball program; some just wanted to use the money for other things. Yet as long as a school formed a team after receiving the subsidy, the authorities did not care how the money was actually spent.

Apart from its financial subsidies, the Department of PE took other important measures that genuinely increased the willingness of schools to organize teams. Accordingly, under-the-table recruiting and bargains were now prohibited.

The Department of PE also enforced the boundary rule, which under LLB regulations was either demarcated by the size of the local population or the number of students. This practice protects league players from being raided by another league. In the past Taiwanese players could move around the entire island because Taiwan observed no boundary rule. Now players were confined to a single county. A county that, if good primary school players graduated, had to establish junior high school teams in order to accommodate them. This requirement increased the willingness of junior high schools to organize teams without fearing that other counties would steal their players. The enforcement of the boundary rule was effective. During the entire 1980s there had been fewer than ten junior high school teams. By 1995 the number had risen to over three hundred.

Still Taiwan partially got around the boundary rule by using entire counties or a municipal city as a league. For example, players in Taipei city, with a population of over two and a half million, could enroll in any school as long as they stayed within the city. At least Taiwanese baseball was headed in a more ethical direction.

Although money and boundary enforcement did lead to a dramatic increase in the overall number of grassroots teams, it did not necessarily mean that the notion of baseball as recreation had supplanted the idea that winning was everything. Nor did these factors mean that a physical culture had begun to take root on Taiwan. Indeed, there was a very real question about sport for all, or subsidy for all to be more exact. Since under this policy schools formed teams because they were paid to do so, would they continue to maintain these squads without state involvement? The answer to this question will be discussed in the next chapter, which examines what happened when the state stopped its funding in 1996.

Détente with the PRC

The most important Taiwanese national policy regarding sports during this period was the rise of steady official contacts with the PRC. Although the three-nos policy had been abandoned in 1987, state contact with the mainland was still taboo. Sports, however, would play a vital role in breaking the ideological barrier.

The political sea change was due to the fact that Taiwan felt that the momentum now lay with the PRC. In 1979 the latter returned to the IOC family and became one of the most formidable sporting nations in the world. As a player in the global sports arena, the PRC was destined to host many international games. If Taiwan could not participate because of its anti-Communist policy, it would miss political and athletic opportunities. A sporting exchange thus would be a chance to break the official stalemate. So in April 1989 the Taiwanese national team stepped for the first time onto the mainland to compete in the Asian Gymnastic Tournament in Beijing. This act opened a new era in Taiwanese sporting history.

Within a year Taiwanese athletes were back on the mainland. Despite the hardline stance of the Ministry of Education, Taiwan decided to take part in the 1990 Beijing Asian Games, but that participation was not without struggle. The main problem was the Chinese translation of "Chinese Taipei," which became an important issue whenever games were held in the PRC. The English word "Chinese" can be translated into Chinese in two ways. One is *Zhonghua*, the other *Zhongguo*. Basically *Zhonghua* means Chinese in the broadest cultural and ethnic sense, while *Zhongguo* refers to China. Therefore the English words "Chinese Taipei" could be translated either as *Zhonghua Taipei* or *Zhongguo Taipei*. Taiwan preferred—and still does—*Zhonghua Taipei*, implying that it is ethnically Chinese but not part of the PRC, which is now synonymous with China. The PRC, however, wanted to use *Zhongguo Taipei*, thus making Taiwan a part of China. IOC President Samaranch, after listening to explanations from both sides, was absolutely baffled and said, "What is the difference between *Zhonghua* and *Zhongguo*? I cannot understand you Chinese people who can make such a big fuss just because of one word."[15] After four rounds of negotiation the PRC's IOC member, He Zhenliang, finally conceded that Taiwan could participate under the name of *Zhonghua Taipei* and signed a document to that effect on April 5, 1989.[16]

Taking part in the 1990 Beijing Asian Games not only signaled that Taiwan implicitly recognized the mainland Communist regime but also indicated a change in the conservative attitude of the Taiwanese military. Originally the Ministry of Defense refused to allow players who were currently serving in the army permission to travel to mainland China. The ministry feared such visits would jeopardize national security.[17] However, several of Taiwan's athletes, among them three baseball players, Lin Chaohuang, Bai Kunhong, and Zhuo Kunyuan, were serving in the military. Other athletes, among them basketball players, cyclists, and shooters, also were serving in the Taiwanese military. So in order to ensure the best outcome for Taiwan, the Department of Defense had to soften its stance. And indeed, Lin, Bai, and Zhuo would prove extremely important in capturing a gold medal at the Asian Games. They and their teammates later became the backbone of the 1992 baseball squad that took the silver medal at the Barcelona Olympics.

Another consideration was a part of the military's rethinking its policy. Objections by the Ministry of Defense would make other international sporting organizations think that the Taiwanese government was allowing politics to dictate sporting decisions. Such a perception might have had grave consequences. Major sporting venues might veto future Taiwan bids to hold international games, which require the free entrance of athletes from all countries.

Premier Hao Bocun, who had been a general in the Taiwanese army, personally endorsed allowing athletes who were active military to play on the national team as special cases.[18] These special cases could go to Beijing with individual identification, a designation meaning that, despite being in the military, the athletes could take part in games held by nongovernmental organizations and play for Taiwan's national honor. As famous shooting athlete Du Taixing said, "I am very glad that the government made the right decision. . . . I am a professional soldier as well as an athlete and know too many mainlanders [referring to the PRC] and foreign athletes. If we can go to competitions held in East Germany and Moscow but are prohibited from going to the mainland, it would be hard for international sporting people to understand."[19]

"Heavy Rewards Bring about Audacious Men"

The Taiwanese government continued its encouragement of its athletes by adopting a policy from long ago. During the period of the Warring States in ancient China, famous politician Shang Yang used heavy rewards to induce audacious men to do things normal people would not do. From this ancient policy came the Chinese proverb "heavy rewards bring about audacious men" (*zhongshang zhixia biyou yongfu*).

Thousands of years later the Taiwanese government used the same method to encourage athletes to win Olympic gold medals. In February 1991 the Ministry of Education announced an important decree, the Guoguang and Zhongzheng Sports Awards, stipulating that athletes would be rewarded financially for winning medals at international games. The amount of money given out depended on the level of prestige associated with the competition. There were three levels, each level containing four grades, with the first level and first grade being the highest.

In 1991 the baseball team was runner-up at the Asian Championship, placing it in the third level-third grade, for which the government gave out approximately $163,000 to the entire team. When in the following year the team won the silver at the Barcelona Olympics, the whole squad, excluding the coaches, was granted $3.88 million. If the team had taken the gold, each player would have been rewarded with a staggering $388,400, totaling $8.16 million for the whole team including the four coaches.

Most Taiwanese athletes and sports experts approved the reward system. A respected former pitcher, Gao Quanrong, said that the "sporting careers of athletes are very short. Moreover, they often abandon their academic study for the sake of exercise. Without an academic diploma and occupational skills, it is difficult for them to have a proper life. The Guoguang Awards are terrific news for those athletes."[20] Retired infielder Lin Minzheng remarked that "now many countries use money as a substantive incentive to encourage athletes to work harder. There is nothing wrong with our following the world trend. Regarding the Guoguang Awards, it is allegedly the highest reward system in the world, showing that the ROC is an economically prosperous country."[21] Outfielder Jiang Taiquan said that "kids who play baseball are economically destitute. Money is an encouragement, from being a breadwinner to buying property or even creating their own business, which could secure future lives. Therefore players would certainly work harder to pursue medals."[22]

Benefiting from rapid economic growth throughout the 1980s and early 1990s, the Taiwanese government had the financial wherewithal to adopt this policy. Obsessed with international success, the government also subsidized national team players who might be attractive to foreign pro clubs. Jiang Taiquan, a three-time Olympian, was given generous allowances by the government in addition to the salary provided by a would-be pro club, the China Times. As a result, his total monthly wages reached $3,940, which exceeded that of most Taiwanese pro players at that time.[23] It should be noted, however, that the government only subsidized a few key players, such as Guoli Jianfu and Luo Guozhang.

Despite the government's professed desire to make the public see baseball as more recreation than competition through the SBL program, Taiwanese officials still regarded winning as uppermost, especially in international tournaments. As such, money was obviously an efficient tool that prompted baseball players to pursue national glory.

Primacy on the National Team

In order to achieve success in international competition, other measures were needed besides the rewards system. It was important to strike a balance between amateur and pro baseball. This balance was achieved through singular leadership, that is, the appointment of Tang Panpan to head both the CPBL and the CTBA. Tang could therefore ensure that the national team was not jeopardized by professional clubs signing talented amateurs. According to Tang, "since international competitions were not professionalized at the time, it was imperative to play for the country. A national team could not be composed of players whom pro clubs were not interested in. Therefore I proposed singular leadership to grab pros and amateurs at the same time. If the two leagues [amateur and professional] were separated, each would pursue its interests regardless of the overall consequences."[24]

Tang's solution to this potential conflict, with strong agreement from the KMT, was for the CPBL to adopt the twenty-four-year-old clause, which stated that pro clubs could not recruit players who were younger than twenty-four. These players then remained amateurs and thus eligible to play on the national team. In other words, players had to retain their amateur status for at least six years after high school graduation before turning professional. The age limit was set at twenty-four because players normally graduated from university at twenty-two and served another two years in the military.

In the United States and Korea national teams were made up of college students with an average age under twenty-two. Japan chose its national team from its amateur industrial league and university students because it did not care about international results. For these countries the pro clubs were not responsible in any direct manner for the talent level of the national team. The average age of players on the Taiwanese national squad, however, before the appearance of pro ball had been over twenty-five. These older players gave the Taiwan team an edge over its younger competitors, and even under the twenty-four-year-old clause Taiwan still retained a small advantage.

When the IBA wanted to lift the restriction on pro or former pro baseball players taking part in international tournaments, the CTBA's stance was resolutely against it. Each time the IBA discussed the issue, Taiwanese representatives rejected the idea completely. The reason was that, if pro players were allowed to take part, the Taiwanese national team, composed of amateur players, could not dominate as it had against the American countries, such as the Dominican Republic, Venezuela, Mexico, and Panama, all of whom have hosts of Minor Leaguers and former pro players whose skills definitely dwarfed those of amateurs. Unless the CTBA drafted pro players from the CPBL, which had its own schedule and whose clubs might not cooperate, the national team could not be competitive. International results were so precious to Taiwan that the CTBA felt it was important to maintain the demarcation between amateurs and pros, even though Taiwanese amateurs had always been trained in a professional manner. But in the end Taiwan lost on this issue, and on September 21, 1996, IBA members voted to allow professional players' participation in international competitions. Although the tide had turned against Taiwan and Cuba, they again stood together, voting no while fearing the IBA decision would compromise their national teams.[25]

The Impact on Amateur Baseball

The Revival of Grassroots Baseball

The government's increasing role in the promotion of baseball, particularly through subsidies from the SBL, allowed grassroots baseball to come back to life. Three levels of SBL—primary school, junior high, and senior high—were launched in 1990, 1992, and 1993, respectively. Since the government provided money and incentives to cover costs, playing baseball was no longer a dead-end activity for children; indeed, it could become a means for upward mobility.

Even girls joined baseball teams. One of the most accomplished was Li Siting, who was a member of the 1992 national championship-winning squad from Lixing Elementary School in Taizhong City. At the

Far East Qualification that year, she hit a home run, becoming the first girl ever to homer in the tournament.[26] The media gave her very little coverage since at the time the country was consumed with professional baseball.

The growth of school baseball was the greatest in the countryside. In urban areas a lesser degree of interest in organizing teams may have been due to a difference in culture and a wider range of possibilities for upward mobility. In the large cities where the examination was common and the competition cutthroat, adults forced their children to do well academically and to shun sports. Although urban baseball programs existed, fewer city schools had them than did rural schools. Additionally, the urban teams were only open to the best players in the region.

The number of rural school teams, on the other hand, was often impressive. For instance, the number of teams in eastern Taiwan, which is far less developed than western Taiwan, is much greater proportionately to the population than of the western portion of the island. Taidong County, especially, where the Hongye legend was born, produced the second highest number of teams on Taiwan. This accomplishment is astonishing because Taidong's population was only around a quarter of a million. The main stimulus for all these teams was that virtually all schools in Taidong had few funds and thus absolutely needed the state subsidies.

The Taidong schools offered their students little besides baseball. No one wanted to teach in these schools because the region was relatively undeveloped. Library and school facilities were also inadequate. In any case, aboriginal parents didn't expect their children to be successful academically in such an environment and didn't push their children to study as hard as Han Chinese parents did. So since aboriginal students lacked the preparation to compete in *liankao* against Han Chinese, their parents thought their children might as well put their hope in baseball.

The SBL affected grassroots baseball by doing more than spending money. By putting an end to under-the-table recruitment at the junior high level, it encouraged these schools to form teams because they no longer had to fear their best players being seduced away. The

SBL's regulations also put an end to the domination at the junior high level of Huaxing, Meihe, and RSEA. These three were no longer able to dominate as they once had because of the SBL's boundary restrictions. RSEA was the first casualty of the SBL because SBL regulations held that teams could not take part in SBL-held tournaments under a sponsor's name, so RSEA had to disband its junior high team as well as its primary school squad.

Though the boundary rule was enforced, it still had a minor loophole. Normally primary school graduates had to go to specific junior highs in their district. But baseball players could circumvent this rule by going to any junior high school they liked providing that it was in the same county. They entered a PE program, which had a curriculum separate from that of the rest of the school and which had its own exams different from those of *liankao*. The national championship could only be won by schools with such a PE-class system; other schools merely played for fun, a concept that was not universally shared by principals and teachers.

Overall the outcome of the SBL's program was impressive. The baseball population soared. During the 1980s there were no more than one thousand Little Leaguers, but by 1994 the total was more than eleven thousand. At the junior high level there were more than forty-five hundred players in 1995, compared to fewer than three hundred in the 1980s.[27]

There Is No Such Thing As Happiness

The SBL did nothing, however, to stop Taiwan from winning the LLB championship. True, the SBL enforced the boundary rule, but this rule was still more lenient than that of the LLB. Thus in 1990 Williamsport witnessed the Shanhua primary school, the most impressive youth team in the tournament's history. On this Taiwanese squad were two giant pitchers, Song Zhaoji and Guo Wenju, who both stood five foot nine and possessed an arsenal of rocket fastballs. Despite boos and abuse from forty thousand American fans, Shanhua beat U.S. East easily, 9–0, while Song struck out 16 of the 20 batters that he faced.

Shanhua was led by coach Wang Zican, nicknamed the "iron-blood manager," the most emotional, explosive, and serious manager on Tai-

wan. Under his guidance the little "professional" players were obedient, self-composed, and unflappable. When Song threw a shutout in
the final game, his reaction was surprisingly calm, shrugging it off with
a "It's nothing." Wang's motto was "baseball is a beautiful sport. As
long as you practice fundamental drills, you can make perfect plays."
It was this perfectionism that made him one of the most formidable
coaches in the baseball world. One slugger, for example, was removed
by Wang just because he made a minor mistake at third base, even
though Shanhua was already seven runs ahead. Glenn Orndorff, Jr.,
the manager of U.S. East, said that "on our team all are players, but on
the Taiwanese teams all are robots."[28]

Wang's greatest achievement, though, did not come at Williamsport
but in the subsequent development of these players, eight of whom
went on to play pro baseball in the domestic leagues. Most importantly, Chen Jinfeng (Chen Chin-feng) was later signed by the Los
Angeles Dodgers and became the first Taiwanese player to reach the
Major League. Five of Wang's players, including Chen, came through
the Shanhua system and represented Chinese Taipei at the 2001 World
Cup, at which the Taiwanese team won the bronze medal.

Such players' successes were not without tremendous toll. Corporal
punishment was often used to discipline players. Yang Sen recalled
that "in one game we were beaten by Gongyuan. Coach Wang could
not control himself and whipped everyone standing in single file. I
was whipped most severely because I made three or four errors. This
is the first time I cried in the ballpark. . . . Although the punishments
hurt very much, they were for our own good. We all called him 'father' behind his back because he was the person closest to us at that
time."[29] Another player, Zeng Hanzhou, said that "I was very naughty
when I was little. In third grade I was kicked out of the classroom by
a teacher. My family had to bring me to Coach Wang to see if I could
be salvaged. If it had not been for Coach Wang's strict management,
I would have been in 'Green Island' [a place famous for locking up
the most notorious criminals in Taiwan]."[30] Zheng Changming, now a
teenage girls' idol, said that "if it had not been for the teacher [referring
to Wang], I would have been in the farm field by now. When players
had baths together, it was time to count the whipping marks. Thanks

to those whippings, however, we were able to develop such a strong baseball foundation."[31]

In 1995 Wang took Shanhua to Williamsport for their second visit. In the finals they crushed U.S. East 17–3, but the semifinal against the Dominican Republic was a nail-biting match that Taiwan won only 1–0. "This is the game that I really thought we could lose," said Wang.[32] One fan was so disillusioned with the Taiwanese team's performance that he wrote an article entitled "Champion and Character" for the Internet. In the article he observes, "Taiwanese players were like robots during the entire match, unlike the Dominican kids, who would hug and cheer each other joyfully when they retired the Taiwanese player, though it was an easy play. But Taiwanese players were stern and motionless. They just could not understand the essence and happiness of the game. After the game one Taiwanese player even flashed his middle finger to the Dominican players."[33]

Despite the continued success of Taiwanese teams at Williamsport and the efforts of the SBL to regulate grassroots baseball, Taiwan still managed to find itself in occasional trouble with the LLB. In 1993 Taiping, the national champions of Taiwan, crushed other countries to earn the right to go to Williamsport. But LLB officials sent a shocking message to Taiwan that Taiping was disqualified and was being replaced by the runner-up. The reason for the disqualification was the discovery that Taiwan had broken another rule on how teams were formed. The LLB required that, if an elementary school has over one thousand students, it needed to field four separate teams; if it had over two thousand, it had to have eight teams. The LLB found out that some Taiwanese schools, among them Taiping that had over three thousand students, had fielded only one team.

Taiping's players were absolutely shocked and saddened by the LLB's decision. Wei Shuzhe, Taiping's catcher, cried on national TV, saying, "we never study and just practice for games."[34]

The depth of the players' disappointment and the forsaking of their academic studies just to win at Williamsport reminded some Taiwanese that winning came with a price tag. As one editorial in *Minshengbao* rightly pointed out, "age-divided champions do not equate with world champions. Therefore we should create a reasonable sporting environment where successes in world champions can be achieved. This is genuine glory. If adults cannot achieve it, it is pointless for little kids to do the face-saving."[35]

The following year Taiwan decided to hold a separate tournament from which the SBL was to select the LLB national team. Although there were only around one hundred schools taking part, some of them were still plagued by irregularities. But most teams abided by the rules. Li-ren captured the national championship and was said to be the weakest national team ever because they lost unexpectedly to Saudi Arabia for the first time in Taiwanese youth baseball history. The CTBA and the Taiwanese Little League authorities believed that it would be difficult for teams to win world championships by adhering strictly to LLB regulations. They therefore reversed the decision that the champions of the SBL would represent the country at Williamsport. The policy change eventually sowed the seeds for Taiwan's pull-out from the LLB in 1997.

Loss of the Limelight

Although student baseball revived dramatically and was still an important tool for the Taiwanese government, the public and the media gradually fell out of love with it, with attention shifting to pro baseball. Fewer and fewer people got up at night to cheer for Taiwanese teams fighting for glory in the United States. Three television channels officially controlled by the KMT had always been passionate in their LLB coverage, whether live or delayed, but they were now fed up with the large expenses of such broadcasts and the low advertising revenues the telecasts brought in. The stations stopped televising student baseball in 1993. The following year the China Broadcast Company permanently discontinued its radio coverage.

Senior baseball also suffered because during this period corporate privatization and financial liberalization were being carried out by the government in order to link to the global capitalist economy. Public enterprises were forced to abandon unprofitable endeavors that contravened the national policy. Thus many companies disbanded their baseball teams, the first being the China Oil Company, followed by RSEA. To add insult to injury, the air force also announced that it was dissolving its team due to a lack of players. Because of ferocious signings by pro clubs, amateur baseball was left virtually without players. Such players as Lan Jianan had to come out of retirement in order to prevent Taipower from folding.

Nor were a lack of players the only problems. There was one amateur game that could not start because of an umpire shortage. An additional irritant was amateur teams being urged to speed up their daytime games in order to accommodate practices for pro clubs, who were preparing for matches at night.

Since all attention was now on pro baseball, there were literally no crowds at amateur matches, even when people could watch three games in one day free of charge. Crowds would be a little larger on weekends, but they were still dismally small. It was increasingly hard to find flocks of students or of company staff rooting for their teams in Division One. Low attendance and apathy were also the norm at international tournaments. In 1988, for example, Gaoxiong held an international tournament called the World Port Cup, which set two records in Taiwanese baseball history: the least ticket receipts and the largest loss on balance.[36] In 1994 Taiwan held the LLB Far East Qualification, which would have had Taiwanese baseball lovers going wild during the 1970s and 1980s. The organizers discovered that people were not interested in the LLB any more. Anthropologist Joseph Timothy Sundeen witnessed the event and commented:

> Past events in Taipei might have attracted as many as 30,000 spectators, but this crowd probably numbered only in the hundreds, and many of these appeared to be friends and family of the players. These contingents were actively involved in supporting their teams, but the rest of the midday crowd fidgeted on their concrete bench seats, ate lunch, baby-sat small children, and otherwise paid only sporadic attention to what was happening on the field.[37]

The results of such apathy was that after 1990 the international amateur competitions were replaced in the public eye by international professional invitational tournaments, which attracted larger crowds thanks to the renowned stars on the field and the high caliber of play.

With enthusiasm for amateur baseball diminished, retaining amateur status to play for the national team was no longer a motivation for players, who were eager to become pros and to earn respectable money in addition to earning popularity. In a sign of the times the Ministry of Education negotiated a new agreement regulating the amateur-pro relationship: players under twenty-three years old, who were not on the national squad, could be signed by pro clubs.[38] Some players aged under twenty-three made excuses to withdraw from the national team and to join pro clubs. As always, it seemed baseball on Taiwan was a game of give-and-take, a characteristic that would continue to be a part of the game as it faced new problems beginning in the late 1990s.

SIX

Multiple Crises, 1996–2001

Despite the appearance of a second professional league, the late 1990s saw much turmoil in the world of Taiwanese baseball. The troubles were many: scandal in the CPBL, foreign recruitment of players, and economic cutbacks for student teams. Amateur baseball was particularly hard hit, suffering a drastic decline in popularity.

Television and Pro Baseball

Ellis Cashmore, a sports media expert, observed that sports and television are a match made in heaven.[1] The CPBL's history, however, shows a love-hate relationship with TV. Live radio broadcasts of important amateur games have always been a tradition in Taiwan. The domain of television, on the other hand, has mainly been international tournaments, not domestic games. So without a track record of live television coverage of domestic games, it seemed daring for the three national TV networks to televise CPBL games. Weekday games started at 6:30 p.m. This starting time put televised games in direct competition with the public's favorite nightly soap dramas, which are the Taiwanese equivalents to America's *General Hospital* and which receive high ratings and generate much advertising revenue. In the opinion of network executives, baseball, unlike the soaps, did not have such market value.

The Chinese Television Service made a breakthrough agreement during the inaugural CPBL season. It was to cover Saturday games live starting at 1:00 p.m. The result was dismal. Fans stopped going to games that were televised, thus avoiding the relentless midday sun, and consequently, only a couple thousand turned up on Saturday. In addition the

Chinese Television Service discovered that the TV ratings were poor. On some occasions games were postponed by rain, and since makeup games didn't fall on Saturdays, the network refused to cover them.

Local cable entrepreneur Qiu Fusheng stepped in. Qiu sensed that pro baseball would become big business and offered to televise league play on his cable channel. The outcome was more than satisfactory, as TV ratings soared, especially during the time of the Elephants dynasty. As a result, TVIS became a genuine sports channel, televising not only domestic games but also those of the MLB and the NPB.

Matters changed completely when the CPBL decided to have open bidding for TV rights in August 1995. CPBL's contract with TVIS stipulated that networks must bid for the TV rights eighteen months before expiration of the agreement. Qiu objected, insisting that he had preferential rights in dealing with the CPBL and should get first shot at any TV deal. After all, TVIS would be an empty channel if it did not televise baseball. Qiu's nightmare of losing the rights was realized when a representative from the Weilai Group, owner of the China Trust Bank, offered a staggering sum of $57 million for the TV rights; this sum was almost seven times higher than projected TV revenues. The offer meant that every club would earn annually $308,000, an amount that would significantly improve the fortunes of the debt-making ball clubs by transforming them into profitable enterprises.[2]

Defeated in both the bidding war and in a subsequent court appeal, the infuriated Qiu retaliated against the CPBL by televising every game in the second half of the 1996 season; his act resulted in lower attendance at the ballparks. Hoping to lure away more of the CPBL market share, Qiu held a high school tournament called *Jinlongqi* (Golden Dragon Flag) to commemorate the first Taiwanese LLB world champion, Jinlong. He wanted to make *Jinlongqi* Taiwan's Koshien, a Japanese competition in which every high school student dreams of participating. TVIS subsidized full transportation expenses for those schools that wanted to take part in the tournament. In addition every game was broadcast live on television and was replayed in the evenings. Broadcasting the tournament was a pioneering event in Taiwanese baseball history since domestic high school games had rarely been televised, especially after the advent of pro baseball.

The Taiwan Major League

The most damaging blow Qiu served to the CPBL was his cofounding with Chen Shengtian of the Taiwan Major League (TML). Chen, owner of Sampo electronics, had been very anxious to become part of the CPBL after witnessing the overwhelming popularity of the league. In 1992 the CPBL announced approval of two new clubs for the following year, but it rejected Sampo on the grounds that it had too many ineligible players. The league told Sampo to apply together with China Trust a year later when the CPBL would be divided into two four-team groups with the acceptance of two more expansion teams.[3] The CPBL, however, reneged on its word by announcing that only one new club was going to be accepted before 1997.

By now Sampo felt like an outcast in Taiwanese baseball. A disillusioned Chen and a disgruntled Qiu made a perfect match with money and a TV channel and declared that they were forming a second pro league. In December 1995 they created the Naluwan Corporation to operate the TML, which commenced playing two years later.

The TML's first task was to find new players. In addition to signing amateur players over twenty-three years old, the TML managed to pry superstars from the opposing league. At the time, players were signed by clubs for life unless the parent club agreed to give them team departure approval, which absolved players of all rights and obligations, thus allowing them to begin a new career with another club. Without this departure approval star players were stuck with one club since there was no free agency system. At the end of 1995, in order to fight for better salaries and working conditions, players organized a Players' Union, which they hoped would give them leverage against owners. Two-thirds of the pro players joined the union, yet it did not make the slightest difference because the owners were too powerful to overawe.

The existence of a second league provided a new opportunity to escape the restrictive CPBL contracts. Chen and Qiu offered lucrative contracts under the table to CPBL players, whose contracts were firmly bound to their parent clubs. In addition ample signing bonuses were provided as long as players went to the TML, either from the CPBL or from amateur teams.

Some CPBL stars could not resist the temptation and accepted money from the TML. One of the franchise players who made the leap was Weichuan's megahurler Huang Pingyang, who was angered that his club reduced his salary after he had surgery for an injury resulting from years of overuse by his coach. Over ten CPBL players admitted receiving money, and nine of them were dubbed the TML jumpers. Wang Guanghui and Lin Yizeng turned down the offer at the last minute, choosing to stay with the Elephants and paying back the money that they had accepted. The defection of the nine jumpers caused shock and left many fans heartbroken and holding deep grudges against the players.

The CPBL clubs did not let the jumpers slip away without a fight and filed lawsuits against them for breach of contract. The district court ruled against the clubs, so Weichuan and Mercury appealed to the High Court, which upheld the ruling. Mercury did not give up, appealing to the Supreme Court, the island's highest court, which remanded the case to the High Court. The latter ruled that the jumper, Kang Mingshan, could not leave his original club at will.[4] Mercury had finally won, but since it disbanded its team in 1999, its victory was meaningless as the previous ruling was revoked without plaintiff.

Meanwhile, the TML continued its search for players by offering money to senior high school students, particularly those spotted at *Jinlongqi*. Because the league still lacked enough domestic players, it allowed four foreign players to be fielded by each team simultaneously. The league clubs signed several famous foreign players, such as Luis Iglesias and Silvestre Campusano, who had played for the CPBL, as well as such former MLB sluggers as Sam Horn. All of these foreign players overshadowed the Taiwanese players, who could not make their names known to fans, except for the jumpers.

After finally rounding up enough players to fill its rosters, the TML looked for ways to attract people to its games. It distributed free tickets in the hopes that those receiving these tickets would like what they saw and return as paying customers.

The league also hit on another way to attract people to the games. It allowed political candidates to step onto the diamond and introduce themselves. The candidates profited because the act gave them a TV audience at very little expense. All they had to do was buy a ticket and some commercial boards at the stadium.[5] The TML benefited because the candidate's supporters, wearing election campaign clothes and cheering for their candidates, came en mass to the game and bought tickets.

Further, in its search for an audience and unlike the CPBL, the TML tried to institutionalize a home-away system under which each club was based in a certain city to attract local fans. However, the attempt failed. Ostensibly local spectators packed the stadiums to root for the home team. Actually they were rallied by county mayors, who had a working agreement with the TML for help in future elections.

Gambling, Match-Fixing, and *Heijin*

All of the TML's efforts to raise attendance through political mobilization, free ticket distribution, and cultivation of local fans did not in the end save Taiwanese pro baseball from a further slump caused by match-fixing. To understand the outbreak of the gambling and match-fixing scandals, one has to have a basic knowledge of Taiwanese politics. Since the 1990s Taiwanese politics has been identified with *hei* (black) and *jin* (gold), referring to gangsterism and big money, respectively. *Heijin* is a combination of business politics, money politics, and mafia politics.

Heijin blossomed under President Li Denghui, who forced out many of the mainlanders in the KMT and brought more native Taiwanese into the party. Li opened up elections to all Taiwanese in order to consolidate the KMT's legitimacy as well as to eliminate the mainlanders' monopoly in the elected bodies of Taiwanese government. In laying the foundation for democracy, Li unintentionally opened the door for mobsters to enter politics. Political scientist Zhao Yongmao commented that "to gangsters an election is one of the important paths of 'laundering' themselves. Once elected, it is not only instrumental in developing above-the-surface enterprises but also consolidating under-the-surface businesses."[6] In the fourth legislative election of 1990 twenty-four percent of those elected had been convicted of crimes. Protected by "big brothers" in the central parliament and provided immunity by their own regional councils, local crooked politicians were able to get away with illegal activities such as betting, drug dealing, and prostitution.

Criminal activities soon invaded pro baseball, whose enormous popularity had attracted the attention of the underworld. Organized gangs soon derived massive profits from gambling operations, which are illegal on Taiwan. Some of these gambling operations were in the hands of local officials, who placed bets on some baseball games. Because the stakes were so high that the bookmakers could not bear losing, some crooked politicians told gangster friends to use money, girls, or intimidation to help fix games. The bookmaker-politicians might even order their friends to kidnap players in order to make them obey.

Not all player involvement in match-fixing was forced. Some players voluntarily sought out gangsters for self-enrichment. These players sometimes even invited criminal associates to help quell factional conflicts within the club.

For years there were rumors of match-fixings and gangster involvement in baseball. Owners, however, only launched quiet internal investigations because they were afraid that public hearings would hurt pro ball's image. At the same time newspaper reporters, though they knew of this dark side of baseball, were intimidated by gangsters and failed to report the game's corruption.

The matter finally came to light in three articles posted on the Mercury Tigers newsgroup bulletin board on April 15, 16, and 27, 1996. The anonymous writer, who many fans speculated was a reporter because of his writing style, made public accusations of match-fixing by some Mercury players in "Mercury Tigers fans, this is the reason to say goodbye, don't go protesting in the ballpark"; "This is the saddest and the last post—Black Tigers Incident"; and "Two and three things about Black Tigers."[7] On May 31 angry Mercury fans gathered in the ballpark before a Dragons-Tigers match. They held banners in Chinese, Japanese, and English protesting the Black Tigers incident. This demonstration was the first ever spontaneously organized by Internet users calling for the expulsion of gangsters from baseball.

The protest did not stop the corruption. Indeed, the first gangster-orchestrated player kidnapping occurred two months later and shocked the general public. On August 2 five Elephants players were abducted and held in a hotel room in Taizhong. Second baseman Wu Fulian was pistol-whipped, and the star pitcher, Chen Yixin, allegedly had a pistol barrel shoved in his mouth. It is believed that a gambling syndicate had lost $125,000 because the Bulls upset the Elephants, some of whose players had been paid to win. The incident led police to station its forces in the dugout the following day.

By now the scandal was completely in the open, and investigators were prompted to dig deeper. The ensuing investigation nearly caused the CPBL's demise. In September Mercury players Luis Iglesias (a Panamanian slugger), Cai Shengfeng, Lin Zhongqiu, and several others were interrogated by the police about match-fixing.

Most damning of all was the interrogation and detention of three China Times Eagles players, Guo Jiancheng, Zhuo Kunyuan, and Gu Shengji, in a probe launched by the Taipei district prosecutor.[8] All three admitted receiving money from bookies to throw games and confessed to investigators that players on the other five teams were also involved. It was the precursor of the infamous Black Eagles incident that snowballed until most of the team was involved. It is believed that Guo's big brother, Guo Jiancai, a police officer, used his position to run betting sites and to make connections with gangsters. Knowing there would be massive profits in pro baseball, he introduced Guo to a syndicate that was protected and abetted by local politicians.[9]

According to former Eagles coach Xu Shengming, his players liked to gamble on *majiang* in which large bets were involved and correspondingly large losses.[10] Additionally, players habitually went to night clubs where they might drop in a single night as much as $1,240, a large sum for people whose salaries were only $7,280 per month. Players with the *majiang* and night club habits became obvious targets for gangsters attempting to tamper with the results of games.[11]

The investigative storm ceased temporarily as the 1997 season got underway. The China Times Eagles, nicknamed the "Violent Eagles" by virtue of the team's many long-range sluggers, won the first-half title. Then on June 20, just one day after their title-winning party, nine Eagles players were arrested and charged with match-fixing, leaving only two domestic Eagles players untouched by the prosecutor. Six other teams had to supply the Eagles with ten second-class players, dubbed the "second-generation Eagles," in order for the club to cope with the second half of the season. Immediately with the end of the season China Times decided to hang up its spikes for good since the team had incurred such disrepute.

During the course of the match-fixing investigation the Mercury Tigers had their own player-kidnapping scandal involving three foreign players, four domestic players, and two gamblers holding a 9mm handgun. "The first slap caught me by surprise. After that, I was really [ticked]. I never actually thought I'd be shot. It was mostly verbal abuse. But before they let us go, they put the gun barrel to our chests and warned us not to tell anyone what had happened. . . . The only thing he [the gunman] kept saying in English was NT$30 million [$922,000]! NT$30 million!" reported Keith Gordon, an American outfielder.[12]

Later Carlos Pulido, signed by the Mercury Tigers in 1998, talked about his chilling experience during his brief stay on Taiwan. "Everything was run by the mob there," he remarked. When invited by a gangster to a hotel, "my legs started shaking. I said I wanted no part of it. I told them I play for my family." They said, "We have 70 percent of the team on our payroll. If you don't throw the game, the guys behind you will be making errors, anyway."[13]

The scandal became so notorious that it spread overseas. The first impression of Jonathan Hurst before coming to the CPBL was "that [Taiwan] is a famous place for gambling!"[14]

In the following year, 1999, Dragons head coach Xu Shengming was attacked by three assailants on the way home from walking his children to school. He was stabbed three times in the hip and thigh, but the injuries were not serious. Xu shouted for help to pedestrians, but no one responded, so he headed home by himself, notifying the club and calling the police before going to the hospital. It was alleged that the mafia had bet on a Dragons game and lost a great deal of money. Huang Lianxing, a mobster in Taizhong, had told his mob brothers to teach Xu a lesson. In the end two of the assailants were caught, charged, and convicted, although they served only light sentences.[15]

In September 1997 twenty-one players and twelve alleged gangsters were tried and eventually convicted of gambling, match-fixing, breach of trust, and intimidation.[16] In the end it was revealed that some of the players willingly became go-betweens, while many were forced to throw games under duress from the mafia. Just before the judge rendered his decision, all the accused players denied their confessions and claimed that they had no connection with gambling. Their recantation did no good, and the verdict stood.

All of the convicted players launched appeals in the High Court, but the cumbersome judicial system took another eight years to reach a final decision in which, apart from one player who was acquitted, all the others received suspended sentences. So although none of the players went to jail, neither could they play pro baseball again.

Prosecutors believed that two powerful local politicians, Xiao Dengshi in Jiayi county and Yan Qingbiao in Taizhong county, were involved in baseball gambling. Some convicted mobsters, such as Lin Guoqing and Li Maofa, were staunch supporters of Xiao and Yan. Testimonies by Guo Jiancheng, Zhang Zhengxian, and Jiang Taiquan were strong enough to convince prosecutors that Xiao and Yan had been behind the whole affair.[17]

The Ice Age in Professional Baseball

The series of gambling and corruption scandals made many fans lose faith in pro baseball. To make matters worse, the arrest and expulsion of several top players hurt the quality of play. Fans were heartbroken and chose not to go to matches. Where CPBL attendance had averaged over five thousand per game before the scandal, it now fell to under two thousand. With low attendance and a tarnished public image, the Mercury Tigers and the Weichuan Dragons decided to call it a day by disbanding at the end of the 1999 season. Despite a street protest staged by Dragons fans to save their club, which was coming off three consecutive championships, the owner announced he had had enough.

The scandals and their aftermath did not ease the competition between the CPBL and the TML, and the tug-of-war between the two pro leagues continued for another seven years. The CPBL regarded itself as Taiwan's sole legitimate baseball organization and never admitted equality with the TML, while the TML used its connections with politicians, who mobilized fans within their constituencies to come to the ballpark, to show that their league was more attractive to fans. At the end of the day, however, both leagues suffered as a result of the gambling scandals and their vicious competition. Thus it is not surprising that no more than two thousand fans, combined, bothered to turn up when the CPBL and the TML played on the same day.

Also at issue was the minimum-age requirement for signing amateurs. The CPBL signed only those over twenty-three (originally it had been twenty-four), while the TML was willing to sign players younger than that age. The governmental sporting body, the Sports Council, was more than willing to broker a truce for the ongoing hostilities over this matter, but both leagues were prepared rather to wage all-out war. For its part the TML completely ignored an agreement signed by the CPBL, the PE Federation, and the CTBA that ruled that students, military servicemen, and would-be military conscripts could not be signed by pro clubs in order to ensure the healthy development of amateur baseball.

In 1998 therefore the TML signed an eighteen-year-old pitcher, Chen Zhicheng, who had not yet served in the army. Chen knew he would be facing a problem two years later when the CTBA and the Ministry of Defense would not allow him to play on the army baseball team, which only accepted amateur players. In other words, he could not practice at all during his military service. But Chen was willing to take the chance that two years of inactivity would not hurt his future career. So on June 20, 1998, he stepped on the mound, marking a watershed event in Taiwanese baseball history by becoming the first military draftee to play for a professional team.

From that point forward owners from the CPBL and the TML vied for talented students, providing them with under-the-table money, the so-called nutritional fees. I was told by a player's sister that, "while my brother was in senior high school, the China Trust Whales remitted money on a monthly basis to his bank account, which we never gave to the club. Basically all the good senior high school players were already 'purchased' by pro teams."[18] Of the two leagues the TML was much more active in this purchasing, signing students through the *Jinlongqi* tournament, out of which some talented youngsters came.

Nevertheless, to counter the TML's aggressive actions, the CPBL also provided certain players with nutritional fees, even causing infighting among them. Xu Shengjie, who had been receiving monthly nutritional fees of $920 from the Mercury Tigers, decided to renege on his word and defected to the Weichuan Dragons. An altercation between the two clubs ensued, but the conflict was soon resolved because they were afraid that, if Xu were not given his choice, he might jump to the rival league. In the end, as punishment for his action, Xu was banned for only half a season. Such a minor penalty implied that players could now exploit the CPBL-TML feud and receive whatever money they wanted.

The signing of young players was probably inevitable even without the CPBL-TML rivalry. The IBA's policy of allowing pro players to take part in international tournaments rendered the CPBL-CTBA gentlemen's agreement obsolete.

Foreign Encroachment

The Globalization of Baseball

The two Taiwanese pro leagues were not the only ones seeing an advantage to the abandonment of the minimum-age requirement. Indeed, Chen's signing opened a floodgate of offers to many young players for pro contracts from the MLB, which for years had been trying to sign Taiwanese talent under the age of twenty. This signing of Taiwanese players of all ages by the MLB was just one example of the globalization of baseball.

There are two views on globalization: one is neoliberalistic, the other neoimperialistic. In the neoliberalist view as proposed by sociologist Ulrich Beck, the world market eliminates or supplants political action, and globalization opens up opportunities and advantages to all states. Within the context of baseball the United States' domination in certain major sports generates enough money to provide opportunities for ballplayers from other baseball-loving countries around the globe. In the neoimperalist view of globalization as put forth by such economists as Martin Khor, Director of the Third World Network, the opening of the market is simply another form of economic imperialism in which world trade is controlled by a few robust economies that leave little or no room for others.[19]

Certainly baseball is a part of globalization. Domestic professional baseball leagues in Western countries are large multinational corporations searching for new markets in which to sell their products. They also are constantly seeking new sources of raw material and pursuing cheap skilled labor. These countries are effectively reducing the skill levels of semiperipheral and peripheral countries because the core states monopolize all of the talented athletes by offering higher salaries and better working conditions. This does not mean that noncore countries cannot obtain good athletes for their own leagues because the logic of the market is conducted under the concept of free movement. Still, noncore nations can only lure second-class or rejected players from core countries as noncore salaries are less than those offered by core countries. This situation is similar to that of free agency, in which the richer clubs get the world's top players while the poorer clubs settle for ordinary players unwanted by the rich ones. Because of the distribution of wealth the asymmetrical exchange is heavily in favor of the global north.

The effects of globalization on baseball are often not good for noncore countries and the players from them. For instance Alan M. Klein, Arturo Marcano Guevara, and David P. Fidler have written that the MLB exploits and mistreats Latin Americans who pursue their dreams in the big show.[20] Further, many countries such as the Dominican Republic and Venezuela are reliant on the MLB, which sets up baseball camps not for the benefit of the host country but in order to attract talented players. In the process the MLB destroys the autonomy of the host country's national baseball. Many of these countries do not have summer leagues because all of the best players either have gone north or are bound by MLB contracts that prevent their playing in domestic pro leagues.[21]

True, winter leagues can exist because they operate during the MLB's off-season, allowing native stars to go back home and prospects to gain game experience. Make no mistake, however, these winter leagues are totally subservient to U.S. baseball.

The only country that resists the U.S. baseball hegemony is Cuba. In Cuba Fidel Castro scrapped pro baseball and replaced it with a purely amateur league, enabling all of the best players to stay in the country and thus making Cuba the best amateur baseball nation in the world. Affected by increasing globalization, though, Cuba has also experienced many defections to the United States, especially by baseball players seeking higher salaries. The current best Cuban pitcher, Jose Contreras, defected in October 2002.

As for professional baseball in Latin America, only Mexico has an autonomous summer pro league, which however only attracts failed American players. In all respects Latin American baseball belongs to the MLB.

The MLB's Impact on Taiwan

Before the 1990s the MLB had absolutely no impact on Taiwan. The Taiwanese only cared about the national team's performances in international tournaments, not about professional American baseball. Although TV occasionally televised MLB games on weekend mornings, not many fans watched them because they seemed so remote.

This Taiwanese indifference does not mean that the MLB was not interested in Taiwanese players. The first of these players was the pitcher Tan Xinmin, who was sent by the Japanese pro club Taiheiyo in 1974 to study baseball. He was assigned to San Francisco's class A team, with whom he had a 9-4 record. As Jack Clark, Tan's teammate, recalled, "he was a very good pitcher. I thought we'd go up through the minors together, but I never saw him after that year."[22] Tan, famous for his knuckleball, mysteriously disappeared from the show and never played pro baseball again. Later, though, he became the head coach of the Mercury Tigers in 1992.

The next closest signing was hard-throwing pitcher Guo Taiyuan, whose fastball, clocked at ninety-seven miles per hour, lit up American and Japanese scouts' eyes. Wayne Morgan, a scout for the Toronto Blue Jays, was confident of signing Guo. The latter gave Morgan a verbal commitment after the 1984 Olympics, at which he struck out twelve from the U.S. team, including Will Clark, Barry Larkin, and Mark McGwire. However, Morgan had to give up on Guo after finding out that the pitcher's brother was receiving under-the-table money from a Japanese pro club, the Seibu Lions, to encourage Guo to sign with it.[23]

Zhao Shiqiang, a cleanup man on the national team, was also on the verge of signing with a MLB club. But he decided to play in the 1984 Olympics first before turning pro. In hindsight this decision was a poor one because his performance in the Olympics was so disastrous that it deterred any MLB club from offering him a contract.[24]

Initially, as a recruiting ground for the MLB, Taiwan was far from perfect. One drawback was that the Taiwanese had a tendency to favor going to Japan, which was near, oriental, and in enough ways culturally similar to Taiwan. The United States was far away and too alien a culture.

More importantly, the MLB wanted—and still wants—to sign foreign players as young as possible so that it could have sufficient time to develop and train them to the major league standard. Older players were a waste of energy and money because their chances of reaching the big show were slimmer than those of younger players. For this reason MLB clubs set up baseball academies in Latin America that attracted youths sixteen or younger.

But compulsory military service was paramount to Taiwan in order to prepare for any possible threat posed by the PRC. It was impossible to escape the draft except for physical reasons, such as obesity, and when players finished serving in the army they were at least twenty-two, which made them too old for and of little value to the MLB.

However, things changed dramatically in 1999 as ongoing globalization intensified and was coupled with Taiwanese domestic change. When the TML decided to put military conscript Chen Zhicheng on the mound, it showed foreign clubs that the Taiwanese government could not prevent young players from signing pro contracts.

Thus in January 1999 the Los Angeles Dodgers announced the signing of a Taiwanese slugger, Chen Jinfeng. It turned out that Chen had already signed a preliminary contract with the TML, who had given the young player under-the-table money estimated at $160,000.[25] Chen immediately needed to face the legal question of multiple contracts. The TML threatened to sue him. The Dodgers contract had come to Chen through Sinon Bulls deputy general manager, Zhang Gaoda, and with his help Chen hastily departed for the United States.[26] Chen later became the first Taiwan-born player to make it in the major leagues in 2002.

Another melodramatic courtship occurred when the Dodgers went after Guo Hongzhi. Guo's signing, again through the efforts of Zhang Gaoda, was a watershed event in Taiwanese baseball history because he was only eighteen years old and had not yet served in the army. At the same time Guo was receiving money from the President Lions, an act that also raised the question of multiple contracts. Zhang used the separation of Guo's parents to affect the Dodgers signing. It was Guo's dad, his legal guardian, who had accepted the money from the Lions. However, the father knew nothing about the Dodgers contract. Zhang had arranged the latter by persuading Guo's mother to put her signature on the contract, even though the father supposedly had final approval of any of his son's contracts.[27] To get Guo to the United States, Zhang had to pull him off the under-19 national team, which was even then preparing for the IBA tournament. This action not only fueled public outrage but was embarrassing to Guo's father. After Guo disappeared from the under-19 team, his dad, not knowing about the Dodgers deal, reported to the local police station looking for his missing son.[28] The saga finally ended with Guo quietly going to the United States to play baseball as a professional.

This deal paved the way for several players to follow in Guo's footsteps. Wang Jianmin (Wang Chien-ming) was signed by the New York Yankees for two million dollars through a student-exchange scheme with Taipei PE College. Huang Junzhong went to the United States with the help of the Boston Red Sox Asian-Pacific scout, who recruited players in southern Taiwan with which he was most familiar. Former TML coach Eric Ireland arranged for Cao Jinhui (Tsao Chin-hui), the first Taiwanese pitcher in the MLB, to play for the Rockies for a little over two million dollars.

The most shocking signing was Luo Jinlong, who was sixteen years old and only a freshman in senior high school. It was another unethical signing made this time by the Colorado Rockies. The entire negotiating process was obscure and opaque. The news source that broke the story was not Taiwanese, but the *Denver Post*.[29] Luo's parents had tried to keep the contract secret because he was participating in the Senior High School Baseball League, whose governing body stipulated that players could not take part if pro contracts had been signed. When the story broke about the Rockies, he was forced to pull out of the tournament.

The implication of Luo's signing was enormous. The MLB apparently could lock up Taiwanese players as young as sixteen, much as it did in Latin America. Some people feared that Taiwanese baseball would be Latinized as a result of Luo. This view was too pessimistic.

Unlike Latin America, Taiwan had its own pro leagues that provided good salaries. Thus players had other options than to accept a MLB club's offer, particularly if it included an unsatisfactory bonus fee. Additionally, unlike poverty-stricken Latin America, Taiwan is wealthy. Consequently, unlike Latin America, Taiwan was not liable to become a training ground for cheap star players. Still no matter the strengths of Taiwan and Taiwanese pro baseball, there is no escaping the undeniable fact that promising prospects will strive to reach the MLB when they are offered a chance.

The objective of the MLB, like other multinational corporations, is to make and enhance profits by keeping costs as low as possible. As Guevara and Fidler demonstrate, there are twelve double standards in the MLB's mistreatment of Latin talent.[30] At least one such double standard applies to Taiwan. MLB teams are prohibited from signing U.S. high school players and from trying to influence a U.S. student into withdrawing from high school or college. Yet they are free to tempt Taiwanese students to abandon school to play pro baseball.

Overall, the MLB hegemony is unchallengeable; even Japan experienced the U.S. power when it lost star players such as Ichiro Suzuki, Hideo Nomo, and Hideki Matsui to the American pro game. Korea also has been through the same process as Taiwan with its high school star players going to the United States. The MLB also caused a controversy over a mainland Chinese player named Wang Chao, with whom a Beijing club had signed a twelve-year contract. The affair was resolved when the Seattle Mariners sent a representative to renegotiate the contract with the Beijing authorities. Only Cuba, which refuses to join the global economic system, has been able to force players to stay in its domestic league, but even it has done so just barely.

The NPB's Impact on Taiwan

Many Taiwanese players also went to Japan to play for both pro and amateur clubs since Japanese salaries were higher and the standard of play far superior to those of Taiwan. The Taiwanese wanted not only to play in the NPB but also to learn advanced skills and techniques, which would be useful if they returned to their homeland.

Although the military obstacle did not prevent Japanese clubs from signing Taiwanese students, it left them absolutely no chance of success. The 1992 Olympic silver-medal-winning star, Guoli Jianfu, was an exception, as he was signed by the Hanshin Tigers, which had a tacit agreement with Guoli.

The military issue became moot when, shortly after pro baseball in Taiwan was established in 1990, the NPB immediately made a goodwill gesture by signing the "Mutual Non-cross-signing Agreement," effective for five years. The agreement ensured that no Japanese pro club would sign CPBL stars and vice versa. This act would maintain player quality on Taiwan.[31] When the non-cross-signing agreement expired in 1995, both sides renewed it the following year at a three-sided meeting of the CPBL, the NPB, and the Korean Baseball Organization. The CPBL also signed a separate agreement with the Korean pro league.

In 1999 controversy arose when the NPB unilaterally revoked the agreement without consulting the CPBL. The reason the Japanese gave for this action was that circumstances on Taiwan had changed drastically with the appearance of the TML. More to the point, this ungentlemanly behavior was triggered by the Dodgers signing Chen Jinfeng. This act took the NPB by surprise but put them to thinking that, "if the MLB can get Taiwanese players, why not us?" Japan now joined with the United States in preying upon Taiwanese talent, and the TML, which had former NPB pitching star Guo Taiyuan as a high-ranking consultant, became an agent for recruiting players for Japan.

After the NPB nullified the non-cross-signing agreement, Seibu immediately signed Xu Mingjie from the TML. The most famous player brokered by the TML was Zhang Zhijia, who earned his fame at the 2001 World Cup by beating Korea and Japan and thus helping Chinese Taipei to the bronze medal. Chen Wenbin, the home run king of the CPBL in 2002, went to the Daiei Hawks in a player-exchange scheme, the first in Taiwan-Japanese baseball history. Perhaps the most unique case, however, was that of outfielder Lin Weizhu, who was able to join the NPB draft by staying in Japan for more than five years, giving him a status equivalent to that of a Japanese player. In February 2004 the Chunichi Dragons made a breakthrough in signing military draftee Chen Weiyin, who went to Japan under a student visa while playing as a professional.

The NPB, just like the MLB, wanted to promote its products and merchandise in other countries by exploring potential markets in affluent areas. Taiwan was a perfect target because of its geographic proximity, its economic robustness, and its cultural similarity. Therefore in 2002 the NPB played two regular games in front of a sold-out crowd on Taiwan for the first time in its history. More fans rooted for the Daiei Hawks than for the Orix Blue Waves because Daiei's manager was Sadaharu Oh, who still held a ROC passport, though he could not speak a word of Mandarin since he was born and raised in Japan. The popularity of these games prompted Daiei to make another trip in 2003, playing in a larger stadium with over twenty thousand seats.

The business strategy behind these games was to get more Taiwanese fans interested in Japanese baseball and to induce them to buy the associated products that would increase the NPB's revenue. One reason for the NPB's search for new markets was the globalization of baseball, which was dominated by the MLB. The American leagues even lured away some Japanese stars, thus resulting in a drop in attendance at NPB games. Further, the inability of most Japanese pro teams to match MLB salaries might, some analysts feared, make the NPB no more than a farm league for the MLB.

The Rise of China

As globalization speeds up, the biggest target for both the NPB and the MLB will eventually be mainland China, which accounts for one-sixth of the global population. According to *Baseball America*, a survey conducted among MLB executives, China ranks as the best untapped source for talent in the world, or so said forty-three percent of the respondents. As Mariners representative Benny Looper observed, the Chinese "are serious about developing it [baseball]. We signed a player there. He had good size and athleticism. One thing that could hurt it is the status of the Olympic sport. That's one of the reasons they're developing baseball—if it's an Olympic sport, they want to be good at it."[32] Not surprisingly, the MLB, the NPB, and the Korean Baseball Organization wanted to have a stake in developing and promoting the pastime within mainland China.

China actually has a long tradition of baseball that dates back to 1863 when a Shanghai baseball club was created. But the sport never really took hold because of domestic turmoil and anti-Americanism. It was not until 1975 when amateur clubs from Kobe, Japan, and Aichi Industrial University visited China that Chinese baseball began to develop.[33]

Over the next quarter century Chinese players have also developed. In 2001 Wang Chao was the first mainland Chinese player ever to be signed by an MLB club.[34] Although a great deal of controversy surrounded the signing, including accusations by the Chinese authorities of unethical behavior by Wang's suitor, the Seattle Mariners, it is the first step for the MLB in gaining a purchase on such a large talent pool.

Sharing almost the same language, history, and cultural background with mainland China, Taiwan should find it easier than Japan to exploit China's potential baseball consumers and market. But the fact is that both are reserved about any exchange. In 1997 when the Chinese national team came to Taipei for the Asian Championship, two sluggers, Luo Weijun and Wei Zheng from Beijing, were scouted by the TML.[35] But the deal fell through because there were too many obstacles.

Although there has been very little club-to-club contact, Taiwanese players and coaches have traveled across the Straits to guide Chinese teams. Badly needing people with baseball expertise and knowledge who can speak the language, China began to lure former Taiwanese pro players as coaches. Lin Xinzhang, mysteriously dismissed as head coach of the Mercury Tigers after the team's fantastic 1990 season, headed to China to instruct the Chinese national team, who nearly beat Taiwan at the 1993 Asian Championship. Some players with gambling convictions, such as Guo Jiancheng, Zheng Baisheng, and Jiang Taiquan, went to coach the mainland's Tianjin Lions, which won three championships in a row after their arrival. As Chinese baseball grows at a steady pace, the volume of exchange will certainly increase.

Rolling Back the State

Pulling out of the LLB

The global outreach of the MLB and the NPB turned baseball into big business, which more or less replaced the notion of state absolutism. And indeed, beginning in the middle 1990s, the ROC decreased its outlay for baseball. This withdrawal of state support would affect Taiwan's grassroots baseball.

Until the mid-1990s Williamsport had been a place that healed social rifts within Taiwanese society, boosted national confidence, mustered overseas Chinese for the motherland, and exposed the Taiwanese to the international spotlight. However, on April 12, 1997, all the heroics and epic struggles came to an end when the Taiwan LLB announced its withdrawal from the parent organization. It was a major decision for the Taiwanese authorities, not only because of the political value of the LLB competitions but also because of the sentimental value of the tournaments in which Taiwan established a baseball dynasty. During twenty-eight years Taiwanese Little Leaguers won seventeen out of twenty-one LLB world series titles.

The CTBA faxed a notice to Williamsport saying, "We can't deny that LLB has played a very important role in popularizing and prospering Taiwan's development of baseball in the past years. . . . However, due to the diversity of social status and culture, we have difficulty in complying with LLB's regulations." Lance Van Auken, spokesman for the LLB, remarked, "'cultural differences.' Those are the words they used. . . . They simply didn't want to have three leagues in the one school. That in itself gives them a distinct competitive advantage." Van Auken went on, "I would think that the general reaction for people might be that the biggest competitor in Little League is out of the way, at least for now. . . . I think this might even pique people's interest. If you take them out of the mix, it might make other people think they have a chance."[36]

Van Auken was right that Taiwan had been violating rules, but the LLB had been traditionally lenient with newcomers in order to foster baseball. For example, the LLB was not fastidious about Taiwan's national all-star team for the first three years because the organization was eager to draw Taiwan into the baseball family. Currently, the LLB is doing the same thing with mainland China, which is gathering together its best players in certain schools. Only when countries begin winning championships does the LLB crack down.

When Taiwan decided to withdraw from the LLB, a spokesman from the Ministry of Foreign Affairs addressed the nation on TV. He stated that because of national integrity and dignity Taiwan reluctantly chose to pull out of the LLB, though it had had great traditions and had produced much glory. This government TV appearance showed how deeply state and student baseball were intertwined. As soon as the government announced the news, many primary schools expressed dismay about their teams not going to the United States. One prominent Taidong school principal observed that withdrawing from the LLB would discourage those players and coaches from being motivated.[37]

This withdrawal did not mean that Taiwanese Little Leaguers stopped traveling abroad. They still participated in tournaments sponsored by such international organizations as the PONY and the IBA. Still the reputation of amateur teams is less than when Taiwan competed at Williamsport.

Even before the sundering from the LLB, student baseball's popularity with the general public had declined sharply as a consequence of the formation of the CPBL in 1990. As a consequence of this declining popularity, the results of these young national teams lessened in importance as much of the baseball-loving audience turned to pro idols.

Williamsport did serve a crucial role in nurturing and popularizing Taiwanese baseball. At the same time, it also brought distortion and ugliness to schools that focused solely on turning out champion players and teams. This must-win attitude still lingers among schools and coaches to this day. It is hard to overstate the success and failure of the LLB, but one thing is certain: Taiwan paid a large price for its LLB membership in terms of attitude toward, values of, and development of the island's baseball.

No Pay, No Teams

Another factor also affected school baseball teams during the 1990s. Hit by an economic slump caused by a global recession that occurred shortly after Chen Shuibian became president in 2000, Taiwan was forced to adopt a limited welfare policy. These money problems proved to be long-term as the Taiwanese economy lingered in its slump.

Sports immediately felt the effect that resulted from the short supply of funds. In 1995 much of the PE budget was cut by the Legislative Yuan, leaving the PE department in the Ministry of Education with no extra money to spend on sports. With this extrinsic incentive gone, a philosophy of "no pay, no teams" prevailed.

The biggest impact was on baseball, which had received the largest percentage of all the sports. The $880 allocated to each team automatically ended, though the $590 disbursement to newly formed teams still existed. As a result, grassroots baseball began to decline once more. The number of school teams dropped dramatically in 1996—from 820 to 557 at the primary level and 332 to 243 at the junior high level—and has never recovered. Analyzing the statistics in depth shows that the poorest and most mountainous areas were hit the hardest. From a peak total of 920 primary school teams in 1994 to a dismal 286 in 2002, there was a sharp decline of 634 school teams, the second most dramatic slump since the 1980s. While junior high school baseball experienced the same stagnation without state funding, the situation was less drastic since not many schools had organized teams because of the pressure of examinations.

The sea change did not undermine baseball development in urban cities where teams were already scarce because urban parents think academic study is more important than sports. The tiny schools scattered in mountainous counties, such as Taidong, Nantou, and Taoyuan, were very passionate about baseball, considering it a means of social mobility. Still those poverty-stricken counties in rural Taiwan were dependent on state subsidies for their baseball programs.

The curtailed sports funding was also reflected in the awarding of the Guoguang Awards, whose rules were amended in 2002 in order to cope with the government's tight budget.[38] According to the newly announced Guoguang Awards and Scholarships, apart from the prize for an Olympic gold, which remained at $294,000, rewards for other competitions shrunk dramatically. The original twelve categories of awards were reduced to nine. Furthermore, youths taking part in age-divided international tournaments, at which baseball teams often lived up to their glorious tradition, could no longer be rewarded with money; they would instead be presented with medals or future career plans depending on their athletic performances. The policy change hit players hard as they devoted virtually all their time to training rather than study. Once athletes ended their sports careers, their options were limited: they could become coaches, get low-paying menial jobs, or simply remain unemployed. Only through achieving good results at international games could they accumulate money for the future, and with little prize money now available, such fortune was unlikely.

Ugliness in Student Baseball

The Contradictory Nature of Civil and Martial

Adding to these three crises faced by grassroots baseball, the traditional cultural contempt for physical exercise remained, as always, an obstacle to the development of the sport. Before the founding of the CPBL, the public had viewed ballplayers as academic failures. The success of the pro leagues had tempered this view, as the public realized baseball could be a means to making a living. Public opinion reversed, however, with the pro gambling scandals that again encouraged people to keep baseball at arm's length.

Baseball indeed seemed plagued by scandal, from the professional leagues down to the elementary schools. Scandal led people to think again that players were uncivilized people with little intelligence. According to a survey done at Dunhua Primary School in 1998, more than one-quarter of parents worried that schoolwork would worsen if children spent too much time playing sports. They believed that, if children got too much exercise, the youngsters would lack energy for their academic work, the avenue to future success.[39]

Thus the various crises, particularly the scandals, only seemed to solidify the suspicion most parents had toward sports. Although some researchers, such as Xu Yixiong, argued that study and exercise were mutually compatible, the traditional notion of "strong body and weak mind" was hard to eliminate. This conception was perpetuated when people saw Taiwanese athletes practice all day without being given time to study.

During the golden era of pro baseball in the 1990s school teams not only mushroomed but were also able to attract academically good students, although admittedly just a few. One baseball commentator, Zhang Zhaoxiong, repeatedly claimed that "baseball-playing kids won't become bad," a sentiment echoed by some parents.

Still it would be naïve to overlook the negative aspects of Taiwanese baseball. Gambling and match-fixing may have filtered down to youth baseball, particularly the *Jinlongqi*. Of the eight annual *Jinlongqi* five have been marred by gambling allegations. Since the tournament is broadcast live on TVIS, it thus reaches a large number of potential gamblers. Bookies have exploited this large pool, and it is rumored that millions of Taiwanese dollars circulate in bets, especially during the closing stages of the event.

In 1996 during the second *Jinlongqi* Pingdong Senior High lost a game by a large margin to Taidong PE school, whose team was composed mainly of second-year students. This loss raised suspicions, and it was later discovered that five players were "invited" by gamblers and told to throw the game.[40] Principal Li Qiyuan was forced to announce on national television that the five players would be expelled, that the school would stop recruiting new players for a year, and that the school would transfer all first-year players to other schools.

Other incidents also came to light of attempts to fix the *Jinlongqi*. During the second tournament Nanying Commercial and Industrial High were intimidated by gamblers, while in the third Pingdong Senior High was again threatened by bookies. In the fifth *Jinlongqi* a Huaxing player received a threatening phone call telling him to throw games. He reported it to the authorities, who eventually discovered that Shi Zhiming, a CPBL player, and Wang Zhongqi, an amateur Taipower player, were involved in the threat. Both were expelled from their parent clubs.[41] Subsequently, Huaxing was under police guard during the tournament. In the sixth *Jinlongqi* parents of Taidong Agricultural and Industrial High players accused the umpires of being bribed by the rival team, which was given many preferential decisions that won the game.[42] In the seventh *Jinlongqi* Nanying shortstop Hu Jinlong received a threatening phone call telling him to be hitless and to make three errors. He told his manager, who reported it to the local police. The next day Nanying won the game 9–0 under heavy police protection.[43]

Apart from becoming involved in gambling and match-fixing, school ballplayers also adopted such pastimes as betel nut chewing, smoking, and drinking, all considered poor habits by the public. All of these failings deterred parents from allowing their children to play baseball because they thought it was a dirty game. As one teacher involved with baseball for many years told me, "during the height of baseball, one player on our team was so bright that with his results he could have entered Taizhong First Senior High. But the gambling scandal changed everything. Only those who are academic failures [now] join the team."[44]

Just as the traditional view of school and academics remains virtually unchanged in Taiwanese society, so does the handling of athletes. What was true in the past remains true today. So now, as in the past, once children enter traditional baseball schools, such as Dongyuan, Fulin, and Shanhua, they inevitably abandon study altogether in order to pursue their professional dreams. At least such abandonment is true beginning in junior high because, with few exceptions, primary schools generally at least pay lip service to academics, requiring players to study. However, when student players advance to junior high, they become unpaid professionals, who spend much less time on study and more on training. One teacher lamented that "there was a pair of brothers on our team. The big brother, who is now entering a junior high, told the little brother that it is better to play in junior high, which means spending only half a day in study and more time on training and does not require homework everyday."[45]

In schools with formal baseball programs players enroll in PE classes, live in dormitories away from their families, train professionally for at least half of each day, and circumvent normal academic requirements. The Taiwanese tend to think it is normal for athletes to give up the right to an education.

In the United States and Japan, however, expectations for student players are totally different. Students need to meet minimum academic requirements before joining a team. "American schools demand that students do well in study as well as in sports. One should never sacrifice schoolwork because of game results. Therefore one has to pass a basic academic threshold before competing with a group of people to be on the team. Consequently, you can see there are many Major Leaguers with high school and college diplomas," said former senior player Jiang Zhonghao, whose son is now studying in an American high school.[46]

Another significant difference between Taiwan and the United States and Japan is that, unlike on Taiwan, a PE major is for those people who want to become teachers. I discovered as a U.S. team interpreter that American players graduate with degrees in sociology, history, economics, and so on but rarely with a major in PE. Conversely, good Taiwanese players going to university all major in PE so that they can concentrate solely on sports.

The PE classes above and within the university are practically independent of the normal educational system and have their own curricula and admissions standards. Below university, each school PE program recruits children from outside its own school district. These programs provide free accommodations and tuition to those they accept. Every subject that PE enrollees study is related to sports. Written examinations are not important; it is rumored that, as long as athletes put their names on an exam paper, they will receive an automatic passing grade. Athletic performance is the only yardstick for progress. If Taiwanese students continue playing baseball as part of their PE class, they either go straight to pro baseball or, as is more likely, falter and find themselves without the education to hold proper jobs.

The separation of baseball-playing students from the rest of the school, particularly their living together in dormitories, sometimes leads to trouble. In 1995 four Xinsheng Junior High baseball players admitted stealing motorcycles and another six used them, fully aware that they were stolen vehicles.[47] Manager Wang Jincheng promised to expel from the team any player involved in the incident, but he later relented and let them stay. The team went on to win the national junior high school title in 1997. Further, three of the four culprits were picked for the 1997 under-16 squad that won the silver medal at the IBA competition.

Nine years later, in a copycat crime, seven Xinsheng Junior High players were caught stealing motorcycles. Their criminal act was excused because the judge at their trial thought that they were good players who would win honor for the country.[48] One teacher offers this explanation for the sometimes bad behavior of young ballplayers:

> Kids who cannot be disciplined were sent to the team, [the parents] asking the manager to take care of them. Kids who have nothing to do apart from motorcycling wildly in the mountains

or chewing betel nuts and those who are illegitimately born and whose mothers have no time to look after them were also sent to the team. They all came to the team from their faraway homes and lived together like brothers and sisters. Sometimes I think a baseball team is like a twenty-four-hour cheap *anqinban* [caretaking class], teaching kids to play as well as providing food and a living. The coach's wife has to prepare over thirty students' dinners each day. Moreover, she has to check their schoolwork, piled up like a little hill. She is more worried than their parents when they get sick or injured. All of this has no remuneration. If they had not come to the team, it is doubtful that they could have received a better living standard and education.[49]

Victory Is the Only Thing

With student baseball out of the limelight one might expect that the Taiwanese win-at-all-costs attitude would disappear. The notion, however, remains firmly a part of Taiwanese student baseball, despite programs designed to promote sports as fun. With sports funds significantly reduced, no school can obtain money to develop its baseball program unless it is one of the top eight teams in the SBL. Other teams are forced to rely on local sponsors or politicians to supply the necessary money. This cash shortage increases the pressure on coaches to win; otherwise, they can face firing or sponsorship withdrawal. Normally, unlike teachers, coaches are hired by *houyuanhui*, supported by parents and local entrepreneurs who are outside the normal educational system.[50] Further, unlike teachers whose jobs are guaranteed by the state, coaches are like any employee who can be let go when results are poor. Thus coaches are classified as gatekeeper or artisan instead of as teachers.

A coach also knows that if he does not produce a winning team, he may lose his job because his principal may abolish the baseball program. A principal can disband a team at will, sometimes even if the team has previously produced good results. Hence a principal is an important factor in deciding a team's future. For example, Guangchun Junior High's principal had supported the team and the coach, but the team was abandoned shortly after a new principal took office. Still some principals want to keep good teams in order to enhance their educational merits and to boost their chances of promotion.

Coaches also face pressure from school officials, parents, and sponsors to win. Because of this demand to win many coaches resort to some unpleasant tactics, such as overusing star players. A favorite method to manage a team is corporal punishment, especially in traditional schools. For the coaches such physical punishment forces players to respect authority and makes them train harder.

Not everyone feels this way about corporal punishment. In 1997 Beinan Junior High's coach Chen Fubin, who beat up a player named Chen Xinhua, was charged by Chen's mother with bodily harm. The coach was sentenced to ten days of penal labor, for which a ninety-two dollar fine was substituted. Two years later Lin Tiansong, coach of Xinsheng Primary School also faced a lawsuit from parents. Lin used the end of baseball bats to hit players' heads and even kicked players and flung them against walls. The affair ended with Lin signing an affidavit promising not to punish players again.[51]

Some players are thankful for harsh treatment, which they feel motivates them to be successful ballplayers. However, ruthless training at one well-known elementary school sparked controversy. In five minutes of footage secretly videotaped by one parent, Shanhua Elementary School's coach Wang Zican was shown slapping four players sixteen times and punching them three times.[52] The tape was released to the public by a local councilor in 2003 and created an uproar and debate over whether physical punishment was justifiable in order to achieve good results. For Wang the argument came down on the side against him, and he was eventually relieved of his coaching duty by the Tainan County Education Bureau.

Physical punishment is really a manifestation of the need to win that still permeates Taiwanese baseball. Island baseball can never grow healthily while this achievement-oriented attitude remains. Many players, often through player overuse, have their careers cut short because of the need to win at all costs. In 1998 Zheng Jiaming, a fifteen-year-old pitcher, used 178 pitches to complete a twelve-inning game, striking out 19 batters. In total, he threw some thirty-two innings in three days. Three years later Zheng again pitched twenty-six innings within four days during the Regional Games. His career ended with surgery to correct damage caused by such overuse. In 2001 Gan Meng-kai, a twelve-year-old player, pitched twenty-six innings over three days. Fourteen innings were thrown on the last day to lead his team to the championship at the Meidengfeng tournament. In later years Gan's performance was well below that of these early years.

No wonder people came to see the "bloody mound" (*lanxie de toush-ouqiu*) as a symbol of student baseball. One teacher, however, pointed out that overuse was not just the coaches' fault:

> Perhaps we can easily blame the manager, who sacrificed players' futures for results. But why do they keep doing it? Because of superior officers, more financial subsidies, fighting for automatic admission to higher institutions [for players], and avoidance of being disbanded due to poor results. I know a manager who was extremely reluctant to let a pitcher throw consecutively. Yet the price was that performances were not as glamorous as before. One day on the way back to school after losing a game, the manager sitting in agony beside the stern-faced principal suddenly turned back, saying to me, "Why is the way back home so far?"[53]

Taiwanese amateur baseball entered its darkest era in 1996. MLB and NPB encroachments and a limited welfare policy contributed to the sharp decline in grassroots baseball. To make matters worse, gamblers extended their influence into student baseball, which had been regarded as a clean game, and match-fixing scandals drove many fans away from the ballparks and deterred little children from playing the sport. Most importantly, the antiphysical culture embedded profoundly in parents' minds also hindered sports development. Some magic was needed in order to revive the national sport that so many people loved. That magic arrived in 2001.

SEVEN

The 2001 World Cup

A Turning Point?

Following the nadir of the late 1990s, Taiwanese baseball experienced a rebirth in popularity beginning in 2001. Factors that contributed to this renaissance were the merger of the two rival professional leagues, the return of Taiwan to the LLB family in 2003, and the many baseball-friendly measures announced by the government. The spark for a renewed popularity of the game was the thirty-fourth World Cup held in November 2001 on Taiwan. It rekindled the fervor and passion of fans, who had lost faith in a sport plagued with gambling, match-fixing, and vicious competition between the two pro leagues.

A Crucial Tournament

At the 2001 World Cup Taiwan hoped to wipe out the humiliations that it had suffered at the 1998 World Championship, at which it placed thirteenth. It also wished to prove itself after its two consecutive failures to qualify for the Olympics. Moreover, pro baseball, haunted by gambling and match-fixing, needed something special to rehabilitate it. The World Cup was a perfect arena to rebuild national confidence and rekindle people's passion. Lin Huawei, who had been head coach of the national team for over three years, was also waiting for the right opportunity to restore the glory of Chinese Taipei last seen when the national team won the 1992 Olympic silver medal.

This World Cup was not without its problems. It was marred by the withdrawal of mainland China, whose sports officials fretted about ROC flags in the stadium. Then the 9/11 terrorist attacks caused the

United States to reconsider the feasibility of sending its national team abroad. Although the MLB forbids its players from taking part in international games because they are under contract to the league clubs, the participation of the United States at the World Cup is paramount since it is a leading baseball nation.[1] The player-abundant United States is always a formidable contender and thus always adds drama to the competition.

Fortunately, the United States agreed to participate with round-the-clock police and military protection. The New York Police Department and the MLB both sent personnel to guard the team. In the final between the United States and Cuba, two Taiwanese SWAT members carrying automatic weapons were stationed just outside the U.S. dugout to ensure maximum safety.

The overall quality of the various World Cup competitors varied. Many nations whose baseball talent was contracted to the MLB were unable to send their best players. So such countries as the Dominican Republic, Canada, and Australia were forced to recruit amateurs.[2] Additionally, many MLB prospects chose not to come. Their agents told them that they risked injuries that might ruin their chances at professional careers. Others, such as the Italian ace pitcher Jason Simontacchi, decided to play in winter leagues, a stepping-stone to the MLB. Finally, some players, especially those from Latin America, chose to make money playing winter ball because there was no financial reward in representing their countries at the World Cup. As a result of all these factors, many World Cup teams were comprised of retired veterans, second-class pros, and amateur players.

Still there were strong teams. As expected, the U.S. fielded an impressive squad. Young prospects, such as Orlando Hudson, Carl Crawford, and Joe Borchard, immediately reached the big leagues in 2002 after the World Cup. Another strong team was Cuba, which defended its title with an aging but seasoned squad. Some of the Cuban players were Omar Linares, Orestes Kindelan, and Antonio Pacheco.

Taiwan also brought an excellent team, which had been preparing for the tournament since September. Coach Lin called up the thirty-eight-year-old slugger Chen Dafeng, who spent his entire pro career in Japan, where he hit a total of 277 homers. The other Japanese recruit was pitcher Xu Mingjie, who won nine games for the Seibu Lions in 2001. Chen Jinfeng was the only American Minor League player included on the squad. The rest of the roster was composed of players from the CPBL, the TML, and the amateur teams, each of which contributed fifteen, two, and four players, respectively.

Chinese Taipei started well, winning consecutively against Italy, France, Nicaragua, and South Africa. Then the Taiwanese faced the United States, which had surprisingly lost to the Dominican Republic and Nicaragua and desperately needed a victory in order to reach the next round.

On the day of the match Chengqing Lake Stadium witnessed the biggest crowd in modern Taiwanese baseball history as more than twenty-three thousand fans packed the ballpark, while thousands more without tickets tried to squeeze in. National flags, emblems, and whistles were everywhere. For most of the American players, who had yet to be called up to the big leagues, it was the first time that they played before such a large crowd. However, before the game started, American players were upset at several overzealous fans holding up pictures of Osama Bin Laden. This fan behavior was not a political statement but merely an attempt to intimidate the visiting squad.

In the end Chinese Taipei lost the game 0–6 after committing five costly errors. Yet they beat Korea in the last game thanks to pitcher Zhang Zhijia and clinched the group title.

The Netherlands was Taiwan's opponent in the quarterfinals. Skipper Lin Huawei sent Cai Zhongnan, nicknamed the "Forkball Prince," to the mound, from which he subdued the Dutch hitters for eight innings. The crisis came in the sixth inning when Chinese Taipei was leading 1–0 after Zhang Taishan hit a solo homer. The Dutch looked certain to score with a man on second base. Kirk Van't Klooster hit a line drive to center field that could have sent the base runner home, but center fielder Huang Ganlin made an acrobatic diving catch to his right to save the day. It was the best defensive play of the tournament. In the end Chinese Taipei won the game 2–0 to enter the semifinals, in which they faced the United States for a second time. At this point in the World Cup many fans were predicting that Taiwan could go all the way and so bought advanced, nonrefundable tickets for the final.

The outcome of the U.S. game was heartbreaking. Taiwanese hitters were absolutely hopeless against American southpaws Jason Stanford, Shane Nance, and Ed Vosberg. The game was decided in the sixth inning when cleanup hitter Joe Borchard hit a massive homer over the center-field fence, leading the United States to a 4–1 victory. Despite losing the game, passionate Taiwanese fans gathered outside the exit tunnel for over one hour while both teams were waiting for their players to finish the drug testing. The fans shouted, "Go, go, Chinese team!" Even the U.S. team deep inside the tunnel could hear the un-flagging chanting and the cheering of the fans.

For the Taiwan national team the moment of truth came in the bronze-medal game against Japan. Ace pitcher Zhang Zhijia shut out the Japanese hitters and allowed only 5 hits, resulting in a 3–0 triumph for Chinese Taipei. Slugger Chen Jinfeng blasted two round-trippers over the fence in the fourth and seventh innings. Thousands of people who could not obtain tickets watched the big screen set up by Taipei city just outside the ballpark. As soon as the game was over, exultant fans shut down Zhongcheng Road just outside of Tianmu ballpark and began parading spontaneously. After six years at a low ebb Taiwanese baseball had recovered its luster. According to a survey conducted by the Sports Council, the thirty-fourth World Cup was an absolute success: over ninety percent of interviewees encouraged the government to host other international sporting events and almost as many thought the World Cup had been helpful in enhancing national prestige.[3]

With the World Cup victory several national team players became overnight superstars. It was a perfect time for pro clubs to publicize themselves and Taiwanese baseball through these stars. So players made a series of public appearances before zealous fans. Handshakes rather than autographs were offered because the CTBA and the professional clubs were afraid that players would become too tired from signing autographs. Much of the attention was focused on Zhang Zhijia, who had beaten both Korea and Japan in the tournament. His celebrity status made him a national icon with whom politicians were eager to become acquainted, especially those running in the upcoming city and county mayoral elections. Zhang was so popular that he released his own pop music CD the following year.

Good as the outcome of the World Cup was it had not met all the expectations of Taiwanese officials. Before the tournament the Sports Council had optimistically hoped that the World Cup would encourage tourism and international publicity, raise community awareness, and increase foreign understanding of Taiwan. Had all these objectives been met, much more money would have accrued from the event. The fact is that only a small number of foreigners knew that the World Cup was being held on Taiwan. Indeed, there was no sign that a single tour group came to Taiwan specifically to see the games. The only foreign visitors to Taiwan for the World Cup were reporters and team delegations.

Additionally, apart from games involving Taiwan, the Cuba versus Japan match, and the finals, all of which attracted large crowds, attendances was dismal. At most of the matches stadium volunteers outnumbered spectators. Ed Vosberg, an American pitcher, said to me during a U.S.–Nicaragua game, "How come no one comes to see the game. I thought many people would come to see us. This is World Cup, isn't it?" On balance, however, despite the low profile of the event globally and the generally poor attendance, Taiwanese baseball certainly benefited and the people who attended enjoyed every minute of the 2001 World Cup.

Merger of the Two Pro Leagues

Total Victory for the CPBL

The World Cup victory had a profound effect on pro baseball and its two feuding leagues. From the outset there had been various governmental and civilian attempts trying to patch up the division and disharmony between the CPBL and the TML. However, the feud burned hot in part because the latter had been very aggressive in luring away CPBL players by providing them with large bonus fees and wages. The nine star jumpers were just the first wave of signings. Zhang Tianlin, Tong Conghui, and Lin Kunhan also defected to the TML while their contracts were still tied to the original league. But the most shocking of all was the departure of Li Juming, nicknamed "Mr. Baseball" because of his exemplary behavior on and off the field. Li had been a starter on the national team for over seventeen years and was on the 1971 LLB squad that crushed the North U.S. squad, led by Lloyd Mc-Clendon. His prowess in center field, in addition to his positive image, made Li a household name.

Li's defection, coupled with the match-fixing shadow and the stabbing of the Dragons' head coach by gamblers, all contributed to the folding of the CPBL's Tigers and Dragons at the end of the 1999 season. The folding of the two clubs witnessed two more players, Huang Jionglong and Chen Gaifa, jumping to the TML.

As discussed in the previous chapter, vicious competition between the two pro leagues also affected amateur baseball. Among other things it contaminated student baseball, to whose players the CPBL and the TML provided under-the-table money in order to secure their signatures lest these prospects be tempted away by the enemy camp.

In 2000 the CPBL began gaining the upper hand when it distinguished itself from the TML by reinstituting the draft, which had been suspended seven years before. For the next several years, in lieu of a draft, clubs offered under-the-table money to amateur and student players. It was the exorbitant costs of these so-called nutritional fees that drove CPBL clubs to resurrect the draft. There was, however, one condition: each club could pick a player that it was paying under the table without fearing that other clubs would grab him. This practice was called the preferential pick. Each club was only allowed one preferential pick, after which players were chosen through a normal draft.

After the draft was restored, Wang Jinyong became the strangest case in CPBL history. He was a preferential player of the Lions and of the Whales, meaning he received money from both, although neither knew about the other's payments. Wang had received a total of $60,460 in nutritional fees during and after his university career.[4] At the draft conference of June 2000 the Lions and the Whales used their preferential picks to choose other players. Wang was then selected by the Elephants, who offered him $90,690 as a bonus fee plus another $21,160 so that he could partially pay back the money he had received from the Lions and Whales. The remainder of what Wang owed was to come out of his bonus fees. Wang's initial response was that the Elephants "should not have used my bonus fees to compensate the

Whales and Lions."[5] In other words, any team that drafted him should be obliged to give out additional money to make up the nutritional fees Wang had received. Wang finally yielded and signed with the Elephants.

Yang Jianfu, drafted in 2003, was the last player on the preferential list. After that, every player would enter pro baseball through a proper, fair, and open draft in which under-the-table money would be forbidden.

With a marked decrease in nutritional fees, the CPBL had a financial edge over the TML, Additionally, the CPBL benefited more than its rival when Chinese Taipei won the bronze at the World Cup because it had fifteen players selected for the team. Zheng Changming's magical defense at shortstop, his homer against the United States, and his good looks attracted many female fans, who followed him and supported his parent club, the China Trust Whales. True, the TML was able to sign the 2001 national squad's megastar pitcher, Zhang Zhijia, but he stayed in the TML a mere two months as a temporary worker before being brokered to Japan's Seibu Lions.

As soon as the season started, average TML attendances slumped to thirteen hundred a game, while the CPBL's climbed to nearly three thousand. The TML had lost the war. Zhao Shiqiang, general manager of the TML, attributed the league's downfall to a biased selection for the national team that left TML players relatively unknown to the public.

The CPBL received a further boost from the Brother Elephants. As discussed earlier, there would have been no pro league without the Elephants, who now provided an important indicator for attendance changes. In 2001 there were already signs of fan resurgence after the Elephants clinched the national title against the Lions. The best-of-seven series between the two clubs was hard fought with the Elephants behind in the series 1-3 at the end of the fourth game. The Elephants finally emerged victorious by winning the final three games and thus claiming the club's first championship since 1994. During the series Elephants fans one-sidedly packed the stadium. When the Elephants won the championship again in 2002, its attendance was boosted significantly.

In the end, with low attendance and shrinking revenues, the TML capitulated and agreed to merge with the CPBL. The four TML teams were to be combined into two teams, Agan and Gida. With the making of two teams out of four, many players and coaches had to be let go. On January 6, 2003, President Chen Shuibian came to witness the historic merger.

The Traitors Clause

The merger had a direct impact on the jumpers, most of whom were coaches in the TML. To CPBL and fans alike the jumpers were traitors, and the defection of these former CPBL members caused profound bitterness and resentment. These feelings linger to this day. I witnessed the hatred aimed at TML jumpers during the games held for selecting members for the 2001 World Cup national team. When men like Hong Yizhong or Pan Zhongwei stepped into the batting box, many fans shouted, "Strike out! Strike out!" When these players did strike out, they were met with cheering from the stands. Even nonjumpers were viewed unfavorably. Although several TML players made the squad, most fans thought the national team should be comprised solely of CPBL players.

After the merger the CPBL took its revenge on the jumpers. In addition to lawsuits filed against them, the CPBL declared them personae non grata, meaning that they could never play in the league again. This exclusion is known as the Permanent Nonemployment policy. There were fourteen players who were permanently banned by the CPBL. Additionally, the nonemployment clause also applied to foreign players who jumped to the rival league.

As a consequence of this blacklisting, ten former coaches and players instantly became jobless with the merger. Although the CPBL–TML merger agreement did not explicitly contain a traitors clause, it had an implicit one in the wording "jumpers cannot be employed indefinitely." In other words, jumpers were shut out for good.

When news of their fate reached the jumpers, all of them agreed that the action was too sudden and too hard to adjust to. Some players, already preparing for the worst, calmly accepted the CPBL's decision, but others were shocked. Lin Kunhan, thirty-five, who still had several years left to play, cried and said, "in foreign countries free agency is normal. But in Taiwan they [free agents] are seen as sinners. . . . How can we face our children in the future?"[6] Despite several conferences held by legislators calling for the repeal of the traitors clause, the CPBL stubbornly clung to its decision.[7] All attempts to aid the blacklisted players failed.

Most jumpers were forced to start second careers. Chen Yixin, Hong Yizhong, Huang Pingyang, and Lü Mingsi transformed themselves into baseball commentators. Li Juming turned from Mr. Baseball to Mr. Coffee, opening a café in Taipei. Zhang Tianlin, who could still play in the outfield, ran a meal-box-selling canteen. In 2004 the traitors clause was finally abolished, and a handful of players were allowed to return to the CPBL as coaches upon the condition that they contribute half of their signing bonus to a grassroots baseball program.

After the Merger

The return to a single-league system meant players' contracts were again firmly bound to the clubs, which could do anything they wanted with salaries. The owners feared that free agency would allow wages to skyrocket and make costs unbearable. Therefore they offered players contracts containing reserve clauses, which gave an owner the right to retain a player's services forever unless he were released. Under these contracts players' wages could even be tampered with in the middle of the season. For instance, Zhang Taishan, the star third baseman of Sinon, signed a four-year guaranteed contract with a monthly salary of $8,280 in January 2000. But in January 2001 Sinon reduced Zhang's salary to $4,870, the team management saying that he was not performing as expected. This reduction was applied even though Zhang's salary was written in black and white on a guaranteed contract.[8]

Not all players were treated so badly. In 2006 Chen Jinfeng, the first Taiwanese to reach the Major Leagues, signed with the Taiwanese Lanew Bears. Since he is a national treasure, he received a very lucrative, six-year guaranteed contract. Unlike Zhang, Chen's performance ensured that his salary remained unchanged.

The postmerger CPBL continued to see good attendance figures, which continued at three thousand per game. Profits were accordingly good. At the end of the 2003 season the Brother Elephants became the first-ever profit-making club in CPBL history, thus demonstrating that professional baseball is not necessarily a charitable industry.

The postmerger pro world also saw the gambling and match-fixing scandal of the 1990s end in 2003 with the Taiwan Supreme Court's finalizing the jail sentence of politician Xiao Dengshi at two and a half years. With this decision the court took an uncompromising stance against gambling.[9]

Unfortunately, gambling and match-fixing did not end with this decision. In September 2005 Xu Weiyue, the prosecutor in charge of investigating gambling and match-fixing operations, was taken into custody for alleged corruption. His arrest followed those of nine runners, who worked for baseball-gambling rings and who were thought to have sent bullets to CPBL players in order to threaten them. In addition one former Sinon Bulls' translator bribed by a runner was also arrested, allegedly for acting as a go-between for the syndicates and the players. Chen Zhaoying, the starting catcher for the Lanew Bears, was interrogated by police, and he and his teammate Dai Longshui were later released by their clubs for match-fixing, as was Macoto Cobras's reserve team coach Cai Shengfeng.

Only a few weeks earlier than this new scandal rumors began circulated that gambling had resurfaced in the league. Fingers pointed at foreign players, and some managers called for foreign players to be banned from the league. The release of Izzy Alcantara was what set the rumors in motion because he was leading the league in home runs and RBIs. The club said he was unmanageable. Whales pitcher Brad Purcell was also released soon afterward for allegedly fooling around with women at a night club. Emiliano Giron was another foreign player who was suspected because of his wildness on the mound. In one game he tossed 5 walks in only 1.2 innings; in another game he threw 2 walks. Whether the rumors were true or whether foreign players were just being made scapegoats, the new gambling and match-fixing scandal was another black mark against the league.

Mainland China: A Magnetic Field?

When the TML jumpers learned that they were banned from playing for the CPBL, they threatened to go to mainland China to help develop baseball there. And indeed, some former Taiwanese pro players have moved to the mainland, which in 2002 launched its first baseball league, the China Baseball League (CBL), with four participating teams, the Tianjin Lions, the Beijing Tigers, the Shanghai Eagles, and the Guangdong Leopards. In 2005 the CBL added two new teams, the Sichuan Dragons and the Hope Stars; now each club played thirty games on a home-away system.

Assisted by Taiwanese coaches, Tianjin claimed the championship in the inaugural season. In the second season the CBL allowed clubs to sign foreign players in order to enhance their squads' skill levels. Tianjin led the way by signing three foreign players, Jeff Harris, Steve Rain, and Edgard Clemente, of whom the latter two had MLB experience. The Korean Samsung pro club also supplied Guangdong with three Korean players. Foreign players made—and continue to make—the CBL more competitive and their games more exciting. At present all four founding CBL clubs have working agreements with Japanese pro clubs, who provide much-needed coaches and players for the league.[10]

Along with the foreign players and coaches are former pros from Taiwan. The successful landing by the CBL of Guo Jiancheng, Zheng Baisheng, and Jiang Taiquan prompted some retired Taiwanese players to explore opportunities in China. In 2003 the Baseball Prince, Liao Minxiong, who had been convicted of gambling and fraud, headed for Shanghai to accept an offer of $2,300 as a hitting coach for the Shanghai Eagles; he was promised $5,000 if he helped the team win the championship.[11] At the same time former China Trust coach He Xinyi became an assistant coach for the Leopards.

Some people were worried about this outflow of talent to China, frightened that it might lead to the mainland beating Taiwan at its own game. However, it would be farfetched to believe that China can be a magnetic field that will attract large numbers of Taiwanese players. As far as salary is concerned, there is little incentive for the Taiwanese to cross the straits: the salaries are too low. Additionally, baseball is a relatively fanless sport on the mainland, which much prefers basketball, soccer, and volleyball. It is these latter sports that attract large crowds and many sponsors, which allow the teams to offer their players high wages. Baseball in China may have potential, but it lacks the necessary support structure right now.

Besides, the CBL rules prohibit Taiwanese from being registered as either domestic or foreign players; they can only work as coaches. The reason for this ban is still unknown. Still there was one exception, Guo Jiancheng, once the closer for Tianjin; he was allowed to pitch because he was a player-manager.

Putting Chinese Taipei on the International Stage

Returning to the LLB

The 2001 World Cup success that so reinvigorated Taiwanese professional baseball was followed by Taiwan's return to Little League Baseball. When in 1998 Peng Chenghao took over the presidency of the CTBA after a fierce battle against the incumbent president, Chen Shengtian, his ambition was to restore Chinese Taipei to its proper international place and become himself the messiah of Taiwanese baseball. During Peng's tenure the national team's international results were good, as seen with the winning of the bronze medal at the 2001 World Cup.

Another of Peng's goal was to return Taiwan to the LLB, which it had pulled out of in 1997. According to the CTBA, Peng received many letters from students and overseas Chinese asking that Taiwan compete once again at Williamsport in order to solidify Chinese sentiment and identity. Another reason for a return to Little League was that a good showing at the Big League competition held by the LLB could help domestic players who wanted to major in PE at universities or colleges.[12]

In requesting a return to Little League, CTBA Secretary-General Lin Zongcheng claimed that "we will act in the future according to LLB demands at Williamsport and won't make any falsifications again."[13] In 2003 Taiwan finally returned to the LLB family. The CTBA held a qualifying competition in which there were sixteen contestants, most of whom still violated LLB rules. Dongyuan Elementary won the national championship, earning the right to play in the Asian qualifier. Dongyuan, a prominent school and team in Taipei city, with a student population of twelve hundred, had eleven players from outside its district, nine of whom were not even from the capital. Thankfully, Dongyuan was beaten by the Korean team 1–4 and by Japan 1–19 and did not have to worry about revealing its ineligible squad to LLB officials.

This renewed bending of LLB rules revealed that Taiwanese officials still persisted in their belief that winning was the only goal of grassroots baseball. This attitude was also revealed in the way the government funded youth baseball. Where the government had instituted large cuts in funding for domestic tournaments, it had not been stingy with money for major international tournaments. The prevailing view continued to be that such tournaments enhance Taiwanese visibility.

Such Taiwanese visibility naturally attracted the attention of the PRC. To such visibility the PRC is extremely sensitive and fiercely opposes it whenever possible. However, although mainland China can block Taiwan's assertion of political sovereignty, it has no leverage against the island in terms of baseball, which Taiwan plays better. Unlike previous KMT administrations that followed the three-nos policy, Li Denghui and Chen Shuibian, both native-born Taiwanese, were eager to increase international involvement and to make the world realize that Taiwan has its own identity separate from that of China and that the island is an independent state, not a part of the mainland.

As part of that endeavor and after a series of strenuous efforts, Taiwan was finally granted the right to host the 1997 Asian Championship for the first time since 1969, despite strong protests from the PRC. After long deliberation mainland China decided to send its national team to gain playing experience. Nevertheless, the tournament was fraught with controversy from the opening game between Taiwan and the PRC. According to the Olympic formula, only Taiwan's delegation flag and anthem could be shown and played during the tournament, while those of the ROC could not.[14] However, the opening match witnessed many ROC national flags flying in the stadium. The representative of the PRC was furious, demanding that the CTBA take action against the violation. The CTBA responded that national flags were spontaneously brought by fans and that it therefore could do nothing about such flags. Being new to baseball and relatively powerless with the IBA, the PRC could do nothing about the flags either, although the animosity caused by the flags of the Taiwanese fans certainly sowed the seeds for events to come.

In 2000 Taipei not only won the right to host the 2001 World Cup but was also granted the right to host the 2001 Asian Championship and the under-19 Asian Championship.[15] The PRC tried to stop these developments, but to no avail. Infuriated at seeing ROC flags again, mainland China pulled out of all three events. The president of the CTBA tried unsuccessfully to persuade the PRC to reverse its decision, which would cause its national and under-19 teams to be demoted to a lower level in Asian competitions because they withdrew without legitimate cause. The PRC, though, was willing to make the sacrifice; after all, baseball is not China's strongest suit. As a result of the PRC's action, the Philippines substituted for mainland China in the World Cup.

The Taiwanese government was encouraged—or perhaps even shocked—by the passion displayed at the World Cup and the subsequent enhancement of Taiwan's international visibility. Bidding to be the host for major tournaments is now high on the national agenda. In terms of baseball the CTBA was able to secure the rights to host the 2003 under-16 IBA tournament, the 2004 under-19 IBA tournament, the World University Baseball tournament, the 2006 Intercontinental Cup, and the 2007 World Cup.

Same Old Story

Taiwan's reemergence on the international baseball scene is built on the old foundation of grassroots baseball. Unfortunately, the nature of the foundation remains unchanged, as does the mindset of the organizers of student baseball. Thus the policy of luring promising players into PE classes at the expense of academic study is basically unchanged. Because of this policy some people dub student baseball players as professional Little Leaguers. A direct effect of the standard PE policy is that students within a school district cannot join their own team unless they are good players.

However, not everyone views the situation as necessarily unfair. One teacher told me that "it is essentially the opposite. It is because most parents don't want their kids to play baseball; that's why we have to look elsewhere."[16]

Beyond concerns about student baseball policy is another troubling matter. The Junior High and Primary School Committee naively thought that rejoining the competition at Williamsport would boost the number of student teams dramatically.[17] In reality grassroots baseball had a more lively development before the advent of the LLB. Striving to be world champions increased the number of teams significantly for only about six years, after which baseball became a sport for only a few.

Ironically, although international success has boosted Taiwanese domestic sports, the bleak fact remains that grassroots baseball continues to fade, as unlike pro ball, youth baseball still waits for a life raft. In part youth baseball's difficulty is cost. Maintaining even a modest youth team on the island costs between $14,700 and $17,600 per year, yet government or local authorities subsidies provide only between $290 and $590 at most, forcing schools to raise funds elsewhere to offset expenses.[18] Facing such expenses, it is not surprising that the capital of Taiwan has only four elementary school teams left, one of which is Taipei American School, a K–12 educational institution serving the Taipei expatriate community.

He Wenlong and Zhang Zhennan, both of whom were mentors of star pitcher Zhang Zhijia, expressed the same opinion: that the government, despite its stated position, does not take sports seriously. The former said that, although he has a master's degree, he is not a PE teacher but rather a contractual worker employed by the Sports Council, which provides salaries below those received by regular teachers and which sometimes cannot pay its employees for up to six months at a time. Zhang, who has been a full-time coach for more than ten years, also argued that, "in addition to lower wages than normal teachers, we don't have merit bonuses, education subsidies, and summer and winter breaks."[19] Islandwide there are around two hundred coaches of this kind. In spite of efforts made by several legislators to institutionalize the coaching system and to incorporate it into the regular educational structure, the laws are yet to be seriously examined.

But the most important factor still hindering domestic sports is the sedentary culture embedded in parents' minds. After the lifting of martial law in 1987, there had been calls for reform of the educational system. Though *liankao* was perceived as the fairest means of entering schools, the outcome was that the entire curriculum was skewed toward subjects that were included on the examination. Thus sports and arts were completely ignored and only practiced by mediocre pupils, who were stigmatized by the public.

In 1994 the Educational Reform Committee was formed with Nobel Prize winner Li Yuanzhe as its chair. The objective was to cultivate well-rounded students, who were good at more than academic study. As a consequence, *gaozhong liankao* and *daxue liankao* were respectively abolished by the government in 2000 and 2001 in order to give Taiwan's schools a healthier environment. The Ministry of Education established a multiple entrance system, which means one can enter senior high school or university through an application process other than examination. During the application process an interviewer will look at a student's extracurricular record, just like in Western educational systems.

The change, however, has yet to alter the sedentary culture. A survey taken one year after the new entrance requirements were put into effect revealed that over seventy percent of parents prefer reinstating the *liankao* system.[20] Further, although the *liankao* system has been jettisoned, parents still use old methods to cope with the new system. As a result, each school department requires certain criteria, such as minimum test scores, in specified subjects—for instance, science, history, and English for political science—along with a good record of extracurricular activities. As in the past parents ask their children to study hard the specified subjects. However, unlike in the past, art, music, and sports have become part of entrance criteria, and consequently, parents follow the old thinking by putting their children into cram schools for these extracurricular activities in order for them to enter the university successfully.

For the moment the Taiwanese educational experiment has not affected grassroots baseball in any significant way. Although children do study at sports cram schools, they mainly concentrate on indoor activities, such as judo, taekwondo, or swimming, and not outdoor sports.

Still the new system is a step in the right direction. Critics may argue that the reforms have put more pressure on children who now not only have to engage in academic cramming but also in art or sports, but the reform shows that some elements of Taiwanese society understand that academic study is not the only criteria to future success.

Not surprisingly, change in attitude is slow in coming. Sports are still viewed by many as activities for academic failures, not for honorable scholars, because under traditional thinking the gap between the civil and the martial is absolutely unbridgeable. Thus, as always, players are deprived of proper education, while other students are denied sporting opportunities.

A teacher at a prominent senior high school in the south gave a vivid description of the management of the baseball team:

> They reside collectively in a classroom, which is very big and not as bad as people thought. Players still sit examinations. But the questions are handed out in advance, and the contents are ridiculously simple. For example, if one person swims 50 meters in 20 seconds, how long will she take to swim 2,000 meters, something like that. We have sporting events held annually at the school. These players are forbidden to take part in any of them because not a single normal student could match them. Thus they can only be umpires, referees, and scorers during the games. On the other hand, they are very simple, innocent, and very funny compared to other students.[21]

The above athletes attended a distinguished school that is famous for its academic achievements, and consequently, the school's principal asked the players to sit examinations. In other traditional schools, however, players sometimes just sign their names to their papers, just as was done in the past.

Ironically, special treatment of players may have led to recent attrition in senior high baseball. The economic recession of the last few years has reduced students' and schools' incentives to organize teams. As mentioned above, the costs for schools to house, train, feed, and educate ballplayers year-round are steep. Additionally, schools also have to buy all the baseball equipment and pay transportation fees. Some schools even provide an allowance to players. Gaoyuan, a famous senior high school, told junior high school graduates that they could enter wearing just underpants, meaning that the school would provide everything else for them. Finally, of course, coaches must be paid.

The expenditures are thus quite substantial, and even more so for a first-class program that may cost over $100,000 per year. The wealthiest school, Gaoyuan, annually lays out over $200,000, which helps give the school field one of the most formidable teams on the island.[22] As a result of such financial demands, schools, especially senior high schools and universities, seek working agreements with private enterprise. Qiangshu High School, for example, receives a great deal of support from RSEA, which donates $150,000 annually.[23]

Since the main purpose for a business supporting a team is advertising, a company asks a school to display commercial logos throughout any tournament that the sponsored squad attends. For example, if Gaoyuan Senior High versus Meihe Senior High were sponsored by Nike and McDonald's respectively, then throughout the game the teams will be called Nike and McDonald's instead of Gaoyuan and Meihe. The danger in commercial sponsorship is that, if the advertising does not produce sufficient results, the company will withdraw its backing.

Such a loss of sponsorship generally means the disbanding of a team because the Taiwanese believe that a team has to be sponsored to be successful. If a team can't be successful, it might as well be disbanded. Nor is this belief unreasonable if one feels the only goal for having a baseball team is winning. Huaxing, for instance, disbanded its under-16 team because the expenses were too high to bear.

First-rate baseball programs are so costly because, in addition to all the normal expenditures, they have to offer generous incentives for good players in order to secure their services. All these benefits to players are necessary privileges under the current system of student baseball, but they are also obstacles to promoting the sport. As the Japanese baseball expert Yang Rongjian commented: "It is strange that many Taiwanese parents don't want to endure any cost in playing baseball. Therefore the government, passionate people, and private enterprises have to undertake the responsibility for covering the expenses. As a result, not only do most children lack the opportunity to enjoy baseball, but it also widens the gap in the future, which makes 'baseball popularization' a dream."[24]

Thus in keeping student baseball a sport for elite athletes, Taiwan has cheated the average student of the thrill of playing the game. Worse, the ROC, schools, and parents do not always serve the elite athletes well either. Instead, they have formed a conspiracy that uses and sacrifices many children in the pursuit of victory. Cheating, scandals, and round-the-clock training remain a part of grassroots baseball culture.

It is true, of course, that the LLB has created an exciting and indelible collective memory for many Taiwanese, as well as for overseas Chinese. To all these parties victories represent the triumph of a great Chinese nation that outmatches any effort on the part of the evil PRC. However, the price to both the reputation of the game and to the players is high.

With the laissez-faire attitude of so many, it is not surprising then that scandal on the local scene also continues to tarnish youth baseball's image. In 2003, for instance, a controversy erupted that involved two Taizhong city elementary schools, Daren and Lixing. Daren defeated Japanese Yaeyama 13–5. After the game, however, Yaeyama raised questions about a player named Chen Hongyi who was listed at four foot ten in the booklet but stood nearly five foot three on the field. Upon confirming that the written listing was an act of forgery, the CTBA swiftly forfeited Daren's qualification and credited Yaeyama with the victory. Daren's coach publicly apologized to the Yaeyama team for the wrongdoing.

Another player-forgery scandal occurred when Lixing used an unregistered player against another Japanese team. Lixing crushed its Japanese opponent, Senshu, 10–5, using starting pitcher Huang Fengyi, who also belted two homers in the game. After checking the videotape, Senshu stated that two players, Huang Pengyi and Huang Lingyi, did not match the pictures in the booklet. Lixing quickly withdrew voluntarily from the tournament, claiming that the team had too many sick and injured players in the hopes that the CTBA would not pursue the matter. But the CTBA soon learned that Lixing had used ineligible players.

In the end the CTBA's technical committee suspended both the Daren and Lixing coaches: neither could coach for three years.[25] Interestingly, the two coaches were brothers.

One Taiwanese reporter conducted a survey of baseball coaches in the Taizhong area and concluded that the motive to recruit ineligible players stemmed from two motives. First, there was schedule congestion: three tournaments were held virtually at the same time. It turned out that three school teams registered for all of the tournaments in order to show how good their baseball programs were. However, none of the school squads were large enough to play so many simultaneous games. Second, coaches were concerned that foreign players were half a year older than their Taiwanese counterparts. Korea and Japan start school in March and April, respectively, while Taiwanese schools begin in September. Knowing that they were short on players and feeling that their foreign opponents had a physical edge, Taizhong coaches were forced to find first-year junior high students to play for them.[26]

What the Taizhong coaches did not understand was what Xie Guocheng Foundation's organizer Huang Min observed: "It doesn't matter whether players are older or teams are stronger. The most important thing is cultural exchange."[27] It seems that, along with the coaches, other Taiwanese cannot grasp that sports can be for sports' sake. This failure in understanding in Taizhong led to the use of fake players.

The dismal state of the grassroots game is compounded by appalling facilities and medical resources. In December 2001 I went to see a junior high game held in Shezidao under the auspices of the Taipei city government. A player collided with the opposing catcher, whose gear caught the runner's ear, causing relentless bleeding. There was no one trained in first aid, though there were three games played that day. The injured player, accompanied by a senior player, had to take a taxi to a hospital.

Game-related injuries are an unfortunate part of any sports, and baseball is no exception. Such a reality, of course, does not excuse the lack of someone trained in first aid at school games.

One of the major sources of injuries among youth baseball players remains overuse. Zheng Qihong and Jiang Jianming are the latest victims of the bloody mound. In 2003 the hard-throwing southpaw Zheng, who was eighteen at the time, had to be carried off the field, suffering from sunstroke and a pulled muscle after pitching thirty innings in nine days.[28] That same year eighteen-year-old Jiang completed four games consecutively in five days, helping Qiangshu to their first major championship in *Jinlongqi*. Within two months he threw ten compete games, eighty-nine innings, and over one thousand pitches. He was fortunate that the soreness of his arm responded to rest. A pro player might throw twice as many pitches as Jiang, but the pro, unlike the school player, has the physical resilience of an adult.[29] Because of the demands placed on players, especially pitchers, it is normal, as one team trainer told me, for them to take Chinese medicine (containing unknown ingredients) before a game in order to recover their stamina quickly in intense competitions.[30]

Overuse is the reason that there has not been a Taiwanese pitcher who has come to the United States and avoided major injury. According to Major Leaguer Cao Jinhui, "pitchers in Taiwan are called to pitch lots of innings in high school and college. That's the environment there, because if you want to win ballgames, you throw your no. 1 pitcher out there. I've pitched up to four times in a single week before. Sometimes four days in a row. This is as a starter, not a reliever. There are nine innings in a ballgame, so after two games, your arm has pretty much reached its limit, and then there's a third game and a fourth game."[31]

Although the 2001 World Cup brought new life to Taiwanese baseball, the event unfortunately did not change public and parental attitudes toward the sport. To alter those attitudes, the entire antiphysical culture has to be changed; otherwise, any incentives, such as the LLB championship, financial subsides, or improvement of the professional league, are doomed to failure, just as in the past.

CONCLUSION

There is no doubt that Taiwanese baseball has both a proud and a sorry history. When I was little, baseball was something that boosted national unity and self-esteem. I recall telling my foreign classmates that the Taiwanese can beat the mighty Americans at their own game. But during my university years I began talking with parents, players, and friends who knew the inside story of baseball, and I learned the cold reality of baseball—the culture of cheating, the scandals, the distortion of history, and the countless people who were injured on the road to Williamsport glory. I was further heartbroken when the club Weichuan, which I had passionately supported since 1982, announced that it was disbanding because the CPBL was plagued by gambling and match-fixing. In a sense writing this book has helped me to come full circle. I came to be objective about what I was studying and writing and to realize that it was important to expose the hard truth about Taiwanese baseball in order for people to reflect on what baseball means to Taiwan.

As the well-known sports sociologist Norbert Elias has observed, through an understanding of sports one comes to understand human society. The converse also holds, and thus insight into Taiwanese baseball can be drawn by analyzing it in the light of political, economic, and cultural context. The Japanese laid a solid foundation for amateur baseball, which should have been an end in itself but instead was penetrated and distorted by the state, the market, and parental forces. As a result the initial motive to play for the sake of playing was compromised and corrupted, thus forcing weaker teams to disband, sportsmanship to sink, and scandals to erupt.

The development of Taiwanese amateur baseball corresponds with the cognitive theory that extrinsic rewards detrimentally decrease intrinsically motivated games.[1] Intrinsic factors are rewards such as getting better, finding excitement and enjoyment, keeping fit, and making friends. Extrinsic motivation is derived from the anticipation of future rewards or approval, avoiding disapproval, or improving one's skills in order to please others. Money, fame, and nationalism all were extrinsic incentives that initially stimulated and subsequently paralyzed Taiwanese amateur baseball. When those extrinsic rewards were withdrawn, as they were in 1975 and again in the mid-1990s, Taiwanese baseball developed into a unique or grotesque form that is markedly different from the sport seen in the United States and Japan.

If all extrinsic incentives are taken away, why do the Taiwanese lack the ability to organize sports voluntarily and spontaneously? The underlying factor is the sedentary culture of Confucianism and its emphasis on examination under which parents discourage their children from physical exercise while encouraging them to study unflaggingly. Taiwanese society is haunted by an ancient Confucian saying: "Those who labor with their minds govern others, and those who labor with their strength are governed by others" (*laoxinzhe zhiren laolizhe zhiyuren*),[2] which presumes that people pursuing sports are simpleminded.

The influence of Confucianism on sports even extends to the overseas Chinese. Steve Gewecke, baseball coach of Los Angeles's Alhambra High School, two-thirds of whose students are Chinese, made an emotional plea to Chinese Americans to participate in sports. The baseball team has fifty players, of which only seven are Asian, four being Chinese. As Gewecke said, "the percentage is absurd. How do you know there will not be a pitcher throwing at 90 mph among those Chinese American students? Academic study is undoubtedly of the most importance, but life is not only about study. Last year one Chinese student came to a baseball tryout and was very impressive. But he was only on the team one day before being told by his parents to pull out in order to spend more time on SAT preparation."[3]

The situation is even worse on Taiwan. According to one statistic, parents in Taipei spent $350 million on cram schools in 2003.[4] Over seventy percent of the general student population was sent to these schools in order to strengthen their foreign language skills, for academic study, and for music and dance. Not surprisingly, only a small fraction of parents, five percent, sent their children to sports camps, despite the abolition of *daxue liankao* in 2001. In other metropolitan areas cramming is also common. As a consequence, grassroots baseball has yet to witness any growth, especially in urban areas.

Of the hundreds of ballplayers I interviewed for this book, Zhou Dexian had one of the most poignant stories. Zhou was a former Mercury Tigers second baseman, whose most cherished memory actually came in 1987 under-19 IBA competition.[5] Batting third in the lineup for Taiwan, he helped his team come back from a 5–1 deficit against a seemingly invincible Cuban squad. He collected 3 hits, and Taiwan went on to win 6–5. His darkest memory came in 1997 when he and six other Tigers players were kidnapped by gangsters early one morning. After the incident he was disappointed with the overall environment of professional baseball and did not want to talk to certain teammates. (I suspect he was referring to teammates connected to gangsters.) Soon after he left the CPBL for good. However, Zhou did not abandon Taiwanese baseball. After earning a master's degree in PE in the United States, he went to Dahan College in Hualian to teach baseball.

When asked why he did not stay in Taipei, he told me that he wanted to foster a healthy baseball environment in Hualian, which is one of the poorest regions on Taiwan. He wanted to instill players with good sportsmanship and teach them that money is not everything. He chose Hualian because graduated high school players in this area have always gone to schools in other counties from which they received better monetary offers. Zhou's journey and his work provide a glimmer of hope for the future of Taiwanese baseball.

Unfortunately, unlike Zhou, too many people choose to overlook the continuous decline of grassroots baseball. This decline is like the sword of Damocles hanging over the country's head. Everyone says that Taiwanese baseball is going to be fine, while in reality it is heading for a dead end. All officials, the public, and parents care about is winning at international tournaments. To their minds such victories will boost amateur baseball. Facts reveal just the opposite. Playing baseball for fun is the real foundation for developing sports, not national success, fame, or money.

It took the Japanese nearly half a century to transform the sedentary Taiwanese into active athletes, only for the process to be reversed when the KMT fled to the island. Still cultural forces are not irreversible; they just need a long time to change when a society is accustomed to accepting thousands of years of tradition. At least in the educational arena steps have been taken toward broadening the public's view of sports. I am still hopeful that traditional thinking will change, especially as new generations appear with different ideas and cultural expectations. It may take a long time to transform the culture, but gradual change is better than no change at all.

APPENDIX ONE

Taiwanese teams in Little League (under-13)

Year	Team	Far East Qualification	Williamsport
1969	Jinlong (Taizhong City)	Champion	Champion
1970	Qihu (Jiayi County)	Champion	Fifth
1971	Juren (Tainan City)	Champion	Champion
1972	Taipei City	Champion	Champion
1973	Juren (Tainan City)	Champion	Champion
1974	Lide (Gaoxiong City)	Champion	Champion
1975	Gushan (Gaoxiong City)	Champion	—
1976	RSEA (Hualian County)	Third	—
1977	Lide (Gaoxiong City)	Champion	Champion
1978	Pingguang (Pingdong County)	Champion	Champion
1979	Puzi (Jiayi County)	Champion	Champion
1980	RSEA (Taipei County)	Champion	Champion
1981	Taiping (Taizhong City)	Champion	Champion
1982	Puzi (Jiayi County)	Champion	Runner-up
1983	Mingde (Gaoxiong City)	Runner-up	—
1984	Fuxing (Pingdong County)	Runner-up	—
1985	Taiping (Taizhong City)	Runner-up	—
1986	Gongyuan (Tainan City)	Champion	Champion
1987	RSEA (Taipei County)	Champion	Champion
1988	Taiping (Taizhong City)	Champion	Champion
1989	Gangdu (Gaoxiong City)	Champion	Runner-up
1990	Shanhua (Tainan County)	Champion	Champion
1991	Daren (Taizhong City)	Champion	Champion
1992	Lixing (Taizhong City)	Runner-up	—
1993	Taiping (Taizhong City)	Champion	—
1994	Liren (Tainan City)	Champion	Failed to finish among the top five
1995	Shanhua (Tainan County)	Champion	Champion
1996	Fuxing (Gaoxiong City)	Champion	Champion

APPENDIX TWO

Taiwanese teams in Senior League (age 13–15)

Year	Team	Far East Qualification	Gary, Indiana (until 1985); Kissimmee, Florida (after 1986)
1972	Meihe (Pingdong County)	Champion	Champion
1973	Huaxing (Taipei City)	Champion	Champion
1974	Meihe (Pingdong County)	Champion	Champion
1975	Meihe (Pingdong County)	Champion	Champion
1976	Meihe (Pingdong County)	Champion	Champion
1977	Huaxing (Taipei City)	Champion	Champion
1978	RSEA (Hualian County)	Champion	Champion
1979	Dongfeng (Taizhong City)	Champion	Champion
1980	Meihe (Pingdong County)	Champion	Champion
1981	RSEA (Taipei County)	Champion	Third
1982	Meihe (Pingdong County)	Champion	Third
1983	Meihe (Pingdong County)	Champion	Champion
1984	Meihe (Pingdong County)	Champion	Runner-up
1985	Meihe (Pingdong County)	Champion	Champion
1986	Huaxing (Taipei City)	Champion	Champion
1987	RSEA (Taipei County)	Champion	Failed to finish among the top five
1988	Meihe (Pingdong County)	Champion	Champion
1989	Meihe (Pingdong County)	Champion	Champion
1990	Meihe (Pingdong County)	Champion	Champion
1991	Meihe (Pingdong County)	Champion	Champion
1992	Hesheng (Pingdong County)	Champion	Champion
1993	Huaxing (Taipei City)	Champion	Runner-up
1994	Zhongshan (Taizhong City)	Champion	Third
1995	Huaxing (Taipei City)	Champion	Fifth
1996	Jianxing (Tainan City)	Champion	Fifth

APPENDIX THREE

Taiwanese teams in Big League (age 16–18)

Year	Team	Far East Qualification	Fort Lauderdale, Florida
1974	National All-star	Champion	Champion
1975	National All-star	Champion	Champion
1976	National All-star	Champion	Champion
1977	National All-star	Champion	Champion
1978	National All-star	Champion	Champion
1979	National All-star	Champion	Runner-up
1980	National All-star	Champion	Third
1981	National All-star	Champion	Champion
1982	National All-star	Champion	Failed to finish among the top five
1983	National All-star	Champion	Champion
1984	National All-star	Champion	Champion
1985	National All-star	Champion	Failed to finish among the top five
1986	National All-star	Champion	Fourth
1987	National All-star	Champion	Champion
1988	National All-star	Champion	Champion
1989	National All-star	Champion	Champion
1990	National All-star	Champion	Champion
1991	National All-star	Champion	Champion
1992	National All-star	Champion	Third
1993	National All-star	Champion	Champion
1994	National All-star	Champion	Champion
1995	Nanying (Tainan City)	Champion	Champion
1996	Gaoyuan (Gaoxiong County)	Champion	Champion

APPENDIX FOUR

IBA under-19 competition

Year	Host country	Gold	Silver	Taiwan
1981	USA	Korea	USA	Eliminated in preliminary round
1982	USA	USA	Taiwan	Silver
1983	USA	Taiwan	USA	Gold
1984	Canada	Cuba	USA	Bronze
1985	USA	Cuba	USA	Bronze
1986	Canada	Cuba	Taiwan	Sliver
1987	Canada	Cuba	USA	Fourth
1988	Australia	USA	Cuba	Bronze
1989	Canada	USA	Cuba	Fourth
1990	Cuba	Cuba	Taiwan	Silver
1991	Canada	Canada	Taiwan	Silver
1992	Cuba	Cuba	USA	Bronze
1993	Canada	Cuba	USA	Bronze
1994	Canada	Korea	USA	Bronze
1995	USA	USA	Taiwan	Silver
1996	Cuba	Cuba	Taiwan	Silver
1997	Canada	Cuba	Taiwan	Silver
1999	Taiwan	USA	Taiwan	Silver
2000	Canada	Korea	USA	Fifth
2002	Canada	Cuba	Taiwan	Silver
2004	Taiwan	Cuba	Japan	Fifth
2006	Cuba	Korea	USA	Fifth

APPENDIX FIVE

Taiwanese players signed by Japanese pro clubs before the CPBL

Name	Position	Year	Club	Came back to play in the CPBL
Tan Xinmin	Pitcher	1974	Taiheiyo	—
Li Zongyuan	Pitcher	1979	Lotte	—
Li Laifa	Catcher	1980	Nankai	—
Gao Yingjie	Pitcher/DH	1980	Nankai	—
Guo Yuanzhi	Pitcher	1981	Chunichi	1997
Guo Taiyuan	Pitcher	1984	Seibu	—
Zhuang Shengxiong	Pitcher	1985	Lotte	—
Lü Mingsi	DH/Outfielder	1987	Yomiuri	1992
Chen Dafeng	Infielder	1988	Chunichi	—
Chen Yixin	Pitcher	1988	Chunichi	1991
Guo Jiancheng	Pitcher	1988	Yakult	1993
Chen Dashun	Infielder	1990	Lotte	1993

Note: Chen Dafeng and Chen Dashun attended Nagoya University of Commence in 1983 and 1985, respectively, thus staying in Japan for over five years to avoid the foreign-players restriction.

APPENDIX SIX

Taiwanese players signed by Japanese and Korean amateur clubs after World War II

Name	Position	Year	Club	Came back to play in the CPBL
Li Zhijun	Outfielder	1981	Kumagai Gumi	—
He Mingtang	Pitcher	1981	Kumagai Gumi	—
Liu Qiunong	Pitcher	1982	Yamaha	—
Huang Guangqi	Pitcher	1982	Yamaha	1990
Lin Huawei	Infielder	1982	Yamaha	—
Lin Zhongqiu	Infielder	1983	York Benemaru	1990
Wu Fulian	Infielder	1984	Toyota	1991
Xu Shengming	Pitcher	1984	Korean club	—
Ye Furong	Pitcher	1984	York Benemaru	1990
Xu Zhengzong	Pitcher	1985	Toyota	—
Zhao Shiqiang	Infielder/DH	1985	Honda	—
Guo Jinxing	Pitcher	1986	York Benemaru	1991
Lin Yizeng	Outfielder	1986	Abe Kigyo	1990
Yang Jieren	Pitcher/DH	1986	Abe Kigyo	1991
Tu Hongqin	Pitcher	1986	Kumagai Gumi	1990
Huang Pingyang	Pitcher	1987	Nittsu	1990
Kang Mingshan	Pitcher	1987	Isuzu	1990
Lin Kunwei	Pitcher	1988	Kawaguchi	1990
Xie Changheng	Pitcher	1988	Isuzu	1991
Chen Mingde	Pitcher	1989	Nikonikodo	1991
Cai Shengfeng	Outfielder	1989	Nikonikodo	1991
Lin Wencheng	Pitcher	1989	Nikonikodo	1991
Wu Sixian	Infielder	1989	Saginomiya	1993
Gong Rongtang	Outfielder	1989	Abe Kigyo	—

APPENDIX SEVEN

Sentences and fines for pro baseball gambling and match-fixing in 1997

Name	Position	Involvement	Charge	Jail sentence	Fine in silver dollars
Guo Jiancheng	Eagles player	Throwing games, go-between	Gambling, breach of trust, fraud	2–6	3M
Zhuo Kunyuan	Eagles player	Throwing games	Gambling, breach of trust	2–6	1M
Gu Shengji	Eagles player	Throwing games	Gambling, breach of trust	2–2	0.4M
Zhang Zhengxian	Eagles player	Throwing games	Gambling, breach of trust	2–0	0.2M
Yang Zhangxin	Eagles player	Throwing games	Gambling, breach of trust	2–0	0.3M
Chen Qingguo	Eagles player	Throwing games	Gambling, breach of trust	2–0	0.3M
Huang Yudeng	Eagles player	Throwing games	Gambling, breach of trust	1–6	0.1M
Cai Minghong	Eagles player	Throwing games	Gambling, breach of trust	0–8, ss 3–0	10,000
Ravelo Manzanillo (Dominican pitcher)	Eagles player	Throwing games	Gambling, breach of trust	Fugitive from justice	—
Zeng Zhengxiong	Eagles player	Throwing games	Gambling, breach of trust, fraud	1–6	0.1M
Chen Gengyou	Eagles assistant coach	Connection with gambling group	Gambling, breach of trust, fraud	1–6	0.1M
Jiang Taiquan	Lions player	Throwing games, go-between	Gambling, attempted breach of trust	1–4	—
Zheng Baisheng	Lions player	Throwing games	Gambling, attempted breach of trust	1–4	—

Name	Position	Involvement	Charge	Jail sentence	Fine in silver dollars
Guo Jinxing	Lions player	Throwing games	Gambling, attempted breach of trust	0–10	—
Wang Guangxi	Eagles player	Throwing games	Fraud, breach of trust	2–0	0.3M
Liao Minxiong	Eagles player	Throwing games	Fraud, breach of trust	1–8	0.1M
Zeng Guizhang	Eagles player	Throwing games	Fraud, breach of trust	2–2	0.4M
Li Congfu	Eagles player	Throwing games	Fraud, breach of trust	2–0	0.3M
Chen Zhixin	Eagles player	Throwing games	Fraud, breach of trust	2–2	0.4M
Chu Zhiyuan	Eagles player	Throwing games	Fraud, breach of trust	0–8 ss 3–0	10,000
Xie Qixun	Eagles player	Throwing games	Fraud, breach of trust	1–6	0.1M
Qiu Qicheng	Eagles player	Throwing games	Fraud, breach of trust	1–0 ss 5–0	30,000
Huang Junjie	Eagles player	Throwing games	Fraud, breach of trust	0–8 ss 3–0	10,000
Wu Junxian	Eagles player	Throwing games	Fraud, breach of trust	0–8 ss 3–0	10,000
Guo Jiancai	Police officer	Connection with gambling group	Gambling, breach of trust, fraud, intimidation	4–0	2.52M
Gao Bonan	Police officer	Connection with gambling group	Intimidation	1–2	—
Guo Wen	Police inspector	Connection with gambling group	Gambling, breach of trust, fraud, intimidation	2–6	1.2M
Liu Xinfa	Police captain	Directing players throwing games	Fraud, breach of trust	1–8	1.2M
Lin Baicun	—	Running gambling site	Gambling	0–10	0.03M
Liu Shuhui	Girlfriend of Guo Jiancai	Managing match-fixing fees	Fraud, breach of trust	0–10	0.03M

Name	Position	Involvement	Charge	Jail sentence	Fine in silver dollars
Lin Guoqing	Xiao Dengshi's crony	Directing game throwing and distributing match-fixing fees	Fraud, breach of trust	3–0	0.02M
Shen Zhezhang	Xiao Dengshi's partner	Running gambling site	Fraud, breach of trust	Innocent	—
Shen Fangda	Xiao Dengshi's partner	Running gambling site	Fraud, breach of trust	Fugitive from justice	—
Wang Zhixiong	Xiao Denghi's	Running gambling site	Fraud, breach of trust	Fugitive from justice	—
Li Maofa	Top figure in Sea Line Gang	Running gambling site	Gambling, breach of trust, fraud, intimidation	5–6	10.02M
Lü Guanxian	Li Maofa's partner	Running gambling siet	Gambling, breach of trust, fraud	3–4	2.02M
Lu Xinjie	Li Maofa's partner	Running gambling site	Gambling, breach of trust, fraud	3–0	2.02M
He Yizhong	Li Maofa's partner	Running gambling site	Gambling, breach of trust, fraud	Innocent	—
Chen Wulong	Li Maofa's partner	Running gambling site	Gambling, breach of trust, fraud, intimidation	4–10	10.02M

Note: SS = Suspended Sentence; 2–6 = 2 years and 6 months; 1 silver dollar = $0.09; M = Million
Source: ROC Department of Justice

APPENDIX EIGHT

Twenty-seven players suspected of match-fixing but released for lack of evidence

Player	Team
Chen Yixin	Elephants
Wu Fulian	Elephants
Li Wenchuan	Elephants
Zhang Taishan	Dragons
Huang Wenbo	Dragons
Chen Dashun	Dragons
Mike Garcia (American pitcher)	Dragons
Huang Zhongyi	Bulls
Lai Youliang	Bulls
Zhang Xiejin	Bulls
Zhang Yaoteng	Bulls
Liao Junming	Bulls
Chen Weicheng	Bulls
Hector de la Cruz (Dominican fielder)	Bulls
Lin Yizeng	Elephants
Chen Yisong	Elephants
Hong Yizhong	Elephants
Ye Junzhang	Dragons
Hong Peizhen	Dragons
Chen Jinmao	Dragons
Huang Qingwen	Dragons
Zhang Wenzong	Bulls
Wang Chuanjia	Bulls
Chen Yancheng	Bulls
Bai Kunhong	Bulls
Huang Shanying	Bulls
Zhang Jianxun	Bulls

Source: ROC Department of Justice

APPENDIX NINE

Taiwanese players signed by foreign pro clubs after the creation of the CPBL

Player	Position	Age	Club	Bonus fee (U.S. dollars)	Signing time
Guoli Jianfu	Pitcher	24	Hanshin Tigers	756,000	1992
Chen Jinfeng (Chen Chin-feng)	Outfielder	21	Los Angeles Dodgers	680,000	January 1999
Guo Hongzhi (Kuo Hong-chi)	Pitcher	18	Los Angeles Dodgers	1.25 million	July 1999
Cao Jinhui (Tsao Chin-hui)	Pitcher	18	Colorado Rockies	2.2 million	October 1999
Xu Mingjie (Hsu Ming-chieh)	Pitcher	22	Seibu Lions (Japan)	850,000	November 1999
Cao Junyang (Tsao Chun-yang)	Pitcher	23	Chunichi Dragons (Japan)	No bonus or transfer fee	January 2000
Chen Qingguo (Chen Ching-kuo)	Outfielder	25	U.S. Independent League	Unavailable	2000
Li Jinhua (Li Chin-hua)	Infielder	23	Mexican Independent League	Unavailable	2000
Wang Jianmin (Wang Chien-ming)	Pitcher	20	New York Yankees	2.01 million	May 2000
Huang Junzhong (Huang Jun-chung)	Pitcher	18	Boston Red Sox	50,000–60,000	October 2000
Luo Jinlong (Lo Ching-lung)	Pitcher	16	Colorado Rockies	1.4 million	October 2001
Yu Wenbin (Yu Wen-bin)	Pitcher	23	Orix Blue Waves (Japan)	420,000	December 2001

Player	Position	Age	Club	Bonus fee (U.S. dollars)	Signing time
Zhang Zhijia (Chang Chih-chia)	Pitcher	22	Seibu Lions (Japan)	1.1 million	May 2002
Wu Zhaoguan (Wu Chao-kuan)	Catcher	18	Seattle Mariners	71,000	September 2002
Chen Wenbin (Chen Wen-bin)	Outfielder	29	Daiei Hawks (Japan)	No bonus or transfer fee	November 2002
Lin Weizhu (Lin Wei-chu))	Outfielder	23	Hanshin Tigers (Japan, drafted)	420,000	December 2002
Hu Jinlong (Hu Chin-lung)	Shortstop	18	Los Angeles Dodgers	150,000	March 2003
Zheng Qihong (Cheng Chi-hung)	Pitcher	18	Toronto Blue Jays	500,000	December 2003
Chen Yongji (Chen Yung-chi)	Shortstop	20	Seattle Mariners	250,000	January 2004
Chen Weiyin (Chen Wei-yin)	Pitcher	18	Chunichi Dragons (Japan)	850,000	February 2004
Huang Jiaan (Huang Chia-an)	Pitcher	18	Seattle Mariners	700,000	April 2004
Geng Boxuan (Keng Po-husan)	Pitcher	20	Toronto Blue Jays	300,000	October 2004
Jiang Jianming (Chiang Chien-ming)	Pitcher	20	Yomiuri Giants (Japan)	700,000	June 2005
Luo Guohui (Lo Kuo-hui)	Outfielder	19	Seattle Mariners	150,000	July 2005
Yang Yaoxun (Yang Yao-hsun)	Pitcher	22	Fukuoka SoftBank Hawks	350,000	October 2005
Lin Yanfeng (Lin Yen-feng)	Pitcher	20	Philadelphia Phillies	100,000	October 2005
Lin Yingjie (Lin Ying-chieh)	Pitcher	24	Tohoku Rakuten Golden Eagles	436,000	December 2005
Ye Dingren (Yeh Ting-jeh)	Pitcher	22	Boston Red Sox	80,000	December 2005
Lin Wangyi (Lin Wang-yi)	Pitcher	17	Boston Red Sox	58,000	December 2005
Yang Zhongshou (Yang Chung-shou)	Infielder	18	Nippon-ham Fighters (Japan, drafted)	873,000	December 2005

Player	Position	Age	Club	Bonus fee (U.S. dollars)	Signing time
Jiang Zhixian (Chiang Chih-hsien)	Infielder	18	Boston Red Sox	375,000	March 2006
Huang Zhixiang (Huang Chih-hsiang)	Outfielder	18	Boston Red Sox	100,000	March 2006
Zeng Songwei (Tseng Sung-wei)	Pitcher	21	Cleveland Indians	385,000	July 2006
Hong Chenen (Hung Chen-an)	Pitcher	18	Atlanta Braves	120,000	July 2006

NOTES

All translations from Chinese to English are the author's.

Introduction

1. During the Japanese colonial era the rulers enforced their own official language policy on Taiwan, and 71 percent of the population was able to speak Japanese fluently. After the KMT took over, it implemented the same policy but changed the language from Japanese to Mandarin Chinese. In 1956 the government mandated that students must speak only Mandarin or risk punishment. The policy was highly successful, and soon 90 percent of the islanders could speak Mandarin fluently. Indeed, many present-day Taiwanese have forgotten their native language.

2. Hughes, *Taiwan and Chinese Nationalism*, 131.

3. Each mainlander on Taiwan had been able to preserve ethnic identity by dividing that identity into two categories, mainlander and Taiwanese. This division was accomplished through the use on identity cards of provincial registration rather than birthplace. Consequently, a bizarre situation occurred in which a Taiwanese's provincial registration could be, for example, Shanghai even though that person had been born in Taiwan and had never been to Shanghai just because the father came from that mainland province.

1. Wooden-Ball Finds a Home

1. Cai, "Riju shidai taiwan bangqiu," 88.

2. Douglas C. Smith, "Foundations of Modern Chinese Education and the Taiwan Experience," in Smith, ed., *The Confucian Continuum*, 7.

3. Latourette, *The Chinese*, 465. See also Miyazaki, *China's Examination Hell*.

4. Zhao, *Changzhong tiyu yundong de huiyi*, 351.

5. Yin, *Taiwan jindai shilun*, 45–46.

6. For further details see Chen, "Houteng xinping zaitai zhimin zhengce zhi yanjiu."

7. Zhang, "Taiwan bangqiu yu rentong," 32. Gao argues that there is another explanation for Sakuma's promotion of the sport: this act was his humble way of repaying the local Taiwanese deity Mazu, who in 1906 had appeared to his ailing wife in a dream and miraculously cured her. Gao, *Dongsheng de xuri*, 40–42.

8. Cai, "Riju shidai taiwan bangqiu," 92.

9. There was a similar situation when the British wanted to promote football in Kashmir. The Kashmir boys were afraid of the "unholy football" made of leather. Furthermore, one boy was taken to the canal and brusquely scrubbed because his face was polluted by the ball. See Mangan, *The Games Ethic and Imperialism*, 184–85.

10. The double school system was discrimination in disguise. At the primary school level students either attended public schools or elementary schools, with the latter being of better quality. Most Taiwanese students were forced to attend public schools since they did not possess the fluency in Japanese language that was required by elementary schools.

11. Abe, Kiyohara, and Nakajima, "Sport and Physical Education."

12. Reaves, *Taking in a Game*, 121.

13. *Tainan Xinbao*, May 26, 1923.

14. Cai, "Riju shidai taiwan bangqiu," 15.

15. Cai, "Riju shidai taiwan bangqiu," 108.

16. *Taiwan riri xinbao*, September 28, 1924.

17. *Taiwan riri xinbao*, September 28, 1924.

18. *Litai tiyubao*, October 7, 2001.

19. The annual high school tournament was created in 1915 by the Asahi newspaper to promote baseball. People compared Koshien to Mecca because every high school students' dream was, and still is, to go on a pilgrimage to the famous Koshien baseball ground.

20. Xie, "Taiwan bangqiu yundong zhi yanjiu," 69–70.

21. Jianong koushu lishi, *Jianong koushu lishi*, 212.

22. Su, *Jiayi bangqiu shihua*, 40.

23. Zeng, "Cong 1931 nian jianong bangqiu."

24. The Tokyo Big Six Baseball League was created in 1925 and consisted of Waseda, Keio, Meiji, Rikkyo, Hosei, and Tokyo Imperial. It sponsored one of the Japanese's favorite tournaments.

25. Xie and Xie, *Taiwan bangqiu yibai nian*, 34–36.

26. *Taiwan riri xinbao*, January 9, 1921.

27. In 1936 seven Japanese professional teams were formed. In 1950 the teams were divided into two leagues; this arrangement remains to this day.

28. Cai, *Riju shidai taiwan chudeng*, 123–41.

29. The most talked about game of the period was a forty-inning, three-day marathon in 1941. On July 26 and 27 Jianong and Taipei Industrial School played eight innings and seven innings respectively before the game was suspended on account of rain. On the third day Taipei Industrial scored first in the top of the second inning. Jianong tied the score in the sixth inning. From that point the game went on and on without another score until Jianong's Shigeo Shibata drove

home Kintarou Hotta for the winning run in the bottom of the twenty-fifth inning. Nishiwaki, *Taiwan zhongdeng xuexiao yeqiu shi*, 506–7.

30. Su, *Jiayi bangqiu shihua*, 25.

31. Zeng, "Chen lunbo koushu bangqiu shi."

2. The Golden Era of Baseball

1. There are two explanations of why the Miaoli players were arrested. In one Xie Yufa was on the team, while in the other members of the squad were acquainted with him. Personal communication with Xie Shiyuan; *Zhongguo shibao*, January 23, 2006; Ma, *Jiaoluo zhongde shengming zhiguang*, 190–95.

2. Wang Zhenhuan, "Taiwan de zhengzhi zhuanxing: cong weiquan tizhi guodu," in Luo and Wang, eds., *Qiji beihou*, 146.

3. According to former soccer player Cheng Ruifu, mainlanders accounted for a higher percentage of the soccer population on Taiwan during this early period.

4. When Chiang Wei-kuo, second son of Chiang Kai-shek, took over the Soccer Association, he ordered in 1980 the construction of Zhongshan Soccer Stadium, which is still the only proper soccer stadium on Taiwan.

5. *Lianhebao*, August 15, 1970.

6. *Minshengbao*, October 13–October 29, 1998.

7. *Taiwan xinshengbao*, October 15, 1952.

8. The Taiwan Provincial Baseball Committee was renamed the Republic of China Baseball Committee in 1955. In 1973 all domestic sporting committees were renamed again. This time the ROC Baseball Committee became the Chinese Baseball Association (CBA), which was subsequently renamed the Chinese Taipei Baseball Association (CTBA) under the Olympic formula in 1981.

9. The only southern corporation to compete with the northern domination was Taipower Electricity, which provided the same financial security as the northern institutions.

10. Dai, "Yushan dijing yu taiwan rentong de fazhan," 123–44.

11. Zhang, "Heku bangqiu wushi nian."

12. Chen, "Taiwan bangqiu yundong," 34–44.

13. Xie and Xie, *Taiwan bangqiu yibai nian*, 84; Zeng, "Weibao weisu 'zhiye bangqiu.'"

14. *Taiwan xinshengbao*, July, 30–August 6, 1968.

15. Gao, *Dongsheng de xuri*, 127.

16. Gao, *Dongsheng de xuri*, 128.

17. Chen, "Taiwan bangqiu yundong," 167–70.

18. *Taiwan xinshengbao*, April 9, 1953.

19. Zeng, "Huang renhui koushu bangqiu shi." A similar narrative can be found in Gao, *Dongsheng de xuri*, 156.

20. Zeng, "Xiaoshi de taiwan bangqiu sai."

21. *Zhonghua ribo*, February 21, 1965.

22. *Taiwan xinshengbao*, November 15, 1954.

23. It took nearly half a century before female baseball flourished again. In 1974 Taiwan's Little League held a female competition. After that event women's baseball again disappeared. However, after the 2001 World Cup held in Taiwan, some women organized baseball teams and were continuing to play up to the writing of this book.

24. *Junguo bangqiu zazhi* 2 (July 15, 1992): 19.

25. *Lianhebao*, August 1, 2004.

3. The Myth of Hongye and the LLB Championship

1. *Taiwan xinshengbao*, February 26, 1968.

2. For a detailed story about Hongye see Wang, *Hongye de gushi*.

3. Zhang, *Zhonghua minguo shaonian*, 33–34.

4. Chen, "Taiwan bangqiu yundong," 92–93.

5. *Lianhebao*, April 5, 1968.

6. *Zhongguo shibao*, August 29, 2004.

7. *Lianhebao*, May 15, 1968.

8. *Lianhebao*, May 22, 1968.

9. *Lianhebao*, May 22, 1968.

10. The upper age for the LLB is twelve. Players over this age are either ineligible or have to compete at a higher level, such as the Senior League.

11. *Taiwan xinshengbao*, February 26, 1968.

12. *Lianhebao*, August 26, 1968.

13. *Lianhebao*, August 28, 1968.

14. *Lianhebao*, August 29, 1968.

15. *Lianhebao*, August 30, 1968.

16. Zeng, "Ling yiduan hongye chuanqi."

17. *Lianhebao*, September 6, 1968.

18. For further details see Anderson, *Imagined Communities*.

19. Horne, Tomlinson, and Whannel, *Understanding Sport*, 178.

20. *Taiwan xinshengbao*, August 28, 1968.

21. *Taiwan xinshengbao*, August 28, 1968.

22. *Taiwan xinshengbao*, August 27, 1968.

23. Although six players were overaged, nine players actually used false names. It is still a mystery why the other three employed pseudonyms.

24. Normally the use of ineligible players would be handled as an internal matter by the Ministry of Education and would result in punishment for a school, sometimes by banning its future participation in baseball. But these three people used photos of bogus players to apply for residence for these players and placed the students' photos in official documents. By doing so, these men were guilty of criminal actions.

25. Administrator Zeng was not satisfied with the sentence and planned to appeal. However, he was dissuaded by arguments that further legal action might compromise national integrity.

26. The documentary about Hongye was filmed by Public TV and was broadcast on November 20, 2001.

27. Gao Yiqun, "Dongtai xiaojiang yibang xiang manshan hongye ya chuiyang," in Zhang, *Zhonghua minguo shaonian*, 23.

28. Upon Taiwan's becoming a member of Little League Baseball, these schools officially became Little League Baseball teams that could play for a chance to go to Williamsport.

29. According to Lin Huawei, a member of 1970 Qihu baseball team, "at that time it was rare for people, even for rich ones, to go abroad. It was exciting when we won the national champion knowing the United States was in sight." Personal interview with Lin Huawei, September 4, 2002.

30. *Zhongguo shibao*, September 7, 1969.

31. One American student said to the press that "this massive scene is only comparable to the one I saw in Boston when people greeted American astronaut [Michael] Collins." *Zhongguo shibao*, September 8, 1969.

32. *Taiwan xinshengbao*, August 27, 1970.

33. *Lianhebao*, September 2, 1971.

34. *Lianhebao*, September 12, 1971.

35. *Zhongguo shibao*, September 30, 1971.

36. Chu, *Taiwan at the End of the Twentieth Century*, 78.

37. *Taiwan dumai xinwen*, September 5, 1991.

38. There was one player, Chen Yixin, who came from the northern part of Taiwan, but he was from Xinzhu county.

39. Lin, "Yundong yu zhengquan weixi," 44–45.

40. Taiwan's performances in the Olympics were dismal, and it was not until the 2004 Olympics that Taiwan won its first gold medal (Hong Kong captured one in 1996). Taiwan also did not fare well in the Asian Games.

41. As John Hoberman observes, in 1987 even culturally homogeneous Switzerland started a wave of sporting chauvinism for nationalistic purposes. See Hoberman, "Sport and Ideology," 15–32.

42. *Taiwan xinwenbao*, September 9, 1969.

43. *Zili wanbao*, September 6, 1969.

44. *Gongshang ribao*, August 29, 1973.

45. Lin, "Yundong yu zhengquan weixi," 48.

46. Chen, *Haiwai taidu yundong sishi nian*, 153–54.

47. Chen, *Haiwai taidu yundong sishi nian*, 154–56; Lin, "Yundong yu zhengquan weixi," 48.

48. Gao, *Dongsheng de xuri*, 181–82.

49. Li was able to circumvent a restriction barring two foreign players on the

field at the same time because he was adopted by a Japanese family and later changed his name to Sogen Miyake.

50. The Milwaukee Brewers offered Zhao a $9,000 signing bonus but asked him to start in Single A ball. Zhao thought the $500 monthly salary too low, so he rejected the offer. But even had he accepted the deal, Zhao would have wanted to play in the 1984 Olympics before going to the United States. *Lianhebao*, January 2, 1983.

51. Li, "Gelei yundong xuanshou dui shaobang de kanfa," 31.

52. Personal interview conducted on July 20, 2002.

53. More recently, in the 2000 presidential election, baseball people, led by mainlander Zhao Shiqiang, chose to back the proindependence candidate, Chen Shuibian, while most basketball players and coaches, many of whom had mainland backgrounds, stood with Lian Zhan and Song Chuyu, both of whom advocated unification policies.

54. The detailed story of this chain's success can be found in Du, "Yonghe doujiang linglei yanjin shi."

55. *Lianhebao*, 1983. This information was provided by a friend, Huang Weihan, who unfortunately did not have an exact date for the newspaper article.

56. *Taiwan xinshengbao*, August 27, 1970.

57. Su, *Jiayi bangqiu shihua*, 66–68.

58. Wu, "Jinnian shaobang wangzuo sheishu," 45–46.

59. Xie, "Ting!," 3.

60. Personal interview conducted on July 20, 2002.

61. I am indebted to baseball expert Zeng Wencheng for this information.

62. Lin, "Cong qihu de shoucuo suo dedao de qishi," 16–17.

4. A Drastic Decline in Baseball's Population

1. *Lianhebao*, October 23, 1973; Van Auken and Van Auken, *Play Ball!*, 175.

2. Zhang, *Zhonghua minguo shaonian*, 24.

3. *Zhongguo shibao*, July 24, 1975.

4. Zhang, *Zhonghua minguo shaonian*, 248.

5. *New York Times*, December 31, 1975.

6. Zhang, *Zhonghua minguo shaonian*, 268.

7. I am indebted to my friend Guozili, who provided this information by going to the library and checking *Lianhebao* concerning the 1976 southern qualification.

8. The police were not the only ones suspicious of this type of examination. Every doctor at Taiwan University Hospital questioned the validity of age examination through the checking of private parts. *Lianhebao*, May 28, 1976.

9. *Lianhebao*, May 21, 1976. Xu Weizhi told the author during an interview conducted on February 10, 2006, that Cao was indeed six years older than his ID card indicated.

10. Zhao did play some baseball in Huaxing High School and went to Gary in 1977, but then he was transferred to another school that had no baseball team.

11. Personal interview conducted on April 13, 2002. Throughout the conversation the interviewee was very reserved about the sensitive questions that I asked. I was surprised, however, at his candor about why Taiwan decided to withdraw from the LLB in 1997.

12. Liao Jincheng and Dai Qingyang did join Meihe in 1980 and helped the team capture the Senior League world series held in Gary that year.

13. Zhang, *Zhonghua minguo shaonian*, 386; Personal interview conducted with Xu Weizhi on February 10, 2006.

14. For instance, the official birthday of current Taiwanese president Chen Shuibian was reported one year later than he was actually born.

15. Personal interview conducted with Xu Weizhi on February 10, 2006.

16. *Minshengbao*, August 28, 1991.

17. Chen, *Feiben de suiyue*, 48.

18. Every year Taiwan crushed Guam by very large margins and only lost once, in 1975.

19. In 1985 the national champion, Meihe, decided to take part in the IBA; generally, however, champion teams chose the LLB as their tournament.

20. *Zhonghua bangqiu zazhi*, May 6, 1990, 56–57; Gao, *Dongsheng de xuri*, 164.

21. *Minshengbao*, December 16, 1999.

22. Gao Zhengyuan and Lin Qiwen argue that the standard of the International Invitation Tournament held in Taiwan was higher than that of the Intercontinental Cup held by IBA. Such a claim is not true because Cuba did not take part because of the KMT's anti-Communist policy, while the United States only sent their community college teams. Only Japan, Korean, the Netherlands, and some Latin American countries sent proper teams. The level of play was not as high as some people like to think.

23. Ironically, several months later Olympic organizers decided to expand the number of participants in the games from six to eight, thus allowing Japan to compete.

24. *Minshengbao*, October 2, 1984.

25. It was not until after 1996 that pro players were allowed to take part in international baseball games.

26. Though Taiwan created a pro baseball league in 1990, it was quite late in doing so as compared with its Asian neighbors. Japan's pro ball dates back to 1936 and Korea's to 1982.

27. TVIS channel interview with Wu Xiangmu conducted in 1995.

28. There was a rumor circulating that the United States deliberately did Taiwan a favor in the hopes that Taiwan could return the favor in the next round. Taiwan did lose 0–7 to the United States the second time around.

29. Liang, "Shehui fazhan quanli yu yundong wenhua de xinggou," 78.

30. Available at telnet://bbs.aidsbbs.net (baseball board, post number 2537, Chinese version).

31. Starting in 1982, the names of Spring and Fall league competitions were changed to the Zhongzheng Cup and the Guoqing Cup. "Zhongzheng" is another name for Chiang Kai-shek, while "Guoqing" means national birthday. It is not known why the names were changed.

32. If the Division Two team won, it could choose either to remain in Division Two or be promoted to Division One. Originally if the team decided to go up, the Division One team had to go down. However, the rule was subsequently changed so that the Division One team could stay put if it lost to the Division Two team. The change was necessary because there were too few Division One teams.

33. Blue and white are the colors of the KMT party flag. If there was a third team, its name would be Chinese Red (*Zhonghua hong*) because blue, white, and red are the colors of the ROC national flag.

34. Zeng, *Dragon Gate*, 88–89.

35. Zeng, *Dragon Gate*, 73.

36. For a comparison of ancient keju and liankao see Zeng, *Dragon Gate*, 98–105; Zheng, *Zhongguo zhengzhi zhidu yu zhengzhi shi*, 57–70; Wang and Lin, *Jiaoyu de kunjing yu gaige de kunjing*, 39–65.

37. Hsu, "Confucianism in Comparative Context," in *Confucianism and the Family*, 62–63.

38. The most bizarre thing in senior high school is that instructors finished teaching three-year courses within two and a half to two years. They then use the remaining time for review and to give countless mock exams. Art, music, and sports are ignored because they are not part of *liankao*.

39. Tan, *Guozhong jiaoyu gaige lun*, 100.

40. *Zhongguo shibao*, July 31, 1982.

41. Personal interview conducted on June 21, 2002; the interviewee wished to remain anonymous.

42. Twenty-two out of thirty-four teams were part of the strong-point school system. One can imagine how few teams would have existed without this program. This dependence on strong-point schools shows how severe the baseball environment was at that time. See Lin, "Yundong yu zhengquan weixi," 72.

43. I am indebted to a former Huaxing player, who wished to remain anonymous, for providing such ample information to me. Personal interview conducted on July 20, 2002.

44. Personal interview conducted on July 20, 2002.

45. I am indebted to my friends Zhang Wenqi and Xiaotang for invaluable information on Tong Renchong, who is also my favorite player.

46. Personal interview conducted on July 20, 2002; the interviewee wished to remain anonymous.

47. *Zhonghua bangqiu zazhi*, May-June 1996, 54–65.

5. The Birth of Professional Baseball

1. *Lianhebao*, November 25, 1981.

2. *Minshengbao*, December 6, 1987. It should be noted that no Taiwanese player who had been signed initially by a Japanese amateur club ever made it to the Japanese pro clubs, who normally signed Taiwanese players as soon as they finished their military service rather than obtaining them from the amateur clubs.

3. *Taiwan xinshengbao*, September 28, 1971.

4. Personal interview conducted on January 10, 2002.

5. *Minshengbao*, August 24, 1999.

6. *Minshengbao*, August 26, 1999.

7. Personal interview conducted on October 28, 2001.

8. *Minshengbao*, March 29, 1988.

9. *Minshengbao*, August 31, 1999.

10. *Lianhebao*, November 12, 1989.

11. *Zhiye bangqiu zazhi* 21 (December 1990): 38.

12. Gong Rongtang, who went to Japan in 1989, was the only player who retained his amateur status until retirement. Gong refused professional temptation because he felt a pro career had no guarantees, so he chose to stay at Cooperative Bank, where he became a manager.

13. Lin, "Yundong yu zhengquan weixi," 97.

14. Zhongxiao xue bangqiu, *Guoxiao liansai*, 1990, unnumbered back cover.

15. Wu and Zeng, *Aoyun changwai de jingji*, 96–113.

16. Privately the PRC media and officials still call the Taiwanese national team *Zhongguo Taipei* so as to downgrade Taiwan to being a mere local province of mainland China. After the takeover of Hong Kong in 1997, for instance, Hong Kong's team became known as *Zhongguo Xianggang* (China, Hong Kong), thus indicating that Hong Kong is a part of China.

17. *Minshengbao*, July 21, 1990.

18. Premier Hao Bocun was a mainlander born in Jiangsu, China. He fled to Taiwan with KMT forces and served in the army for fifty years. He was appointed premier by President Li Denghui in 1990, stepping down in 1993. In Taiwan's political system the president, elected by general election, is the head of state and the armed forces, and appoints the premier, who forms the cabinet and runs the day-to-day affairs of the government.

19. *Minshengbao*, August 3, 1990.

20. *Zhonghua bangqiu zazhi* 8 (August 1992): 17.

21. *Zhonghua bangqiu zazhi* 8 (August 1992): 17.

22. *Zhonghua bangqiu zazhi* 8 (August 1992): 17.

23. *Zhonghua bangqiu zazhi* 3 (March 1992): 12–16.

24. Personal interview conducted on January 10, 2002.

25. Fifty-six members voted yes, seven members voted no, and two members

abstained. The five other members voting against the proposal were Brazil, Panama, Puerto Rico, Malaysia, and Japan. *Zhongguo shibao*, September 22, 1996.

26. *Lianhebao*, August 3, 1992.

27. Zhongxiao xue bangqiu, *Guoxiao liansai*, 1994, unnumbered back cover; Zhongxiao xue bangqiu, *Guozhong liansai*, 1995, unnumbered back cover.

28. *Minshengbao*, September 1, 1990.

29. "Bama buyao de xiaohai," January 23, 2002; available at http://www.ctba .org.tw/discuss/view.asp?messageid=11883&board=world.

30. *Minshengbao*, November 7, 2002.

31. *Minshengbao*, November 7, 2002.

32. Available at telnet://bbs.aidsbbs.net (baseball board, post number 3726, Chinese version).

33. Available at telnet://bbs.aidsbbs.net (baseball board, post number 3729, Chinese version).

34. *Lianhe wanbao*, August 12, 1993.

35. *Minshengbao*, August 14, 1993.

36. Gao, *Dongsheng de xuri*, 241–42.

37. Sundeen, "A Kid's Game," *Journal of Sport & Social Issues* 25, no. 3 (August 2001): 260.

38. *Zhongguo shibao*, January 2, 1995.

6. Multiple Crises

1. Cashmore, *Making Sense of Sports*, 193–211.

2. *Zhonghua bangqiu zazhi* 48 (December 1993): 100–103.

3. *Lianhebao*, January 13, 2003.

4. *Lianhebao*, June 2, 1999.

5. *Zhongguo shibao*, April 30, 1999.

6. Lin, "Heijin zhengzhi yingxiang," 22.

7. Available at telnet://bbs.aidsbbs.net (baseball board, post number 23253, 23254, and 23255, Chinese version).

8. *Zhongguo shibao*, January 30, 1997.

9. *Zhongguo shibao*, February 21, 1997.

10. *Majiang* is a game of Chinese origin that uses tiles made of bone or plastic and bamboo. It bears a resemblance to Western rummy card games.

11. Xu Shengming gave a lecture on professional baseball at Aletheia University, Taipei, June 3, 2003.

12. The whole story is available at http://www.usatoday.com/sports/baseball/ bbw/sbbw7528.htm.

13. Souhan, "Baseball's Frontier."

14. Personal interview conducted on April 22, 2002. I am indebted to the Brother Elephants.

15. Taizhong District Court, Criminal Verdict 2000 Yi Number 3466, January 29, 2002.

16. Another twenty-seven players were suspected by prosecutors of throwing

games, but the evidence was insufficient to bring them to trial. *Ziyou shibao*, August 26, 1997.

17. *Zhongguo shibao*, February 5, 1997.

18. Personal interview conducted on June 21, 2001; the interviewee wished to remain anonymous.

19. For more on globalization see Held and McGrew, *The Global Transformations Reader*; Baylis and Smith, *The Globalization of World Politics*.

20. For further information see Klein, *Sugarball*; Guevara and Fidler, *Stealing Lives*. It should be noted, however, that Klein is critical of Guevara and Fidler's work. The criticism and countercriticism are available at http://www .onlyagame.org/features/2003/03/resteallive.asp and http://www.onlyagame.org/ features/2003/04/contersteal.asp. See also Alan M. Klein, "Trans-nationalism, Labor Migration, and Latin American Baseball," in Bale and Maguire, eds., *The Global Sports Arena*, 183–205; Regalado, "Latin Players on the Cheap," *Indiana Journal of Global Legal Studies* 8 (2000): 9–20.

21. The Dominican Republic and Venezuela do have summer leagues, but they are set up by the MLB for the benefit of its rookie prospects.

22. Reaves, *Taking in a Game*, 147.

23. Callis, "Clubs Have Turned to World-side Scouting," *Baseball America*, November 29, 1993. The story is available at http://www.baseballamerica.com/today/ features/worldscout0125.html.

24. Gao, *Dongsheng de xuri*, 205–6.

25. *Zhongyang ribao*, January 5, 1999.

26. The LA Dodgers had a working relationship with the Sinon Bulls at the time.

27. *Zhongyang ribao*, July 14, 1999.

28. *Zhongyang ribao*, July 13, 1999.

29. *Denver Post*, October 9, 2001.

30. Guevara and Fidler, *Stealing Lives*, 175–76.

31. Japanese high schools, universities, and amateur clubs were not part of the restriction. Thus some Taiwanese senior high players, such as Shi Zhiming, Lin Weizhu, and Wu Renrong, transferred to Japanese schools in 1995 unhindered by the agreement.

32. Available at http://www.baseballamerica.com (visited on December 20, 2002).

33. Chen, Liang, and Du, *Zhongguo bangqiu yundong shi*, 45–46

34. The first China-born person to play in the MLB was Harry Kingman, son of American Congregationist missionaries who worked in China. He made his MLB debut in 1914.

35. *Zhongshi wanbao*, May 26, 1997.

36. *The Associated Press*, April 16, 1997.

37. *Taiwan ribao*, April 12, 1997.

38. *Minshengbao*, March 27, 2002.

39. Zhang, "Touhao, yeyao zhuangzhuang," *Guanghua zazhi* 22, no. 4 (April 1997): 8–19.

40. *Zhongshi wanbao*, February 2, 1997.

41. *Zhongyang ribao*, January 5, 2000.

42. *Dachengbao*, January 24, 1999.

43. *Lianhebao*, January 14, 2002.

44. Personal contact through telnet://bbs.aidsbbs.net on July 5, 2000.

45. Available at telnet://bbs.aidsbbs.net (baseball board, post number 19464, Chinese version).

46. Chen, "Bielai wuyang jiang zhonghao."

47. *Ziyou shibao*, September 30, 1995. Taidong county mayor Chen Jiannian went to Xinsheng personally in order to discover how the team was managed.

48. *Lianhebao*, July 14, 2004.

49. Available at telnet://bbs.aidsbbs.net (baseball board, post number 19428, Chinese version).

50. *Minshengbao*, December 3, 2002.

51. *Minzhong ribao*, February 12, 1999.

52. The footage was shown on national TV on August 14, 2003.

53. Available at telnet://bbs.aidsbbs.net (baseball board, post number 19462, Chinese version).

7. The 2001 World Cup

1. There have been two exceptions to Major League players taking part in international games. The first was the Dodgers allowing their ace pitcher Park Chan-ho to play for South Korea in the 1998 Asian Games. The Dodgers apparently agreed to Park's participation because then he could be exempted from compulsory military service if Korea won the gold medal, which it subsequently did. The other exception, of which the MLB did not initially know, was the 2000 Pan American Games, at which several Panamanian Major Leaguers, such as Carlos Lee, Olmedo Saenz, and Einar Diaz, played for their national team. However, when MLB authorities discovered that these players were in the tournament, it forbid them from taking part in the finals.

2. One senior Dominican figure, Hector-Tino-Pereyra, for instance, even demanded that his nation cancel the trip because the head coach could hardly find any players for the World Cup.

3. *Zhongguo shibao*, December 22, 2001.

4. The Whales started giving nutritional fees of $380 monthly to Wang in July 1997, and the Lions offered him the $880 a month commencing in 1998. Subsequently, Wang borrowed an additional $880 every month from the Lions. *Minshengbao*, June 26, 2000.

5. *Dachengbao*, June 29, 2000.

6. *Lianhe wanbao*, February 11, 2003.

7. *Lianhe wanbao*, January 8, 2003.

8. *Lianhebao*, January 28, 2001.

9. *Zhonghua ribao*, August 22, 2003.

10. Tianjin has a working relationship with the Yokohama Bay Stars, Shanghai

with the Kintetsu Buffaloes, Beijing with the Yomiuri Giants, and Guangdong with the Hiroshima Carps. Liu, "Fenbie yu meiri xingcheng hezuo guanxi."

11. *Dongsen xinwenbao*, October 15, 2003.

12. *Minshengbao*, February 6, 1999.

13. *Minshengbao*, January 12, 2002.

14. At the 1996 Atlanta Olympics, for instance, one Taiwanese was arrested after waving a ROC flag in the spectator stands while cheering for a Chinese Taipei player, Chen Jing, in the table-tennis finals.

15. The Philippines should have hosted the 2001 Asian Championship, but it was forced to forego the privilege because of domestic turmoil.

16. Personal contact through telnet://bbs.aidsbbs.net on July 15, 2001.

17. *Dongsen xinwenwang*, January 31, 2003.

18. *Zhongyangshe*, November 20, 2001.

19. *Zhongguo shibao*, November 21, 2001.

20. *Lianhe wanbao*, January 27, 2003.

21. I am indebted to an English teacher, Xu Yashu, who was studying for a master's degree at Warwick University in 2003, for providing me this invaluable information on July 22, 2003.

22. *Minshengbao*, August 13, 2001.

23. *Ziyou shibao*, December 14, 2004.

24. Yang, "Riben guoqiu qiangsheng de mimi."

25. *Lianhebao*, January 8, 2003.

26. *Litai tiyubao*, January 8, 2003.

27. *Litai tiyubao*, January 12, 2003.

28. *Lianhebao*, July 31, 2003.

29. *Minshengbao*, January 19, 2003.

30. Personal communication, July 31, 2003.

31. Kuo, "Q&A with Colorado's Tsao."

Conclusion

1. Gill, *Psychological Dynamics of Sport*, 149.

2. The proverb is from Mencius, who was a staunch follower of Confucius.

3. *Taiwan ribao*, February 6, 2003, LA edition. *Taiwan ribao* is in Chinese characters but is published in both Taiwan and Los Angeles; each edition has different contents. I am indebted to the contributor Zhong Mengwen, who was the Boston Red Sox's Pacific Asian scout.

4. *Minshengbao*, November 19, 2003.

5. Personal interview conducted on November 19, 2005.

BIBLIOGRAPHY

Abe, Ikuo, Yasuharu Kiyohara, and Ken Nakajima. "Sport and Physical Education under Fascistization in Japan." *InYo: Journal of Alternative Perspectives* (June 2000). http://ejmas.com/jalt/jaltart_abe_0600.htm.

Allison, Lincoln, ed. *The Changing Politics of Sport*. Manchester: Manchester University Press, 1993.

———. *Taking Sport Seriously*. Aachen: Meyer & Meyer, 1998.

Anderson, Benedict. *Imagined Communities: Reflections on the Origin and Spread of Nationalism*. New York: Verso Books, 1983.

Bale, John, and Joseph Maguire. *The Global Sports Arena: Athletic Talent Migration in an Interdependent World*. London: Frank Cass, 1994.

"Bama buyao de xiaohai." Chinese Taipei Baseball Association. http://www.ctba.org.tw/discuss/view.asp?messageid=11883&board=world.

Baylis, John, and Steve Smith. *The Globalization of World Politics: An Introduction to International Relations*. 2nd ed. Oxford: Oxford University Press, 2001.

Beck, Ulrich. "What is Globalization?" In *The Global Transformations Reader: An Introduction to the Globalization Debate*, edited by David Held and Anthony McGrew. Cambridge UK: Polity Press, 2000.

Cai Zhenxiong. *Riju shidai taiwan chudeng xuexiao tiyu fazhan shi*. Taipei: Shida shuyuan, 1995.

Cai Zongxin. "Riju shidai taiwan bangqiu yundong fazhan guocheng zhi yanjiu: Yi 1895 (Mingzhi 28) nian zhi 1926 (Dazheng 15) nian wei zhongxin." Master's thesis, Taiwan Normal University, 1992.

Cashmore, Ellis. *Making Sense of Sports*. 2nd ed. London: Routledge, 1996.

Chambers, Simone, and Will Kymlicka, eds. *Alternative Conceptions of Civil Society*. Princeton NJ: Princeton University Press, 2002.

Chappell, Robert. "Sport in Developing Countries: The Role of Physical Education as Part of Sport for All." In *Cultural Diversity and Congruence in Physical Education and Sport*, edited by Ken Hardman and Joy Standeven, 229–37. Aachen: Meyer & Meyer, 1998.

Chen Jiamou. "Taiwan bangqiu yundong fazhan zhi yanjiu (1945–1968)." Master's thesis, Taidong Normal College, 2002.

Chen Mingcheng. *Haiwai taidu yundong sishi nian*. Taipei: Zili wanbaoshe, 1992.

Chen Shizheng. "Bielai wuyang jiang zhonghao" (Long Time No See, Jiang Zhonghao). Fanshuteng. http://sports.yam.com/show.php?id=0000004083.

Chen Xianming, Liang Youde, and Du Kehe. *Zhongguo bangqiu yundong shi.* Wuhan: Wuhan chubanshe, 1990.

Chen Xiaoyu. *Feiben de suiyue: Lin yizeng.* Taipei: Minshengbao, 1995.

Chen Yanhong. "Houteng xinping zaitai zhimin zhengce zhi yanjiu." Master's thesis, Danshui University, 1986.

Chu Jou-juo. *Taiwan at the End of the Twentieth Century: The Gains and Losses.* Taipei: Tonsan Publications, 2001.

Cohen, Jean L., and Andrew Arato. *Civil Society and Political Theory.* London: MIT Press, 1994.

Dai Baocun. "Yushan dijing yu taiwan rentong de fazhan." In *Guojia rentong lunwenji.* Taipei: Taiwan lishi xuehui, 2001.

Deankin, Nicholas. *In Search of Civil Society.* Basingstoke UK: Palgrave, 2001.

Du Zongbo, "Yonghe doujiang linglei yanjin shi" (Another Kind History of Yonghe Doujiang). Qimou. http://home.kimo.com.tw/peckerkimo/doc/drink/drink.htm.

Echevarria, Roberto Gonzalez. *The Pride of Havana: A History of Cuban Baseball.* New York: Oxford University Press, 1999.

Gao Zhengyuan. *Dongsheng de xuri.* Taipei: Minshengbao, 1994.

Gernet, Jacques. *A History of Chinese Civilization.* Cambridge UK: Cambridge University Press, 1982.

Gill, Diane L. *Psychological Dynamics of Sport.* Champaign IL: Human Kinetics, 1986.

Guevara, Artuo J. Marcano, and David P. Fidler. *Stealing Lives: The Globalization of Baseball and the Tragic Story of Alexis Quiroz.* Bloomington: University of Indiana Press, 2002.

Guo Zhengliang. *Xin zhengzhi chufa.* Taipei: Guobao Guoji, 2000.

Hardman, Ken, and Joy Standeven, eds. *Cultural Diversity and Congruence in Physical Education and Sport.* Aachen: Meyer & Meyer, 1998.

Held, David, and Anthony McGrew, eds. *The Global Transformations Reader: An Introduction to the Globalization Debate.* Cambridge UK: Polity Press, 2000.

Hoberman, John. "Sport and Ideology in the Post-Communist Age." In *The Changing Politics of Sport,* edited by Lincoln Allison, 15–32. Manchester: Manchester University Press, 1993.

Horne, Johan, Alan Tomlinson, and Garry Whannel. *Understanding Sport: An Introduction to the Sociological and Cultural Analysis of Sport.* London: Spon, 1999.

Hsu, Cho-yun. "Historical Setting for the Rise of Chiang Ching-kuo." In *Chiang Ching-kuo's Leadership in the Development of the Republic of China on Taiwan,* edited by Shao-chuan Leng, 1–31. New York: University Press of America, 1993.

Hsu, Francis L. K. "Confucianism in Comparative Context." In *Confucianism and the Family*, edited by Walter H. Slote and George A. DeVos. New York: State University of New York Press, 1998.

Hughes, Christopher. *Taiwan and Chinese Nationalism: National Identity and Status in International Society*. London: Routledge, 1997.

Jamail, Milton H. *Full Count: Inside Cuban Baseball*. Carbondale: Southern Illinois University Press, 2000.

Jarvie, Grant, and Joseph Maguire. *Sport and Leisure in Social Thought*. London: Routledge, 1994.

Jian Yongchang. *Zhonghua bangqiu shiji*. Taipei: Self-published, 1993.

Jianong koushu lishi bianji weiyuanhui. *Jianong koushu lishi*. Jiayi: Guoli jiayi nongye zhuanke xuexiao xiaoyouhui, 1993.

Jordan, David K. "Filial Piety in Taiwanese Popular Thought." In *Confucianism and the Family*, edited by Walter H. Slote and George A. DeVos. New York: State University of New York Press, 1998.

Keane, John. *Civil Society: Old Images, New Visions*. Cambridge UK: Polity Press, 1998.

Klein, Alan M. *Sugarball: The American Game, the Dominican Dream*. New Haven CT: Yale University Press, 1991.

———. "Trans-nationalism, Labor Migration, and Latin American Baseball." In *The Global Sports Arena: Athletic Talent Migration in an Interdependent World*, edited by John Bale and Joseph Maguire, 183–205. London: Frank Cass, 1994.

Kuo, Paul. "Q&A with Colorado's Tsao." Major League Baseball. http://colorado.rockies.mlb.com/NASApp/mlb/col/news/col_news.jsp?ymd=20030822&content_id=494010&vkey=news_col&fext=.jsp&c_id=col.

Latourette, Kenneth Scott. *The Chinese: Their History and Culture*. New York: Macmillan, 1962.

Lee, David Tawei, and Robert L. Pfaltzgraff Jr., eds. *Taiwan in a Transformed World*. Washington DC: Institute for Foreign Policy Analysis, 1995.

Leng Shao-chuan, ed. *Chiang Ching-kuo's Leadership in the Development of the Republic of China on Taiwan*. New York: University Press of America, 1993.

Li Miao. "Gelei yundong xuanshou dui shaobang de kanfa: wangyang bulao you weiwan ye." *Tiyu shijie wenzhai* 47 (1972): 31.

Liang Shuling. "Shehui fazhan quanli yu yundong wenhua de xinggou—Taiwan bangqiu de shehui lishi wenhua fenxi (1895–1990)." Master's thesis, National Zhengzhi University, 1993.

Lin, Cheng-yi. "ROC Defense Programs and Priorities: Current Assessment and Future Projections." In *Taiwan in a Transformed World*, edited by David Tawei Lee and Robert L. Pfaltzgraff Jr. Washington DC: Institute for Foreign Policy Analysis, 1995.

Lin, Chien-yu. "Baseball and Politics in Taiwan's Three Political Regimes, 1895–2002." PhD diss., Brighton University, 2003.

Lin Jianqi. "Heijin zhengzhi yingxiang gonggong gongcheng zhi yanjiu." Master's thesis, Donghai University, 2001.

Lin Qiwen. "Yundong yu zhengquan weixi: jiedu zhanhou taiwan bangqiu fazhan shi." Master's thesis, Taiwan University, 1995.

Lin Xianzheng, "Cong qihu de shoucou suo dedao de qishi." *Tiyu shijie wenzhai* 31 (1970): 16–17.

Liu Ailin. "Fenbie yu meiri xingcheng hezuo guanxi: zhongguo bangqiu jieshi shanglei." Zhonghua wang. http://sports.china.com.

Liu Guoshen, *Dangdai taiwan zhengzhi fenxi*. Taipei: Boyang wenhua, 2002.

Luo Jinyi and Wang Zhangwei, eds. *Qiji beihou: jiegou dongya xiandaihua*. Hong Kong: Oxford University Press, 1997.

Ma Tengyue. *Jiaoluo zhongde shengming zhiguang—dangdai taiwan chiren liezhuan*. Taipei: Rizhen chubanshe, 1997.

Mallett, Ashley. *Lords' Dreaming: The Story of the 1868 Aboriginal Tour of England and Beyond*. London: Souvenir Press, 2002.

Mangan, James A. *The Games Ethic and Imperialism: Aspects of the Diffusion of an Ideal*. London: Frank Cass, 1998.

Mann, James. *About Face: A History of America's Curious Relationship with China, from Nixon to Clinton*. New York: Knopf, 1998.

Miyazaki, Ichisada. *China's Examination Hell: The Civil Service Examinations of Imperial China*. New Haven CT: Yale University Press, 1981.

Morris, Andrew. "Baseball, History, the Local and the Global in Taiwan." In *The Minor Arts of Daily Life: Popular Culture in Taiwan*, edited by David Jordan, Andrew Morris, and Marc Moskowitz. Honolulu: University of Hawaii, 2003

Nathan, Andrew J., and Helena V. S. Ho. "Chiang Ching-guo's Decision for Political Reform." In *Chiang Ching-kuo's Leadership in the Development of the Republic of China on Taiwan*, edited by Shao-chuan Leng. New York: University Press of America, 1993.

Nishiwaki, Yoshitomo. *Taiwan zhongdeng xuexiao yeqiu shi*. Taipei: Self-published, 1996.

Reaves, Joseph A. *Taking in a Game: A History of Baseball in Asia*. Lincoln: University of Nebraska Press, 2002.

Regalado, Samuel O. "Latin Players on the Cheap: Professional Baseball Recruitment in Latin America and the Neocolonialist Tradition." *Indiana Journal of Global Legal Studies* 8 (2000): 9–20.

———. *Viva Baseball! Latin Major Leaguers and Their Special Hunger*. Chicago: University of Illinois Press, 1998.

Riordan, James, and Robin Jones. *Sport and Physical Education in China*. London: ISCPES, 1999.

Scholte, Jan Aart. "The Globalization of World Politics." In *The Globalization of World Politics: An Introduction to International Relations*, edited by John Baylis and Steve Smith. 2nd ed. Oxford: Oxford University Press, 2001.

Slote, Walter H., and George A. DeVos, eds. *Confucianism and the Family*. New York: State University of New York Press, 1998.

Smith, Douglas C., ed. *The Confucian Continuum: Educational Modernization in Taiwan*. New York: Praeger, 1991.

Souhan, Jim. "Baseball's Frontier: Venezuela Fertile Ground for Twins." *Star Tribune*, January 14, 2003. http://www.startribune.com/viewers/story .php?story=3589893.

Stotz, Carl E. *A Promise Kept: The Story of the Founding of Little League Baseball*. New York: Zebrowski Historical Services & Publishing Company, 1992.

Su Jinzhang. *Jiayi bangqiu shihua*. Taipei: Lianjing, 1996.

Sun Jianzheng. "Tiyu jizhe dui shaobang de kanfa: caifang liunian yougan." *Tiyu shijie wenzhai* 47 (1972): 27.

Sundeen, Joseph Timothy. "A Kid's Game? Little League Baseball and National Identity in Taiwan." *Journal of Sport and Social Issues* 25, no. 3 (August 2001): 251–65.

Tan Yuquan. *Guozhong jiaoyu gaige lun*. Taipei: Taiwan shangwuyin shuguan, 1989.

Taylor, Jay. *The Generalissimo's Son: Chiang Ching-kuo and the Revolutions in China and Taiwan*. Cambridge MA: Harvard University Press, 2000.

Vale, Pete. "South Africa and Taiwan: Pariahs, International Redemption, and Global Change." In *Taiwan's Expanding Role in the International Arena*, edited by Maysing H. Yang. New York: Sharpe, 1997.

Van Auken, Lance, and Robin Van Auken. *Play Ball! The Story of Little League Baseball*. State College: Pennsylvania State University Press, 2001.

Van Auken, Robin. *The Little League Baseball World Series*, Charleston SC: Arcadia, 2002.

Wang Huimin. *Hongye de gushi*. Taipei: Minshengbao she, 1994.

Wang Zhenwu and Lin Wenying. *Jiaoyu de kunjing yu gaige de kunjing*. Taipei: Guiguan, 1994.

Weller, Robert. *Alternate Civilities: Democracy and Culture in China and Taiwan*. Boulder: Westview Press, 1999.

Whiting, Robert. *You Gotta Have Wa*. New York: Vintage Books, 1990.

Wu Jingguo and Zeng Yifang. *Aoyun changwai de jingji: Wu jingguo de wuhuan shiyue*. Taipei: Tianxia yuanjian, 2001.

Wu Zhongfan. "Jinnian shaobang wangzuo sheishu." *Tiyu shijie wenzhai* 45 (1972): 45–46.

Xie Guocheng. "Ting! Shaobang zhuanjia tan ruhe fuzheng shaobang fengqi." *Tiyu shijie wenzhai* 38 (1971): 3.

Xie Jiafen, "Taiwan bangqiu yundong zhi yanjiu (1920–1945)." Master's thesis, Zhongyang University, 2005.

Xie Shiyuan and Xie Jiafen. *Taiwan bangqiu yibai nian*. Taipei: Guoshi chubanshe, 2003.

Yang Congrong. "Wenhua jiangou yu guomin rentong: Zhanhou taiwan de zhongguohua." Master's thesis, National Qinghua University, 1992.

Yang, Maysing H., ed. *Taiwan's Expanding Role in the International Arena*. New York: Sharpe, 1997.

Yang Rongjian. "Riben guoqiu qiangsheng de mimi" (The Secret Success of the Japanese National Sport). Qiuhun. http://playballx.com/taiwan/Marines/marines012.htm.

Yergin, Daniel A., and Joseph Stanislaw. "The Woven World." In *The Global Transformations Reader: An Introduction to the Globalization Debate*, edited by David Held and Anthony McGrew. Cambridge UK: Polity Press, 2000.

Yin Zhangyi. *Taiwan jindai shilun*. Taipei: Zhongwen, 1986.

Yu Junwei and Zeng Wencheng. *Taiwan bangqiu wang*. Taipei: Woshi chubanshe, 2004.

Zeng Kangmin. *Dragon Gate: Competitive Examinations and Their Consequences*, London: Cassell, 1999.

Zeng Wencheng. "Chen lunbo koushu bangqiu shi" (The Baseball Oral History of Chen Lunbo). Fanshuteng. http://sports.yam.com/show.php?id=0000010152.

———. "Cong 1931 nian jianong bangqiu dui kan riju shidai taiwan bangqiu fazhan" (Examining Taiwanese Baseball Development from the 1931 Kano Baseball Team). Fanshuteng. http://sports.yam.com/show.php?id=0000010420.

———. "Huang renhui koushu bangqiu shi" (The Baseball Oral History of Huang Renhui). Fanshuteng. http://sports.yam.com/show.php?id=0000012924.

———. "Ling yiduan hongye chuanqi." Fanshuteng. http://sports.yam.com/show.php?id=0000010891.

———. "Weibao weisu 'zhiye bangqiu'" (The Weibao "Professional Team"). Fanshuteng. http://media.justsports.net.tw/spo_demo/digital_baseball.asp?m_3_id=78.

———. "Xiaoshi de taiwan bangqiu sai—Minsheng bei bangqiu sai" (The Vanished Taiwanese Competition—Minsheng Cup). Aizi BBS Station. telnet://bbs.aidsbbs.net. Baseball America. http://www.baseballamerica.com; Baseball Reference. http://www.baseball-reference.com; Fanshuteng. http://sports.yam.com/show.php?id=0000012187; Judicial Yuan. http://jirs.judicial.gov.tw/FJUD/FJUDQRY01-1.asp; Major League Baseball. http://mlb.mlb.com/NASApp/mlb/index.jsp.

Zhang Jingguo. *Zhonghua minguo shaonian qingshaonian qingnian bangqiu fazhan shishi*. Taipei: Self-published, 1983.

Zhang Like. "Taiwan bangqiu yu rentong: yige yundong shehuixue de fenxi." Master's thesis, Qinghua University, 2000.

Zhang Ming. "Heku bangqiu wushi nian" (The Fifty Years of Cooperative Bank Baseball). *Taiwan Xinshengbao*. Date unknown.

Zhang Qiongfang. "Touhao, yeyao zhuangzhuang—MQ! Shidai lailin." *Guanghua zazhi* 22, no. 4 (April 1997): 8–19.

Zhao Tianci. *Changzhong tiyu yundong de huiyi*. Tainan: Changrong High School, 1975.

Zhao Yongmao. *Taiwan diqu heidao yu xuanju zhi guanxi*. Taipei: Geming shijian yanjiuyuan, 1994.

Zheng Qinren. *Shengsi cunwang niandai de Taiwan*. Taipei: Daoxiang, 1989.

———. *Zhongguo zhengzhi zhidu yu zhengzhi shi*. Taipei: Hedao chubanshe, 1996.

Zhongxiao xue bangqiu yundong liansai choubei weiyuan hui. *Gaozhong bangqiu yundong liansai baogao shu*. Taipei: Ministry of Education, 1990–2005.

———. *Guoxiao bangqiu yundong liansai baogao shu*. Taipei: Ministry of Education, 1990–2005.

———. *Guozhong bangqiu yundong liansai baogao shu*. Taipei: Ministry of Education, 1993–2005.

Zhuang Jingyan. *Tainanshi zhigao wenjiaozhi*. Tainan: Tainan city government, 1959.

Zimbalist, Andrew. *Unpaid Professionals: Commercialism and Conflict in Big-Time College Sports*. Princeton NJ: Princeton University Press, 1999.

INDEX